Ellen Glasgow

Ellen Graham
Anderson –

Ellen Glasgow
New Perspectives

Edited by Dorothy M. Scura

Tennessee Studies in Literature
Volume 36

The University of Tennessee Press • Knoxville

TENNESSEE STUDIES IN LITERATURE
Editorial Board: D. Allen Carroll, Don Richard Cox, Allison Ensor,
Richard Finneran, Nancy Moore Goslee, Marilyn Kallet, Norman Sanders.

"Tennessee Studies in Literature," a distinguished series sponsored by the Department of English at The University of Tennessee, Knoxville, began publication in 1956. Beginning in 1984, with Volume 27, TSL evolved from a series of annual volumes of miscellaneous essays to a series of occasional volumes, each one dealing with a specific theme, period, or genre, for which the editor of that volume has invited contributions from leading scholars in the field.

Inquiries concerning this series should be addressed to the Editorial Board, Tennessee Studies in Literature, Department of English, The University of Tennessee, Knoxville, Tennessee 37996-0430. Those desiring to purchase additional copies of this issue or copies of back issues should address The University of Tennessee Press, 293 Communications Building, Knoxville, Tennessee 37996-0325.

Frontispiece: Drawing of Ellen Glasgow by Ellen Graham Anderson. Courtesy Anderson Family Papers (#38-96-A), Manuscripts Division, Special Collections Department, University of Virginia Library.

The paper in this book meets the minimum requirements of the American National Standard for Permanence of Paper for Printed Library Materials. ∞   The binding materials have been chosen for strength and durability.

 Printed on recycled paper.

LIBRARY OF CONGRESS CATALOGING-IN-PUBLICATION DATA

Ellen Glasgow: new perspectives/edited by Dorothy M. Scura.—1st ed.
        p.   cm.—(Tennessee studies in literature; v. 36)
ISBN 0-87049-879-7 (cloth: alk. paper)
    1. Glasgow, Ellen Anderson Gholson, 1873-1945—Criticism and interpretation.
    2. Women and literature—Southern States—History—20th century.
    I. Scura, Dorothy McInnis.
    II. Series.
PS3513.L34Z6534   1995
813'.52—dc20   94-18726
                                           CIP

✹

For Michael, Debbie, and Jennifer
in admiration of their grace
and humor and courage

Contents

Acknowledgments

I acknowledge, with appreciation, the support of the John C. Hodges Better English Fund of the English Department, University of Tennessee. For other generous support in preparation of this volume, I thank several people: Martha E. Cook, friend and colleague, for her diligence in obtaining the drawing of Ellen Glasgow by her cousin, Ellen Graham Anderson; Catherine Rainwater for other collegial support; Peggy Dunn for assistance in checking quotations; Caroline Maun for help with proofing and indexing; and Norma Meredith for help with all aspects of manuscript preparation.

For permitting the publication of "Ideals," originally published in *Hearst's International* combined with *Cosmopolitan* 80, no. 1 (Jan. 1926): 24–29, 140, 142, and eight letters from Ellen Glasgow to Louise Chandler Moulton, now in the Library of Congress, I thank Ms. Margaret Williams, Director, acting for the Richmond Society for the Prevention of Cruelty to Animals, beneficiary of the Estate of Ellen Glasgow. The drawing of Ellen Glasgow by Ellen Graham Anderson in the Anderson Family Papers (#38-96-A), Manuscripts Division, Special Collections Department, University of Virginia Library, and an undated handwritten note by Ellen Glasgow, Papers of Ellen Glasgow (#5060), Manuscripts Division, Special Collections Department, University of Virginia Library are used with permission of the Library and the University of Virginia and with my appreciation to Michael Plunkett, Curator of Manuscripts and University Archivist. The portrait of Ellen Glasgow on the cover is from a pastel portrait on ivory in the collections of the Virginia Historical Society, Richmond, and is reproduced with permission of the Virginia Historical Society, Richmond, Virginia, and with appreciation to Nelson Lankford and Sara Bearss.

Introduction

For what we call the woman's movement is a revolt
from a pretense of being—it is at its best and worst
a struggle for the liberation of personality.
—Glasgow, *New York Times*, 30 November 1913

[T]hough the chief end of the novel is to create life,
there is a secondary obligation which demands that fiction shall,
in a measure at least, reflect the movement and tone of its age.
—Glasgow, *A Certain Measure*, 1943

Ellen Glasgow was born April 22, 1873, in Richmond, Virginia, and died there in her home at 1 West Main Street on November 21, 1945. Her parents were Anne Jane Gholson and Francis T. Glasgow. The eighth of ten children, Ellen Glasgow was connected through her mother to many of the distinguished families of Tidewater Virginia such as the Randolphs, Blands, and Taylors. Her father came of Scottish stock from western Virginia. For many years he was manager of the Tredegar Iron Works, which was owned by his uncle, General Joseph Reid Anderson. Ellen Glasgow identified with her gentle, Episcopalian mother and rejected her stern, Presbyterian father, but readers of her novels recognize the influence of both strains—cavalier and puritan—on her fiction as well as her personality.

Glasgow received very little formal schooling, but read books in her father's library and as a young woman was guided in wide reading by her sister Cary's husband, Walter McCormack, a Charleston lawyer.

Works cited in this introduction are to be found in the bibliography, pages 235-37.

In independent study she gained knowledge of science, philosophy, economics, cultural theory, and literature—evident in the texts of her fiction. A precocious child, she found her vocation young, or, as she explained in *The Woman Within*, "At the age of seven my vocation had found me. . . . I was born a novelist, though I formed myself into an artist" (41). "Only a Daisy," printed in Godbold's biography, is her first short story, written when she was seven years old.

At twenty-four, she published anonymously her first novel, *The Descendant* (1897), and she continued to publish regularly for the rest of her life. Nineteen novels, a volume of poetry, a collection of short stories, a collection of prefaces to thirteen of her novels, and two collected editions of her novels appeared during her lifetime. Posthumously published were her autobiography, *The Woman Within* (1954), and her last work of fiction, *Beyond Defeat* (1966). She was a serious and committed artist who received positive reviews of most of her books; nevertheless, she frequently wrote books that sold well. Five of her novels, for example, were best-sellers—*The Deliverance* (1904), *The Wheel of Life* (1906), *Life and Gabriella* (1916), *The Sheltered Life* (1932), and *Vein of Iron* (1935).

Her apprenticeship ended with her tenth novel, *Virginia* (1913), the very best of her early work and the first novel to feature a woman protagonist. Although she began her career in her twenties, her finest novels were published when she was in her fifties and early sixties. Beginning in 1925 with *Barren Ground*, and continuing with *The Romantic Comedians* (1926), *They Stooped to Folly* (1929), *The Sheltered Life* (1932), and *Vein of Iron* (1936), Glasgow produced her most significant work. In her old age she was much honored—receiving, for example, the Howells Medal in 1940, awarded every five years by the American Academy of Arts and Letters, and the Pulitzer Prize in 1942. She was awarded honorary degrees by the University of North Carolina, University of Richmond, Duke University, and the College of William and Mary.

This collection of fifteen essays is the second volume of critical articles published on Ellen Glasgow and her work. *Ellen Glasgow: Centennial Essays*, edited by M. Thomas Inge, was published in 1976, three years after Glasgow's hundredth birthday; now, *Ellen Glasgow: New Perspectives* appears two years before the centennial anniversary of the publication of Glasgow's first novel, *The Descendant* (1897). In the nineteen years between the two volumes, the critical landscape of Glasgow scholarship has changed considerably.

Two important scholarly books have presented new interpretations of her work: Julius Rowan Raper's *From the Sunken Garden: The Fiction of Ellen Glasgow, 1916–1945* (1980) and Linda Wagner's *Ellen Glasgow: Be-*

yond Convention (1982). In addition, three reference works have been published: Edgar E. MacDonald and Tonette Bond Inge's *Ellen Glasgow: A Reference Guide* (1986) provides annotated secondary bibliography on Glasgow from 1897–1981; Julius Rowan Raper's *Ellen Glasgow's Reasonable Doubts: A Collection of Her Writings* (1988) brings together unpublished short works as well as published works that appeared in scattered places; and Dorothy M. Scura's *Ellen Glasgow: The Contemporary Reviews* (1992) reprints critical reviews of Glasgow's work published in her lifetime.

For many years Glasgow was regarded as a transitional figure in Southern letters, a writer who published books in the time between Thomas Nelson Page and William Faulkner. She was an outsider, an anomaly, a Virginian who did not quite fit the context of the Southern Literary Renaissance. Often she was characterized as a precursor of that great movement even though her finest work was published between 1925 and 1936, absolutely concurrent with the Renaissance.

As critics in the last decade or so have begun to look closely at the work of women writers, Glasgow's work is being re-visioned. When considered in the context of women writers, she is often accorded a significant place in the canons of American and of Southern literature. Beginning with Anne Goodwyn Jones's seminal *Tomorrow Is Another Day: The Woman Writer in the South, 1859–1936* (1981), which addresses the ways in which seven women writers dealt with the concept of Southern womanhood, Glasgow has been included in a number of important critical books focusing on women writers. In *After the Fall: The Demeter-Persephone Myth in Wharton, Cather, and Glasgow* (1989), Josephine Donovan argues that Glasgow's works depict woman's fall from the "cloistered hothouse" of the mother's garden to a "Darwinist social jungle" where man governs. Lucinda H. MacKethan's *Daughters of Time: Creating Woman's Voice in Southern Story* (1990) includes Glasgow along with Zora Neale Hurston and Eudora Welty in her central chapter in this study, which traces the development of a distinctive woman's voice in Southern fiction.

In *Female Pastoral: Women Writers Re-Visioning the American South* (1991), Elizabeth Jane Harrison analyzes Glasgow's evolving use of pastoral in novels from *The Battle-Ground* (1902) to *Vein of Iron* (1936). Elizabeth Ammons, in *Conflicting Stories: American Women Writers at the Turn into the Twentieth Century* (1991), discusses Glasgow along with Anzia Yezierska and Edith Summers Kelley with respect to the depiction of "hunger" and "anger" in their works. In *Fiction of the Home Place: Jewett, Cather, Glasgow, Porter, Welty, and Naylor* (1992), Helen Fiddyment Levy traces in Glasgow's novels a movement from the male-centered city to the loving community close to the land created by Kate Oliver at Hunter's Fare in Glasgow's last fiction, *Beyond Defeat*. Will Brantley focuses on autobiographical works in *Feminine Sense in Southern Memoir* (1993) to show a liberal tradition in the work of women writers of the South; Glasgow is treated along with Eudora Welty in a chapter entitled "Writing the Sheltered Life."

Although the subjects of these book-length studies are varied—southern womanhood, female voice, pastoral, anger, liberalism—the approach of the scholars is in each case informed by recent critical interest in issues of gender. In this present collection of essays, too, topics range broadly over Glasgow's life and work, and scholars choose varied approaches in essays, but the view of most of the authors is shaped in some respect by feminist criticism. Ellen Glasgow is receiving careful scrutiny and a central place in American and Southern letters by critics as her work is approached from a feminist perspective. This is entirely appropriate, for Glasgow not only participated briefly in the woman's movement in the early part of the century but she wrestled in all her novels with the role of women—all kinds of women—and with the values of the patriarchal culture that permeated her world.

There is some irony, too, in the feminist discovery of Glasgow's work when one considers that Glasgow began her career at the end of the nineteenth century with an anonymously published novel, thought by critics to have been written by a man. She did not find her writing voice as a woman until sixteen years and nine books later with *Virginia*. Then, with *Barren Ground* in 1925, the story of Dorinda Oakley, a strong surviving woman, Glasgow began the most productive period of her career.

These essays focus on many topics and include some interesting new material. Martha E. Cook has found a "new" short story, "Ideals," originally published in 1926 in *Hearst's International* combined with *Cosmopolitan* and reprinted in this volume. "Ideals" brings to fourteen the number of known Glasgow short stories. Cook speculates intriguingly that there may be more Glasgow work not yet located: "We may know less about the boundaries of Glasgow's canon than we thought." In her essay, Cook connects the heroine of "Ideals" to other Glasgow characters such as Virginia Pendleton Treadwell and Dorinda Oakley, as well as connecting the story to the work of Kate Chopin and of Sylvia Plath.

Nancy A. Walker and Susan Goodman each focus specifically on Glasgow's autobiography in their essays. Walker looks at *The Woman Within* in the context of recent scholarship on the genre of autobiographical writing and proposes that *The Woman Within* presents "the process of fashioning a self capable of standing as the artist." The objective truth of the work is not as important to the reader as is developing "an understanding of the value and necessity of self-creation in a world that did not readily bestow selfhood on women writers." Goodman also calls upon critical studies of autobiography as she makes a fascinating comparison of Edith Wharton's *A Backward Glance* and Glasgow's *The Woman Within*. She finds surprising similarities in the two writers' works and lives. Each writer, however, reacted differently to the writings of Freud, and these reactions are manifested in each one's autobiography: Wharton emphasized public matters, focusing upon social realism rather than psychological truth, while Glasgow emphasized the private woman within.

Essays by Terence Allan Hoagwood and Stephanie R. Branson consider Glasgow's poetry and her short stories, work that has not received the critical attention paid to her fiction and autobiography. In a groundbreaking analysis, Hoagwood studies Glasgow's volume of poetry, *The Freeman and Other Poems* (1902), and proposes that "an ironized point of view, elaborated with considerable poetic artifice, produces . . . an impressively unified poetic volume." He connects ideas expressed in the poetry to Glasgow's autobiography and to her fiction and points out that Glasgow's poetic vision is "a socially critical vision that is at once profound, bitter, submerged, and subversive." Branson looks at three stories of the fantastic—"Dare's Gift," "The Past," and "The Shadowy Third"—from *The Shadowy Third and Other Stories* (1923), exploring why Glasgow referred to herself as a "verist." She terms the three short stories "feminist fictions," concluding that Glasgow was more experimental in short fiction than she was in novels.

The final ten essays in this volume focus on Glasgow's novels. Connecting an earlier text with a later one, Lucinda H. MacKethan proposes that "*The Battle-Ground* and *Vein of Iron* both envision a design that can be called matriarchal." MacKethan defines a matriarchal design as one with "a structure of relationships based on sharing rather than competitiveness, on negotiation rather than self-assertion, and on integration rather than exclusion." Betty Ambler and Ada Fincastle, according to MacKethan, both "struggle against a dying, but still powerful patriarchal southern ethos."

In her article, Pamela R. Matthews reprints eight heretofore unpublished Glasgow letters written in 1905 and 1906 to the writer Louise Chandler Moulton. Blair Rouse's *Letters of Ellen Glasgow* (1958) includes only seven letters from this period, so this new correspondence is noteworthy. Matthews is interested in Glasgow's friendships with women and in the narrative implications of women's friendships in the woman-centered plot of *The Wheel of Life* (1906), a novel that has received little critical attention. She asks readers to re-vision Glasgow's life and "confront the implications of a woman's life centered emotionally on other women."

Virginia, which has received significant critical attention, is the subject of two new approaches. Phillip D. Atteberry argues that narrative structure and not the subject of the novel is the feature that distinguishes *Virginia* from Glasgow's earlier work. According to Atteberry, the novel employs "tonal contrasts and structural counterpoints that qualify every presentation and question every assertion." Francesca Sawaya looks at *Virginia* in terms of economics, gender, and genre. She concludes a complex argument by asserting that the novel "is a naturalist text," but one "that puts into question the naturalist project in relation to race and sex, puts into question the naturalist project through sentimentalism—its opposite and its double."

In the first of two essays on *Barren Ground,* Julius Rowan Raper proposes that Glasgow has not been recognized appropriately for bringing the psychological complexity of modernism to her characters in the 1920s. Drawing upon Glasgow's life, he analyzes, explains, and reconciles the problem of the often completely contrasting interpretations of Dorinda as either victim or victor. As Raper explains in this rich essay, "The side-by-side existence of Dorinda's mythic success and her psychological failure creates the almost electric arc that gives the book its power and enigmatic interest." Next, Margaret D. Bauer sees Dorinda as victorious at the end of *Barren Ground.* Comparing the texts of that novel and *Gone With the Wind,* she finds an astonishing number of parallels and proposes that the ambiguous ending of Margaret Mitchell's novel is illuminated by considering it along with the ending of Glasgow's novel; thus Bauer concludes that *Gone With the Wind* ends in a moment of triumph—not defeat—for Scarlett O'Hara.

Caroline King Barnard Hall writes with spirit and verve of Glasgow's sparkling comedy, *The Romantic Comedians.* Hall analyzes Judge Honeywell as well as the female characters and points out connections between the novel and T. S. Eliot's *Waste Land.* As Hall explains, "Glasgow weaves into her novel a texture of nostalgia and correcting wit, of wistful longing for pre–World War I values and clear understanding of their present irrelevance, of old male standards and new female iconoclasm."

Two essays that directly reflect current movements in critical theory focus on works generally considered Glasgow's finest. Linda Wagner-Martin draws upon Julia Kristeva's concepts of women's worlds and time to illuminate *The Sheltered Life.* She shows how Glasgow depicts the inner life of characters "through deft structuring, ironic yet seemingly straightforward dialogue, and an indictment of the patriarchy—

complete with its love of linear time." Catherine Rainwater demonstrates that Glasgow's well-documented interest in animals was profound as well as philosophical. She proposes that a "semiotic network of animal references unites nearly all of her novels, especially *Barren Ground* and *Vein of Iron*." By reading these animal signs in the two novels, Rainwater opens new layers of meaning in the texts.

Appropriately, the last essay in this collection focuses on Glasgow's last two works of fiction, *In This Our Life* and *Beyond Defeat*. Echoes of earlier essays are present in Helen Fiddyment Levy's discussion of a female-centered homeland, of the paternalistic and hierarchical family, and of the urban wasteland of Queenborough. Levy argues that *Beyond Defeat* embodies Glasgow's "final philosophy," and her last work shows that the novelist "at last found refuge in a visionary pastoral home place presided over by an elder wise woman, an American icon."

As we approach the centennial of the publication of Ellen Glasgow's first novel, we also approach a centennial of Glasgow criticism. For almost ten decades, critics have read her large body of work and responded with interpretation and evaluation. Her work has offered solid material for the literary historian, for the New Critic, for the textual critic and the bibliographer and the biographer, for the psychological critic, and for others. Recently published books and this collection of essays reveal the growing significance of the shaping influence of feminist criticism. Ellen Glasgow's words about feminism in the epigraph to this Introduction remind the reader that her own view of this movement was intellectual and personal, a challenge to the woman within. Perhaps her words about the novel in the epigraph may appropriately be applied to these essays: May they create thoughtful new ways to look at Glasgow's life and art, for they surely reflect—in a measure, at least—the critical movement and tone of the 1990s.

PART I

A New Glasgow Story

Ideals

Ellen Glasgow

She belonged to that magnanimous generation of women who married men to reform them. The older members of the community called such injudicious philanthropy "true womanliness," and praised it in proportion to the absence of rectitude in the reformed or unreformed husband. Only her mother, having attained the ripe wisdom which is the fruit of unhappy experience, murmured with mild Victorian firmness:

"John Henry is not a safe man to marry, Lydia."

"He will be safe with me," rejoined Lydia, who had the spirit as well as the face of a reformer of men.

"He drinks too much, Lydia."

"He won't drink with me, mother."

"He plays cards for money."

"There won't be enough money to play cards for after we're married."

"He"—Mrs. Westcott hesitated, for she was late Victorian, and in Virginia even the late Victorian was later than it was in most other places—"he has not a—a nice way with women." This was as near as a Virginian of her period, who called neither the moralities nor the immoralities by their right names, could bring herself to allude to the facts of sex before any woman who was still young enough to profit by the allusion. Though this was only twenty-five years ago, those twenty-five years have made the world safe for many more experimental failures than democracy.

"He has a nice way with me, mother," retorted Lydia, with the uncompromising logic of one who knows what she wants if not what she is talking about.

"Wild men make their wives very unhappy, Lydia," insisted Mrs.

Westcott, who, unlike Lydia, was burdened with the disadvantages of complete knowledge.

"He won't be wild after we're married, mother."

"Many men are, dear."

Lydia shook her head, a pretty head it was, with a brown bang cut straight across her forehead above the dove-like gray of her eyes. "But John Henry is different," she returned resolutely.

"All men are different when they are in love," sighed Mrs. Westcott; and picking up one of her husband's socks from her work-basket, she patiently ran her needle round the edge of a hole which had not been worn there by constant treading in the thorny path of monogamy.

"Then John Henry will always be different, for he will always love me," Lydia said with a serene though exasperating confidence in the power of her charm.

"How can you tell, my child?" inquired Mrs. Westcott, looking up from her darning.

"I know because he has sworn it to me," answered Lydia, which sounds hopelessly simple-minded even for the Victorian era.

Lydia was young then, so young that her parents, uniting the protest of the virtue that has suffered from vice with the firmer remonstrance of the vice that has suffered from virtue, were able to postpone the threatened disaster. At the end of five years, when her wedding clothes, selected with such passionate care, were already in the house, when the music had been chosen and "The Voice That Breathed O'er Eden" was being practised, very low, by the choir of the church, when the wedding-cake had been ordered and was actually in the oven—at this poignantly crucial instant, grim reality had stalked over the flowery carpet of destiny. John Henry had shot a man in sudden rage over an idle game of cards, and a few months later he had gone to prison for twenty years instead of to the marriage altar.

Even then Lydia, though with waning confidence in the power of charm over other people's characters, would have married him; but, displaying a consideration he had never revealed before, he had, not without tears in his eyes, released her from her engagement. When, overcome by his tears, she had refused to be released and had promised to wait for him, he had gone away with one of those commemorative gestures which express so much while they accomplish so little.

Justice was a sterner matter then than it is now; prisons, even twenty years ago, were more realistic places; and it seemed to Lydia that the very quality of living was harder to endure. John Henry's sentence, which might have been shortened by docility, was lengthened by insubordination, and for twenty years Lydia had waited in what seemed to her a prolonged heartache, an unalterable hush of remembrance.

Though she was only forty-five, she had had the misfortune to fall between two eras, and she had tried, with the discouragement which always accompanies such efforts, to lap over from the period when self-sacrifice was a virtue into the period when self-sacrifice had become merely the Freudian stepfather of all the vices. Twenty-five years ago, even twenty years ago, she had been an ideal, and she suffered now from the feeling that she had lingered on into an age when ideals had gone hopelessly out of fashion. Yet, notwithstanding the hard white light of the modern world, something of that lost illusion, of the tender grace of a day that is dead, still clung to her from a youth which had read Tennyson and practised the more delicate virtues.

In her own way, which was so different from the way of Elizabeth, her orphan niece who lived with her, she was not without a saintly beauty of feature, though time had robbed her of her girlish color and sparkle. For she had spent twenty years of her life, the best years, as her mother used to remind her, waiting for the man she had failed to reform to come out of prison. In the grave old house of her parents she had lived as quietly as a nun in a convent. Nothing had changed since he went away, nothing except Elizabeth, who had been a small girl then and who was now a handsome and determined young woman, very intelligent and a little too noisy for Lydia's secluded tastes.

For the rest, he would find things when he came back just as he remembered them. Even the soft color of her dresses and the prim arrangement of her hair, with the square bang falling like a veil above her dove's eyes, were unaltered. The house, like herself, she knew, was too stately, perhaps, for the hurrying years, and, like herself, it was a trifle worn and thin and reminiscent of ideals that were outlived.

Twenty years of consecration, of nun-like sanctity of thought and feeling, of vicarious expiation and regret, did not leave one untouched. There were delicate lines, as faint as the marks of butterflies, round her eyes and at the corners of her pale mouth, which drooped in an expression of weary acquiescence. Her cheeks were too thin, and so was the slender, veined throat beneath the narrow band of black velvet—the necklace of lost illusions, Elizabeth called it. Color, vivacity had been drained out of her face as out of her life. Yet there were times, Elizabeth said, and Elizabeth was too modern to try to spare anyone's feelings, when she was still as lovely as ever. Not as young, of course, but lovely in a rare and distinguished fashion which youth, as long as it was only youth, could never hope to possess.

"I shall wait and hope," she had said to him at the last, just before they took him away; and she had waited and hoped as long as she could keep hope alive in her heart. Even when hope was over, she had still waited. Life had drifted past her; people had married or died in her family; wars had been fought and won or lost; false literary or political gods had been placed upon altars and then broken to pieces; an era had changed and the standards she had served had changed with it; but still she had waited and still she had tried to keep the breath of faith where hope had been in her heart.

Four times every year she had left the old house and gone into the city to the prison; and four times every year she had looked into a face which reminded her of features seen dimly beneath running water. The same face and yet different! As fluid as time or as memory.

At first, in those dark days of the ancient history of prisons, the stripes had changed him beyond all outward recognition. She could not see his face, she could not see his soul for the stripes that covered him. Then, with modern ways, the stripes had gone and that look of a thing tormented had faded slowly out of his eyes. The semblance of peace had come into them in the last ten years, the expression of a man, she felt with a breaking heart, who had become not only inarticulate but insensible.

They had had so little to say to each other—for what can one say in prison?—and as the years went on, they found that even that little grew less with every difficult visit. Gradually silence widened between them, like the stream that became a river in the poem of her girlhood, and the wider and deeper it flowed, the more impossible she found it to stretch out her hand to him or to remember the glimpse of his face in the distance. Yet she had never failed in those twenty years. Even when her mother lay dying, even when she herself had risen from a bed in the hospital and the doctor had told her it was dangerous for her to go to the prison, never once had she failed him!

"You have turned your whole life into a prison," her mother had said to her before she died. "You have made yourself a prisoner in the past."

"Ten years more," Lydia had responded. "Even if he isn't pardoned, there will be only ten years more of waiting."

"But he will come out an old and broken man. You must remember that, Lydia," Mrs. Westcott had murmured with the relentless veracity of one who is piously dying.

Lydia had smiled her smile of hidden knowledge. "We shall have grown old together. We have always been together."

"You mean in sorrow?"

"No, I mean in spirit. I have never lost him in spirit."

In those twenty years, before and after her mother's death, it seemed to her that she had learned all there was to know about waiting. For the first months she had felt as if time were an animate thing that was torturing her. The minutes crawled over her like spiders, and struggle as desperately as she could, she could not shake herself free of them. Instead of passing over, they seemed to stick to her, and even after they were dead she felt that they still clung to her flesh.

In the early days of her sorrow she was never quiet, running always in an ineffectual endeavor to escape from this crawling suffocation of time. Over the house; out into the garden; up the long white road that led into the village; back again to her flower-beds; and from the flower-beds into the darkened rooms of the house. She worked at the hardest tasks she could find, digging, planting, watering her flowers, which might have been of paper for all the sweetness and bloom they shed for her. Twenty years of emptiness ahead of her! Twenty years of waiting, and she was only twenty-five! She was only twenty-five with marriage and motherhood snatched out of her life!

This was in the beginning. Gradually, as the relentless years passed, the sharp pain was dulled, though until the very end that single nerve of longing had never ceased entirely to ache. Five years dragged by and there were fifteen still ahead of her—fifteen years of waiting for a freedom that meant the end of her youth. At thirty she was at her loveliest, and even her cloistral devotion could not keep other men completely out of her life.

There was one for whom she might have cared if he had come earlier; but it was too late after she had given her love and her promise. Her pure brow, her winged eyebrows above the dove's eyes, were the visible signs of her spirit; and in her own generation she had been reverenced for the very qualities of soul which had cost her the sympathy and even the comprehension of the generation that had come afterward.

When ten years had gone the torment of the nerves became gradually calm. Waiting, which had been active torture, settled into a passive expectancy. Four times a year she still visited the prison, and on these visits she smiled and talked with an artificial vivacity which she dropped like a veil as soon as she reached home again. Little interests came into her life; friends who mattered enough to be missed when they went away; Elizabeth's school days and the children who came to play in the garden; seed catalogs in the spring and the planting of borders; bird baths in the grassy squares and the birds that came back to drink from them; the garden club that was formed in the neighborhood; watching

Elizabeth's friends at croquet or tennis and serving tea out-of-doors in the summer-house. Little interests, but they filled her days between thirty and forty.

And more than all there was, she never lost sight of this, the supreme consolation of being faithful to an ideal. In being faithful to an ideal she had herself developed into an ideal for the people around her. The women of her own age treated her with the tender solicitude which the sentimental South bestows upon its perpetual widows. The deference she inspired was the deference accorded to the old or to those who wear a crape veil as a winding-sheet for youth and happiness. It was a life of sorrow, of sanctity, of self-denial, of vain expiation; but it was a life that held its own sweet and terrible recompense.

"She is so faithful," sighed the women of her generation, clustering loyally round her, for faithfulness in women, which was the only faithfulness they regarded as within nature, was a virtue they esteemed only a degree less than chastity. There was solace for her loneliness in the thought that if she served an ideal she also embodied one.

Waking in the night she would stretch out her empty arms in the fragrant darkness of spring and murmur brokenly, "She is so faithful." She had sacrificed her youth, her beauty, her happiness, even her unborn children, on the altar of an invisible perfection, and in return she had won the right to her epitaph, "She was so faithful." That was the reward of her constancy, and who shall say that, as long at least as the Victorian fashions lasted, the reward did not suffice?

Fifteen years dropped away one after one, as noiselessly as petals from the fruit-trees in her garden. Her mother died; Elizabeth grew into a woman and filled the house with the pleasure-seeking, mannerless youth of her age. Older friends were crowded into the background; Lydia herself was crowded presently into the background. There was no room for regret, still less for faithfulness, among the breathless activities of the ever-rising generation.

Then the war came; and when it was over the very virtues had changed not only their names but their aspects. Even love had been dethroned from its immemorial place among the eternities. The Great War had been fought, she felt, on her spirit; and in the end the legions of darkness had conquered.

She was vanquished, and nothing remained but the battle-field. Not an ideal was left alive in the world, and it seemed to her that the one buried deepest beneath the assault of material things was the ideal of constancy. Like smoke the perpetual widows of the South had vanished into the sunlight. Even the women of her own period, the women who had consecrated Lydia's life to an unattainable pattern of perfection, even these women appeared to have discarded, in the excitement and adventure of war, all reverence for mourning as the outward sign of an invisible grace. Though they lagged behind Elizabeth and her group in their impassioned revolt from the categorical imperative, they were becoming openly skeptical of the canonical virtues. And at last, in the romantic maelstrom of the middle forties, she was caught and flattened out between two epochs.

It was at this time, when the long waiting drew to an end, that she took up the game of patience as an escape from the insurgent selfishness of the younger generation. It was the only way that she could retreat, even for an hour, from the depressing pleasures of youth; for during these latter years Elizabeth's friends were seldom absent and when they were present they were never silent. The gracious habit of self-effacement was as alien to Elizabeth's group as were those antiquated amenities which had kept the surface of life smooth and pleasant. These energetic young people were not only without reverence; they were without sentiment and without courtesy as well.

Elizabeth had shot up into a dark, robust, flashing girl, with an intrepid gaze and a full mouth which she painted a violent crimson. Though she looked fragile she was, in reality, as hard as iron; and twenty-five years before she would have been promptly arrested if she had appeared in the village street. It was true, Lydia emphasized this whenever it was possible, that the girl had her fine points. She was honest, kind-hearted, truthful within reasonable bounds; and notwithstanding her aversion from sentiment, she was genuinely fond of her aunt.

Elizabeth it was, assisted by her friends, who drove Lydia to patience, but having once discovered the value of the game as a refuge, the elder woman resorted to it now as she had once resorted to her garden before tumultuous youth overflowed its seclusion. As the years passed Lydia grew to love her solitary diversion, for it became gradually the only retreat which democracy had left safe for her.

Then, after eighteen years of waiting, while she sat over her cards one afternoon, there came the telegram which told her that he had been released.

At the breakfast table Elizabeth was sprinkling sugar over her oatmeal. She looked very handsome in her dress of grass-green linen, and she had as usual put on her small round hat, scarcely larger than a bathing-cap, before coming down-stairs. Her golf-clubs, brightly polished, were already in the hall, for she would start for the country club as soon as she had hurriedly eaten her breakfast.

Though she was sympathetic with her aunt, her sympathy was the detached, inattentive kind which one accords to a religion or a philanthropy. To a girl so blooming, so buoyant, so deeply concerned with her own mind and her own mind alone, it was impossible that Lydia, enmeshed in her faded romance and her old-fashioned loyalties, should appear more than half animate. Yet even Elizabeth, though she was ignorant of it, had helped to place Lydia in the becoming, if antiquated, frame of another century. After all, it is easier to respect than to comprehend, and Elizabeth's grasping youth was not lacking in an artistic appreciation of relics. It was beautiful, she felt, to have one about; it was as distinguished as having a genuine Gilbert Stuart or Thomas Sully hanging on one's wall. She was sincerely proud of what she called Lydia's "old-fashioned romance"; but she made no effort to conceal the truth that, though she did not fail in her admiration of relics, she rejoiced nevertheless that destiny had not enshrined her in the picturesque niche of the past.

"I think it's perfectly lovely the way you've given your whole life to a memory, Aunt Lydia," she said.

The hand that Lydia stretched out to the coffee-pot trembled. "But it isn't only a memory," she answered. "I've always had something to look forward to. I always think of the future."

"For twenty years to think of the same person!"

"I loved him very much, you know," sighed Lydia, unaware that she had spoken in the past tense, while she drew a long breath as if her loyalty were dying for lack of air.

This was one of the moments—there had been many such moments—when it seemed to her that she was imprisoned like a wax wreath under one of the glass globes of the nineteenth century. They had kept her there under glass because they enjoyed showing her off; and she had been too passive, too waxen in her conventionality, to break the globe and escape while she was still young. She had been condemned for life, she felt without knowing that she felt it, to an ideal; and the kind of public sympathy which is as strong as public obloquy had made her confinement a solitary imprisonment.

"We don't love like that in these days." Elizabeth echoed her aunt's sigh as accurately as she could attune her ringing voice to so plaintive a note, and she added with conviction: "You are so faithful."

"Twenty-five years ago when my character was formed, women were supposed to be faithful. It was," Lydia conceded, not without a tincture of bitterness in her thoughts, "almost the only thing they were permitted to be."

"Only twenty-five years ago!" laughed Elizabeth. "Isn't it wonderful," she demanded triumphantly, "what the World War has done for women?"

"Yes, I imagine the war has changed things even more than we real-ize. People used to say that feeling is always the same everywhere and in all periods; but I dare say they were mistaken. There are fashions in emotions as well as in virtues."

Again Elizabeth laughed, not unkindly but because it was as natural for her to laugh over sentiment as it had once been for Lydia to weep over it.

"Great passions have gone out of fashion," she said lightly. "The way we look at it now is that, with so many other things to do with your time, a whole life is too big a price to pay for a single experience. We want variety, not just to go on playing one tune on the same string of a harp. I suppose a great many women felt as you did twenty-five years ago, only the South always clings longer to its tombstones than any other part of the country. If there had been more women like you even here you wouldn't have been such a rarity." She hesitated an instant and then went on with the reckless cruelty of youth: "You've given your whole life to a man who wasn't worthy of you, Aunt Lydia. If he had been worthy of you, he'd have kept out of prison for your sake."

A pallid flush suffused Lydia's features. "He had a high temper," she answered, while her throat beneath the narrow black-velvet band worked convulsively. "The quarrel was about me, and he had a demon of jealousy. We were to have been married in three days and I ought to have been more careful."

"But I always heard the quarrel was over a game of cards." There was genuine surprise in Elizabeth's voice.

"Everyone thought so. He—he never let the truth come out at his trial."

"Then it must have gone harder for him."

"I was afraid of that. I tried to tell the truth, but he denied it, and nobody, not even his own lawyer, believed me. They said I was trying to shield him. But it was the truth. That is why—that is one of the reasons why I have—why I have—" Her voice trailed off into an echo.

"I understand." In spite of her hard youth and her artificially colored mouth, Elizabeth looked as if she did understand. "But he oughtn't to have been jealous. If he loved you, he might have trusted you."

"Men can't always control their impulses."

"Men!" jeered Elizabeth indignantly, and she continued with deri-sion: "Well, if they couldn't in the past, they'll jolly well begin to in the future. Suppose you'd run amuck and killed a woman from jealousy, do you imagine he'd have given up his youth waiting for you outside the wall of a prison?"

"Men are different."

"Then it's time women were becoming different too," retorted Elizabeth, who was as natural within as she was artificial without. "As man to man," she demanded abruptly, "haven't you ever wanted to smash your glass case and get out?"

A quiver ran over Lydia's features and her eyes saddened to a wounded look. There were moments when she knew that Elizabeth was indecorous and feared that she was immoral; yet, notwithstanding this knowledge and these fears, she was never able entirely to resist the unbridled honesty of the girl's attitude. "The only thing that matters in life," she added limply, "is to be true to your ideals."

"I know, but I asked you if you never got tired and wanted to smash things."

"Being tired doesn't make any difference."

"It makes all the difference there is."

"People made it as easy for me as they could," Lydia resumed with an evasive sweetness. "Everyone was so kind."

"Yes, I've heard grandmother say that you were like a widow who was never permitted to take off her weeds."

"I always felt that our marriage was only postponed."

"Postponed for twenty years? Well, I'm as glad as I can be, Aunt Lydia, that your waiting is over, and I hope he will appreciate all the sacrifices you've made for him. It makes me cry to think of your wasted youth; but I suppose you may look forward to a long and happy old age."

A happy old age! That was how her belated romance appeared to the ardent imagination of twenty. Yet at forty-five she did not feel old; she felt, indeed, surprisingly young, as if she were the artless product of a less sophisticated point of view. In all her forty-five years she had never learned as much about life as Elizabeth had discovered before her twentieth birthday.

"And is he really coming this afternoon?" inquired the girl, who knew it already but imagined she was pleasing her aunt by repeating the question.

"So he wrote me. He said he would come on one of the afternoon trains and walk up from the village."

"Which one? I might meet him."

"He doesn't want to be met. He—he sounded almost as if he were afraid of it."

"Poor old boy," rejoined Elizabeth, not unkindly. "It must be rather rotten. Worse than Rip Van Winkle because he had been asleep all the time. I suppose he'll want to shy off from us at first. We must make him feel that we don't see anything queer about him." At least Eliza-

beth had no prejudice against prisons. She was, Lydia confessed reluctantly, as destitute of moral prejudices as it was possible for a healthy
and hearty young woman to be.

When breakfast was over and Elizabeth had whirled away to her
golf, Lydia cut the spring flowers in the garden and after she had ar-
ranged them in the dim drawing-rooms, went up-stairs to prepare herself for the meeting. As the end of her long waiting approached she
felt tremulous and depressed and, in spite of her efforts, she could
arouse no happy expectancy in her thoughts. Her face looked wan in
the mirror, and she wondered if he would find her even more changed
than she had appeared on her last visits to the prison.

Well, twenty years are too long. It is impossible to expect anything,
any bloom, any sweetness to last twenty years. Standing there, she tried
to remember the way he had looked when he had left her three days
before they were to have been married. She tried to bring back his
smile, his gaiety, his youth; but she found herself recalling him as she
had seen him in prison clothes; the coarse gray shirt hardly rougher
than the texture of his skin; the grim furrows that made his face look
as if it were cast in iron; the closely clipped hair which showed grizzled
and dry wherever it was not rubbed away; the hard, glazed eyes staring, not at her, but beyond her, into vacancy. A cold hand clutched her
heart. Yes, twenty years are too long.

In the afternoon she put on a dress of lavender crêpe—even in her
youth she had not been one for gay colors—and went down-stairs to
watch in the garden. Would he come straight up the white turnpike or
by the winding road which was called after Catlett's Mill? Lilacs were
in bloom, among them the double white lilacs her mother had loved.
Purple and black pansies edged the brick border round the bird-bath
and robins were flitting over the bright grass in the walks. The garden
was like a picture, and because it was like a picture she felt that she
could not sit still in the center of it. After twenty years of stillness she
longed suddenly for change.

Going up on the porch she watched the two roads again until watching them became harder to endure than the radiant silence of the garden.
Over and over a question was beating against the wall of her mind. Would
he come by the turnpike or over the old bridge at Catlett's Mill? In a little
while this fearful expectancy, this breathless waiting which seemed to
shrink from the thing it expected, made her nerves jump with apprehension, and leaving the porch she went into the cool drawing-room.

"I might as well try to distract my mind," she thought, and sat down
resolutely to a game of patience at the card-table, which was placed where
the light fell through the front window. Here, just by bending her head

sideways, she could still catch a glimpse of the turnpike trailing off amid the soft spring foliage into the powder-blue of the hills on the horizon.

At tea time Elizabeth blew in like a brightly colored flower and demanded: "Hasn't he come yet, Aunt Lydia?"

"No, dear, I'm looking for him every minute."

"May I tell William to bring tea? I'm starving."

"Yes, order tea. There's a special cake I made myself, an orange one. We needn't cut it until he comes. He—he used to like it."

Elizabeth darted out to take off her hat, and when she came back she spoke in a strained whisper. For all her arrogant sophistication a stranger would have thought that her lover, not Lydia's, was approaching.

"I think he is coming, Aunt Lydia. There is a man walking up the drive. Can you recognize him?"

Pale to her lips, Lydia glanced out of the window and shook her head. "I—I can't see, Elizabeth. My eyes are failing. But—but it must be John Henry."

"Would you rather I'd go out?" asked Elizabeth quickly, eager, for once in her selfish life, to be helpful. "There's the bell now. I'll have tea in the pantry if you'd rather see him alone."

Lydia reached out and clutched her and there was a desperate appeal in her frail grasp. "No, stay. I don't want to be alone. I don't want to be alone at first," she insisted tremulously.

Through a gray film she saw William hastening to the front door; she heard a sound in the hall; a slow, heavy step over the polished threshold; and she thought hurriedly, "I didn't know he would be like this. I didn't know he would be like this."

Her hand was taken heavily but limply, and she heard as if she were in a dream, as if she were in another life, Elizabeth's voice speaking meaningless words. "Aunt Lydia has been wonderful. You can never know how wonderful she has been. She is so faithful." The words strangled her as if they were in her throat, and she longed to cry out that she had not been faithful to this, not to this, but to something different—oh, utterly different!

At the sight of him standing there before her in new clothes, from his hat which was too small to his boots which were too large, standing there so dreadfully ceremonious, as if he belonged to some inferior class, it seemed to her that the glass globe under which she had lived for twenty years was shattered in pieces. In all her dreams of his return she had imagined him coming out wasted, broken, crushed and tragic, but not simply inferior. That was what prison had done to him. It had disciplined him into the appearance and bearing of an upper servant.

And this was worse than prison clothes, was worse, she realized, than any agony. It wasn't that he was old. He didn't strike her, in that instant of meeting, as being older than she had expected, and the thought shot through her mind: "It isn't age that happens to you in prison; it is worse." Some coarsening material was spread over the man, body and soul, as if he had undergone a process of thickening, of gradual decay. He was heavier, not only physically, but, she knew even before he spoke, mentally as well, and he appeared—there was no other word for it, she told herself despairingly—congealed, just as if the plastic substance of spirit had settled into some hard and permanent shape. There was a terrible patience about him, the patience of middle age which is denied the serene wisdom of maturity.

While they sat down and she turned to the tea-table, an intolerable pity pervaded her heart. Her own inadequacy overwhelmed her with humiliation; yet she was powerless to withstand it; she did not even wish in her suffering heart to meet the occasion triumphantly. After twenty years of waiting the hour for which she had longed so passionately had dissolved like a bubble. If only she could escape before her dream had materialized into an actual event.

Dread was the only emotion that remained in her heart, and this dread filled her with self-reproach and with an aching sympathy which she was powerless to express. "If I wasn't faithful to him, to whom was I faithful?" she found herself asking, and could find no answer in the past. Twenty years of devotion to what? To nothing. Just emptiness— just a dream that could never come true because it had no counterpart in reality. For so long she had been an ideal that she had lost the capacity, she had lost even the inclination, to become anything else.

He had sat down heavily, glancing carefully at the seat before he trusted his weight to it, and she saw that he had acquired a pathetic caution in the years of his imprisonment. In the old days he had been impetuous, venturesome, hot-headed; but now he appeared to have been drilled into a model of all the depressing virtues. He might, she thought, with bitter humor, have been a vestryman on Sunday morning, so conventional, so immaculately correct he had become on the surface. On the surface, she repeated. Was there something else, something more human and impetuous beneath? Or was there merely the same methodical, well-disciplined set of attributes in his soul?

"The garden is so lovely this spring," Elizabeth rippled on in a voice that sounded as hollow as the hour in which Lydia was living. After all, Elizabeth had her good points, and though she was ill-mannered on occasions, she was a sport, every inch of her. "When we've finished tea, we must show you the lilacs. Aunt Lydia reminds me every spring that lilacs are your favorite flowers."

He bowed with ceremonious politeness. "Yes, I'll be glad to smell lilacs again," he replied, agreeably enough, though his face did not alter.

Already she had noticed that his face never altered from its wax-like immobility; that it seemed to have lost irrevocably the power of recording any change of expression. His features were lowering in their heaviness, yet she realized that this lowering was unintentional, and she suspected that he was not even aware of it. The face of a stone mountain could not have appeared to her more permanently settled in its impassive remoteness.

"He doesn't want tea," said Elizabeth, visited by one of her brisk and playful ideas. "No male thing but a mollycoddle ever really likes tea. Haven't you got some of that old Madeira, Aunt Lydia?"

Yes, there was a bottle in the sideboard, and the keys of the sideboard were in William's keeping. One had to keep wine locked up now since prohibition had prevented drinking and put a premium on stealing. In the old days the servants never thought of taking wine from the sideboard; but now only William could be trusted not to empty the bottle as soon as one turned one's back.

"Here's an orange cake," the girl began again more brightly after the Madeira was brought and the amber wine-glasses filled. "We'll drink your health in grandpa's favorite wine, and then Aunt Lydia will cut you a slice of your favorite cake. You see, she never forgets anything."

"What would she have done," Lydia asked herself mutely, "without Elizabeth?" The younger generation might be both indecorous and immoral; but it was impossible to deny that it possessed an ingenuity of mind and a competence of manner which were superior to the feeble strategy and the fumbling tactics of the womanly woman of her own period. It knew, among other things, how to deal with a crisis; especially, Lydia reflected dispassionately, how to deal with the crises of other people. Elizabeth was dealing with this particular one better than she herself was able to do; but that might be simply, the older woman pursued with whimsical pathos, because it wasn't Elizabeth's funeral.

He had accepted the wine, she observed, with obvious relief, and she remembered, what she ought never to have forgotten, that twenty years ago the South had not adopted afternoon tea. Then nobody ever offered tea to a caller; but her mother, until her death, had punctiliously served old Madeira and slices of orange cake to her afternoon visitors. Strange, how the break of so small a custom could mark the burial of an era!

Confused but grateful, he sat there with his coarse red hands, in which the veins stood out like cords, clutching the slender stem of the wine-glass. How proud she used to be of his hands, and she recalled with a pang the way she had kissed them when he said good-by twenty years ago. Well, memories like that were only what her mother used to call "nails in a coffin."

"Yes, this is the same Madeira," she said with a laugh which contained a choked-back sob. "We have still a few bottles left for great occasions. For very great occasions," she repeated with hollow brightness, and saw that Elizabeth tossed an encouraging smile to her.

Picking up the knife, Lydia cut down into the orange cake with a firm, deep stroke. When she raised her lashes she saw that his gaze was fastened on the cake and that there was the look in them with which a famished dog watches food.

"I feel as if I could never get enough of sweet things," he said suddenly, and his voice was husky with longing.

A shiver ran over her. What unspeakable pangs he must have endured to have reduced his desires to that solitary quivering nerve of appetite! All those twenty years she had thought of his imprisonment as a spiritual martyrdom; but she realized now that the spiritual part of it had surrendered long ago—how long ago, she wondered?—to the physical torture. His chief torment had been not the longing for her, but the crude hunger for the ordinary pleasures of life. Sweet things! The craving of the palate had been sharper even than the denial of love.

While he ate and drank she watched him compassionately, but the compassion was that of a nurse, not of a lover. Though he was greedy, she saw that he tried to conceal his greediness, that he made an effort to preserve the stiff ceremoniousness of his manner. "How can I live through it?" she thought; and looking up met Elizabeth's sympathetic and yet slightly mocking eyes.

What did Elizabeth think of her now? Did she suspect, with her blade-like intelligence, that the long delusion of twenty years was at an end, that the ideal had crumbled like a deserted wasp's nest? Did the girl despise her because she could feel nothing, nothing but dread, but aversion, and because she lacked even the courage of her pitiful failure? Did Elizabeth realize now that there had never been any ideal, that there had been nothing except the vanity of faithfulness to an empty past which a generation of women had hidden under a sham of crape?

"Another slice?" Elizabeth was asking with her frank laugh. "You mustn't spoil your appetite for dinner, you know. We dine at seven and there's strawberry ice-cream unless I'm mistaken in the kindness of Aunt Lydia's intentions." Still laughing, she made a daring face at her aunt. "Now, you needn't scold me because I've betrayed your secret. Secrets, like the ladies in 'Jurgen,' which Aunt Lydia won't read," she added gaily, "exist only to be betrayed."

How like Elizabeth that was to be ashamed of her kindness and boast of her vulgarity! And had she really betrayed Lydia's secret? Fear seized the older woman and then passed quickly beneath a wave of inexpressible weariness. She would have given her life to feel; yet she could feel nothing, not even a quiver of disappointment. Had she dedicated herself for so long to unrealities that she was helpless in the presence of actual events? There were minds, she knew, that were incapable of dealing with the objective world, minds that were at home only in the fourth dimension which is beyond mortal experience. Had she become like that at the end? Could she respond only to the dream lover? Could her love, her tenderness, her passion even, be awakened only by an impalpable image?

Well, however it was, she could not change, she could not help herself now. It was too late to begin over again. The years which had starved his appetite into a famished craving for sweets had etherialized her temperament until she had lost all contact with the substance of life. Her world, she realized suddenly, with a blinding flash of insight, was a world of fabrication. Yet it was none the less the only world in which she felt that she belonged. Even if he had been different, even if twenty years had left him unchanged, it would still have been impossible for her to bridge the gulf between the dream and the actuality.

And all the time she felt, with the sharp anguish of a suddenly unbandaged vision, that he sat there in his heartrending patience, staring down, like a rapt child, at the slice of orange cake, while he held the delicate plate in his awkward hands, as if his fingers were all thumbs and he was trying to recover the right way of holding fragile china. If only she could feel anything! If only she could help him! But she could not feel, she could not help either him or herself. She had felt too much when he was not there; in the long surrender of her soul she had lost the force of will which might have saved her in the supreme crisis of life. If she was unreal now, it was because she had never from the beginning been anything else.

Presently Elizabeth stood up. "I told the girls to come over in the garden for tennis," she said. "There they are at the gate, so I'll leave you and Aunt Lydia together. I know you will have all the silence of twenty years to make up." She caught her aunt's eye and added hastily, "Unless, of course, you would rather come out and watch us play. It is a glorious afternoon out-of-doors."

Having placed his wine-glass precisely in the center of his plate, John Henry put the plate on the table and stood up slowly and cautiously while he looked doubtfully from Elizabeth to Lydia and then back again to Elizabeth. Was he afraid of moving too quickly, or was it, Lydia asked herself, simply that his joints had hardened like his features into the mold of the prison? His impassive face had not changed, but there was a flicker in his eyes when he glanced at the girl, the same flicker of suppressed youth with which he had watched the orange cake while it was cut. In a flash the knowledge came to Lydia that for him also the moment was not without its dull tragedy. What he wanted was not the youth of twenty years ago, but the living youth, the youth that he had never known, of today.

"Would you like to watch the girls play?" she repeated. "Or would you rather sit indoors and hear about the people you know?"

Again he turned from her to Elizabeth, and the flicker of interest brightened into a flame of wonder or admiration. "I'd like to watch the girls," he replied, almost eagerly. "I feel as if I could never get enough of young things."

Elizabeth met her aunt's eyes with her mocking gaze which was so artless and yet so incredibly wise. "You are coming too, aren't you, Aunt Lydia?"

"Not yet, dear. Take him with you. I'll come presently."

"Well, I'll take him, of course." A frown of exasperation wrinkled the girl's forehead. "He can sit on a bench in the sunshine, but I think you ought to come with him."

There was a note in Elizabeth's tone which made Lydia want to laugh or to cry. It made no difference which; one would do as well as the other.

"Not now, a little later. I like to watch you play, but—but I've something more important to attend to."

At this Elizabeth laughed, and her laugh was one of relief. "Oh, I know, you want to go back to your housekeeping. You've just thought of something perfectly delicious you forgot to order for dinner."

John Henry turned and looked at her. "You will come in a little while, won't you, Lydia?" he asked as solemnly as if he were addressing the prison board.

"In a few minutes, yes. Go with Elizabeth."

As they went out, she rose from her chair and walked slowly across the room which looked on the bowers of lilacs and the grassy squares where robins were still flitting back and forth in the soft afternoon sunlight. She felt tired; she felt unutterably old, as old as the last century; but she felt, she realized presently, a relief that was infinite. Though she was old, she was herself again; she was not an ideal; she was not any longer merely the living embodiment of an outgrown virtue. The weight of another epoch had fallen from her shoulders, and she stood erect and dauntless for the first time in twenty years. Never again would she crawl back under her glass case; never again would she merit the epitaph, "She is so faithful." For twenty years she also had been in prison, but she had found her perilous freedom at last.

Turning away from the window, through which merry voices were floating, she went over to the card-table and, smiling happily, swept the cards to the floor with the first unrestrained gesture of her life. A sense of release like a strong wind swept through her being. She felt the stirring of inanimate forms within, as if the wax flowers of her soul were warming at last into living bloom. In that one instant of spiritual liberation she saw a vision of the future which was like a new world rising out of the dim chaos of the old.

Youth, denied, suppressed, defeated, edged the vague outline of that promised land with the enkindled glory of adventure. She forgot that she was middle-aged and remembered only that she had never lived. Not love, not motherhood, but simply the freedom to be herself, appeared to her as the crown and the fulfilment of life. She saw herself a happy wanderer with the alluring wide world before her. She saw countries of gold and ivory and exotic perfumes; she saw horizons that melted like dawn into the purple mist of tropical seas. All the strange places and the ardent enterprises that she had missed in her youth!

"I can go now. I am free. I am no longer tied," she thought wildly, with her enraptured gaze on the vision.

"Aunt Lydia! Aunt Lydia!" Faint at first as a distant bell and then ringing loud and clear in her ears she heard Elizabeth's voice. "Poor Aunt Lydia! She had waited so long for her happiness!"

"Something has happened," she thought, and again before the girl reached her, "something has happened!" Walking as if she were asleep she moved through the French window and down into the garden, where she met Elizabeth running toward her.

"Oh, poor Aunt Lydia, you must be brave! You must be braver than ever!" cried the girl while the tears ran down her face. "Not dead. Oh, no, it isn't as bad as that. But he is ill. It came so suddenly while he was watching the girls. Paralysis, the gardener says. Yes, one of the boys has rushed off in the car for the doctor. Oh, Aunt Lydia, Aunt Lydia, after you had waited so long!"

Running ahead of the girl, Lydia turned the corner of the rose-arbor and reached the square of grass by the bird-bath, where John Henry was still sitting on a green bench, with his feet in a border of pansies and his eyes, with their dreadful gravity, turned to the sky. Robert, the gardener, was bending over him; his collar had been already loosened, and his ill-fitting clothes appeared to accentuate the intolerable appeal of his helplessness. While she stood there watching the confused efforts to revive him, she felt that she was turning slowly to wax again after her brief hour of bloom. Pity as terrible as passion was closing over her spirit.

A hand pushed her aside, and a doctor hurried by to the motionless figure on the green bench. Elizabeth's arms were about her, and there sounded in her ears, like the sobbing of waves on a distant beach, the faint echo of that public sympathy in which she had been submerged and suffocated in her youth.

"She has waited so long. She has been so faithful," chanted the Greek chorus of destiny.

For an eternity she heard nothing but this tragic refrain. Then Elizabeth spoke in the clear and determined accents of one who is merely the mouthpiece of the invisible Powers.

"It isn't the worst, Aunt Lydia. Even if he is never well again, he will live a long time for you to take care of him."

Affectionate, noisy, admiring, they closed in about her. Though she longed to cry out: "But this was not what I meant. I haven't waited for this," she felt suddenly that she had become as inarticulate as an image. She had had her moment and it was over. For forty-five years she had been only what they had expected her to be, and it was too late now to break away from the pattern into which she had grown.

"If anything can keep him alive it will be your beautiful faithfulness, Miss Lydia," murmured the young doctor, whose father had been in love with her twenty-five years ago.

She smiled faintly her smile of perfect acquiescence, and it was upon this smile, she felt, that the glass globe shut down forever.

Note

This story was originally published in *Hearst's International* combined with *Cosmopolitan* 80, no. 1 (Jan. 1926): 24–29, 140, 142, and 144. Two-color illustrations by W. Smithson Broadhead appeared on pages 24–25, 26–27, and 29. The story has apparently never been reprinted.

※

Ellen Glasgow's "Ideals"
A "New" Story from the 1920s

Martha E. Cook

The January 1926 issue of *Hearst's International* combined with *Cosmopolitan* magazine lists a tantalizing group of authors on its cover, headed "All These." At the top of the list, obviously designed to attract the newsstand browser, is the name of Ellen Glasgow, followed by Irvin Cobb, Fannie Hurst, Ring W. Lardner, W. Somerset Maugham, and others. Glasgow's contribution, apparently never reprinted, is entitled "Ideals"; the text of the short story is illustrated by W. Smithson Broadhead. The opening two pages, emblazoned with the phrase "A New—and Totally Different—Story by the Author of 'Barren Ground,'" show an attractive young woman, dressed in current fashion, with golf clubs slung over her shoulder, and an older woman, also attractive, clad in soft clothing of no particular style, with gardening shears and a basket of just-cut flowers; both gaze toward the reader. The illustration is labeled "Elizabeth, of the new century, and Lydia, of the old" (25). Broadhead, a British artist popular with *Cosmopolitan* editors in the 1920s and 1930s, was an excellent choice for Glasgow's work, since he was gifted at capturing the spirit of a text and could portray characters of all social classes with skill (see, for example, his illustrations for A. J. Cronin's *The Stars Look Down*, serialized from June through November 1935).

Notwithstanding Glasgow's own statements about her lack of interest in and talent for short fiction, and despite critics' and scholars' staunch proclamations for decades about her ceasing to publish short stories with "Romance and Sally Byrd" in *Woman's Home Companion* for December 1924 (see, for example, Godbold 134), this text provides the reader with further indication of what Glasgow could accomplish within the limits of the genre. "Ideals" is important in several ways, not the least being to serve as a reminder that we may know less about the boundaries of Glasgow's canon than we thought. She published seven stories in *The Shadowy Third and Other Stories* (1923). A previously unpublished story, "The Professional Instinct," was edited by William W. Kelly for publication in *Western Humanities Review* in 1962. Richard Meeker collected these and four others in a 1963 edition; the same twelve are listed as "Stories in Periodicals" in Kelly's 1964 bibliography of Glasgow's works (116–18).

Julius Rowan Raper, in a 1977 article in the *Southern Literary Journal*, later incorporated into his book *From the Sunken Garden: The Fiction of Ellen Glasgow, 1916–1945* (1980), refers to "thirteen short stories" (53), apparently adding Glasgow's first known published story, "A Woman of To-Morrow" (*Short Stories*, 1895). He later reprinted it in *Ellen Glasgow's Reasonable Doubts: A Collection of Her Writings* (1–14). Now we add a story from thirty years later to a list of works of short fiction that we may find important for their own merit as well as for light they shed on other works by Glasgow. Raper has convincingly argued that from Glasgow's "experiments in characterization" in her short fiction "emerged the psychological insight that distinguishes the novels she began to publish with *Barren Ground* in 1925 from those she wrote before 1916" (53).

No evidence to date would lead the critic or scholar to seek out *Hearst's International* combined with *Cosmopolitan* for this date—or any other—to track down a "new" Glasgow story. What we know would lead one to assume that searching volumes of this publication could only prove futile. Ellen Glasgow wrote, for instance, to her agent, Paul Revere Reynolds, in 1917 regarding the publication of "Dare's Gift": "Please get me the largest price you possibly can—even if it has to go to the *Cosmopolitan*. I couldn't appear in *Hearst's Magazine* or in some others" (Colvert 195). Glasgow's reluctance to be associated with *Cosmopolitan* in that era is understandable. Frank Luther Mott explains in *A History of American Magazines* that in *Cosmopolitan*, which William Randolph Hearst had purchased in 1905, "the dominant subject in every number from 1912 until 1918 was sex—sex in society, sex in adventure, sex in mystery" (4:497).

Glasgow's antipathy to *Hearst's Magazine* of those years probably stems not from its fiction, which Mott calls "outstanding" (4:501), but from the controversial political views of William Randolph Hearst (see, for example, Carlson and Bates 188–93). Glasgow was able to place "Dare's Gift" in the prestigious monthly *Harper's Magazine* for February-March 1917, though it did not pay as much as the Hearst-owned *Good Housekeeping* (Colvert 195), in which she published two stories,

"Thinking Makes It So" (February 1917) and "The Past" (October 1920). After Hearst took over *Good Housekeeping* in 1911, it became "popular as a fiction magazine" (Mott 5:133).

Years later, in 1932, Glasgow wrote to Daniel Longwell about a possible deal for a serial: "I simply cannot see myself or my book in *The Cosmopolitan.* All my life at a sacrifice, I have stood against the commercialization of my work" (*Letters* 117). Not only did she not want to publish her novels serially—she seems to have turned down an offer of $20,000 in 1930 for a serial (Colvert 196)—but in 1925 *Cosmopolitan* had merged with *Hearst's International* and carried both titles for many years. However, in a note in Glasgow's papers at the University of Virginia, there is one comment that on close reading reveals that while Glasgow had at times made the choice to publish in magazines such as *Hearst's,* at other times she had made sacrifices rather than do so: "I have never, since I preferred to go without things rather than win them by means I regarded as distasteful, been obliged to submit myself or my way of writing to the popular magazines or the moving pictures" (undated note, Papers of Ellen Glasgow). [In *Ellen Glasgow and the Woman Within,* E. Stanly Godbold, Jr., recalls Glasgow's brief encounters with the film industry (214, 287).]

From our perspective late in the twentieth century, such matters as an author's having published in popular periodicals of the nineteenth and twentieth centuries, as many serious women writers did, bear less relationship to the quality of fiction than literary critics once believed. The lines between literature and popular culture have blurred; the reading audience has likewise become more meaningful to the literary critic, especially in reader-response criticism. I was delighted to uncover this story in *Cosmopolitan* and am tantalized by the possibility of others yet undiscovered.

The most interesting aspect of this "new" story from the Roaring Twenties is that, despite a contrived plot, Glasgow uses modernist techniques to portray the theme of entrapment through her protagonist. "Aunt Lydia" to her niece Elizabeth, "Miss Lydia" to the young doctor, she is an important addition to the works in Glasgow's canon that are of particular interest to the feminist critic.

"Ideals" opens with a recounting of Lydia's past, a sad, generally predictable tale of love for a man who "is not a safe man to marry" by one who "belonged to that magnanimous generation of women who married men to reform them" (24). On the eve of the wedding, "when the wedding-cake . . . was actually in the oven," John Henry shot a man and was sent to prison for twenty years (25). Lydia waits and hopes, reaching after ten years "a passive expectancy" (28). Learning that John Henry is being released after eighteen years, she confesses to Elizabeth that rather than having shot his victim in a fit of anger over a game of cards, as everyone has believed, John Henry had lost his temper in a jealous quarrel over her (140). Lydia, aided by Elizabeth, prepares for John Henry's return. To her dismay, she realizes that his time in prison has not changed him in any dramatic or romantic way; rather, "It had disciplined him into the appearance and bearing of an upper servant" (142).

After an agonizing scene in which John Henry betrays the coarseness of his desires after years of imprisonment—"I feel as if I could never get enough of sweet things" like the orange cake made from Lydia's mother's recipe (142) and "of young things" like Elizabeth (144)—the climax and denouement come quickly. He accompanies Elizabeth to watch her young friends playing tennis. Lydia, alone inside the house, realizes that she can release herself from her commitment to John Henry and move forward with her own life. At that moment Elizabeth rushes in with the news that John Henry has collapsed. Rather than die and leave Lydia with her freedom, "he will live a long time for you to take care of him," as Elizabeth proclaims with unsuspecting irony (144).

Early in the story Glasgow describes Lydia as having "had the misfortune to fall between two eras" (25). Though John Henry offered to release her from any vows, she chose to wait. She was viewed in the past as "an ideal," living the circumscribed life of "a nun in a convent" (25, 26). Now she sees herself as existing in "an age when ideals had gone hopelessly out of fashion" (26). Though she has aged, she is "lovely in a rare and distinguished fashion which youth, as long as it was only youth, could never hope to possess" (27). Earlier Lydia romantically believed she and John Henry "shall have grown old together." After a period of frenetic activity, she has succumbed to "the supreme consolation of being faithful to an ideal" and settled into life in a circumscribed space, with limited activity and a stagnant set of ideals. Glasgow clearly wants her reader to compare Lydia to the Civil War widows who might still be seen in the South of the 1920s. Perhaps her epitaph will be "She was so faithful," the phrase she and others repeatedly apply to her character (28).

Attitudes change after World War I, when "Not an ideal was left alive in the world" (28). Lydia, unchanging, dresses in the same soft colors and wears her hair in the same prim style of her youth (very effectively depicted in Broadhead's illustrations); Elizabeth, in sharp contrast, is described as "a dark, robust, flashing girl, with an intrepid gaze and a full mouth which she painted a violent crimson" (28). Yet Glasgow seems to reverse the stereotyped attitudes of the Victorian lady and the Jazz Age flapper. Lydia's Victorian mother says to her *fin de siècle* daughter, surprisingly, "You have made yourself a prisoner in the past" (28). In the next generation Elizabeth unpredictably at first views her aunt as a static but admirable object like "a genuine Gilbert Stuart or Thomas Sully hanging on one's wall" (29).

After relying on conventional metaphors of convents and prisons for more than half the story, Glasgow cleverly introduces her most powerful symbol of entrapment. Lydia and Elizabeth discuss John Henry's imminent return: "'I loved him very much, you know,' sighed Lydia, unaware that she had spoken in the past tense, while she drew a long breath as if her loyalty were dying for lack of air" (140). This last phrase, "dying for lack of air," anticipates the controlling image of the text:

> [I]t seemed to her that she was imprisoned like a wax wreath under one of the glass globes of the nineteenth century. They had kept her there under glass because they enjoyed showing her off; and she had been too passive, too waxen in her conventionality, to break the globe and escape while she was still young. (140)

Glasgow skillfully utilizes this image through to the closing passage of the story. Though the niece, Elizabeth, has earlier respected Lydia's devotion to the absent John Henry, she later exclaims, "As man to man, . . . haven't you ever wanted to smash your glass case and get out?" (140). While Lydia waits for John Henry, she plays the card game patience (a common term for solitaire, especially in England), which she has taken up to while away her solitary hours. Finally he appears. At first glance of his "new clothes, from his hat which was too small to his boots which were too large, . . . it seemed to her that the glass globe under which she had lived for twenty years was shattered in pieces" (142). When John Henry leaves after tea to accompany Elizabeth outside, the story seems to reach its climax. Lydia has an epiphany: "Though she was old, she was herself again; she was not an ideal. . . . Never again would she crawl back under her glass case" (144).

Glasgow then uses the ironically named game of patience to allow Lydia a grand gesture: "she . . . swept the cards to the floor with the first unrestrained gesture of her life. . . . She felt the stirring of inanimate forms within, as if the wax flowers of her soul were warming at last into living bloom." She looks to the "future"; she thinks, "I am free" (144). As Glasgow's powerful words reveal, reinforced by Broadhead's masterful illustration (29), Lydia's patience is at an end. She is ready to stop playing cards and start living.

But Glasgow is too much the realist, the ironist, to allow the story to conclude here. Lydia is called outside; when she views John Henry collapsed in a state of paralysis, she feels that she is "turning slowly to wax again after her brief hour of bloom" (144). When the young doctor invokes "your beautiful faithfulness," Glasgow reveals the true irony of Lydia's belief that she can escape her entrapment: "She smiled faintly her smile of perfect acquiescence, and it was upon this smile, she felt, that the glass globe shut down forever" (144). Surely 1920s readers sensed the oppressiveness of duty and other ideals of the Victorian era as Glasgow described this icon of that age. Perhaps no other image could sum up the repressiveness of the period of Lydia's youth—and Glasgow's— more effectively than this glass case, enclosing not even once-living flowers but waxen ones.

The editors of *Cosmopolitan* call attention to the differences between the story "Ideals" and Glasgow's most recent novel, *Barren Ground* (1925), as I have indicated above. One could list many ways in which the story is indeed "Totally Different" (24); perhaps this phrase serves as a warning to the careful reader not to expect the same kind of freedom that Dorinda Oakley achieves. However, the two texts raise similar questions about women's choices and what forces determine their actions. After Dorinda is jilted by Jason Greylock, she is able to take charge of her life; years later she chooses to nurse Jason in his last illness. Glasgow describes Dorinda after Jason's funeral as "suffocated, . . . buried alive beneath an emptiness" (506). However, after a night of mental and physical pain caused by her desire to "live over the past again and live it differently," Dorinda looks out over her land and thinks she will "find happiness again" (506, 509). Glasgow makes Dorinda's suffocation temporary, while entrapment is Lydia's past and her future.

Encountering the story "Ideals" in 1926, loyal followers of Glasgow's fiction might also have identified a common theme of waiting to be found in the novel *Virginia* (1913). Dorothy M. Scura has made a strong case for the relationship between *Virginia* and Glasgow's comments on feminism, particularly the woman's suffrage movement (see especially 36–37). Like the character Virginia, Lydia in her mid-forties is perceived as old. Rather than the ambiguous ending of the earlier novel, with Virginia's son's return, the story closes with a conclusive image of entrapment.

A reader who had enjoyed "The Artless Age," published in the *Saturday Evening Post* for 25 August 1923, would recognize Glasgow's hand in "Ideals" at once. In both, Glasgow portrays flappers of the Jazz Age in a sympathetic way, seeming to respond positively to their youth and exuberance and not to focus on a loosening of manners and morals. In this way "Ideals" is closely related as well to the novel *The Romantic Comedians*, published the same year, with Glasgow's surprisingly warm portrayal of Annabel Upchurch. However, "The Artless Age" uses irony lightheartedly, so the ending of "Ideals" might have come as a shock. In this story Glasgow is willing to offer some hope of freedom for young women like Elizabeth, but not for those from an earlier generation. By the end of the decade, she had become more cynical about the lack of responsibility exhibited by women who were granted such freedom, as we see in the characterization of Milly Upchurch and Mary Victoria Littlepage in *They Stooped to Folly* (1929).

If "Ideals" is indeed Glasgow's final work of short fiction, it gives us an important perspective on her maturity from the time of "A Woman of To-Morrow," in which she naively envisions her female protagonist becoming "an Associate Justice of the Supreme Court" (11), or "Between Two Shores" (*McClure's Magazine*, February 1899), where the protagonist willingly entraps herself in a relationship with a man who has committed a murder, believing that therein lie true fulfillment and happiness. In the later text of "Ideals," of course, we see that Lydia has lost all illusions, though in the end she seems incapable of violating society's traditional expectations of women.

"Ideals" provides an important example of Glasgow's treatment of mature women characters, especially in the novels of the 1920s in which such characters are sometimes seen to speak for Glasgow. They respect tradition, but do not condemn change. There is Corinna Page in *One Man in His Time* (1922), who is governed by "that irresistible instinct for things as they ought to be" (310). Glasgow has her reject her unworthy suitor, John Benham (easily identified with Glasgow's own suitor, Henry Anderson), and resolve to go on with her life.

Glasgow's characterization of Lydia is actually more complex than that of Corinna or of Amanda Lightfoot in *The Romantic Comedians*, who "belonged to that fortunate generation of women who had no need to think, since everything was decided for them by the feelings of a lady and the Episcopal Church" (143). Amanda has long loved Judge Gamaliel Honeywell, who has married two other women and at the close of the novel is lusting after another, the youngest of all.

There are also parallels between Lydia and a minor character in *They Stooped to Folly*. Louisa, spinster friend of Virginius Littlepage and of his deceased wife, the aptly named Victoria, has come to understand the contrast of the new freedom of the postwar decade with the "deceit" of the days of her Victorian girlhood. She believes she has "lived through the ages of waiting" (331); yet at the conclusion of the novel, she seems doomed to looking after Virginius's daughter, Mary Victoria, and her expected child.

There may be another connection between Ellen Glasgow and her creation Lydia, one that might have been sensed by a few close friends and relatives of Glasgow's at the time of the publication of "Ideals." It is possible that Glasgow here conveys her entrapment by her loss of hearing through Lydia's entrapment by her sense of duty. Glasgow writes, for example, in her spiritual autobiography, *The Woman Within,* "there was no escape from that closing barrier of deafness which held me, imprisoned, with my sorrow and my memories. Not for a solitary minute in time could that wall of silence be broken through or pushed back into nothingness" (195). While Lydia is enclosed spiritually, emotionally, rather than physically, the image of the glass globe may have held a double meaning for its creator.

In "Ideals," Ellen Glasgow at first appears to be writing a new story of women who came of age in the Victorian period. She may actually have considered revising the traditional view, allowing her protagonist to escape the glass globe of duty and faithfulness. However, in the end Glasgow is not willing to grant Lydia the release that Kate Chopin gives to Mrs. Mallard in her turn-of-the-century "Story of an Hour." Believing herself freed by her husband's death, Mrs. Mallard collapses and dies when he reappears; onlookers mistake her grief for joy. Instead, Glasgow utilizes a powerful modernist technique to create the entrapment from which Lydia cannot escape. One of Glasgow's literary descendants, Sylvia Plath, creates a comparable symbol in her 1963 novel, *The Bell Jar.* At its conclusion, Plath's protagonist, after being trapped literally by madness in an institution and symbolically under a bell jar, walks through an open door, a symbol of at least the possibility of freedom for women in a new age. But to Glasgow there is no open door for Lydia in the 1920s.

Works Cited

Carlson, Oliver, and Ernest Sutherland Bates. *Hearst: Lord of San Simeon.* New York: Viking, 1936.

Colvert, James B. "Agent and Author: Ellen Glasgow's Letters to Paul Revere Reynolds." *Studies in Bibliography* 14 (1961): 177–96.

Glasgow, Ellen. *Barren Ground.* Garden City: Doubleday, 1925.

———. *The Collected Stories of Ellen Glasgow.* Ed. Richard K. Meeker. Baton Rouge: Louisiana State UP, 1963.

———. "Ideals." *Cosmopolitan* 80.1 (January 1926): 24–29, 140, 142, 144.

———. *Letters of Ellen Glasgow.* Ed. Blair Rouse. New York: Harcourt, 1958.

———. *One Man in His Time.* Garden City: Doubleday, 1922.

———. *The Romantic Comedians.* Garden City: Doubleday, 1926.

———. *They Stooped to Folly.* New York: Literary Guild, 1929.

———. Undated note. Papers of Ellen Glasgow (#5060), Manuscripts Division, Special Collections Department, University of Virginia Library.

———. "A Woman of To-Morrow." *Ellen Glasgow's Reasonable Doubts: A Collection of Her Writings.* Ed. Julius Rowan Raper. Baton Rouge: Louisiana State UP, 1988. 1–14.

———. *The Woman Within.* New York: Harcourt, 1954.

Godbold, E. Stanly, Jr. *Ellen Glasgow and the Woman Within.* Baton Rouge: Louisiana State UP, 1972.

Kelly, William W., ed. *Ellen Glasgow: A Bibliography.* Charlottesville: UP of Virginia, 1964.

Mott, Frank Luther. *A History of American Magazines.* Vol. 4, *1885–1905.* Cambridge: Harvard UP, 1957.

———. *A History of American Magazines.* Vol. 5, *Sketches of Twenty-One Magazines, 1905–1930.* Cambridge: Harvard UP, 1968.

Raper, Julius Rowan. *From the Sunken Garden: The Fiction of Ellen Glasgow, 1916–1945.* Baton Rouge: Louisiana State UP, 1980.

Scura, Dorothy M. "A Knowledge in the Heart: Ellen Glasgow, the Women's Movement, and *Virginia.*" *American Literary Realism* 22.2 (Winter 1990): 30–43.

PART II

Autobiography

The Romance of Self-Representation
Glasgow and *The Woman Within*

Nancy A. Walker

One overwhelming theme in recent studies of autobiography—which have themselves been overwhelming in number—is what autobiography does *not* tell us: that is to say, the truth. This is not simply a postmodernist commentary on the elusiveness of truth itself, but rather a recognition that in all forms of autobiographical writing, even the most personal, such as the letter or diary, the moment a reader becomes possible, the writer becomes creator rather than mere recorder, shaping the telling—by means of selection, omission, arrangement, style, and emphasis—to construct a self that is to some degree fictive. To shape what the reader will thus "know" is an act of power. But the act of power collides with and is complicated by a kind of powerlessness that has taken on particular meaning in a post-Freudian age: the inability to know fully one's own "self"—and, indeed, a calling into question of the very notion of unitary selfhood. Thus Shari Benstock writes:

> Autobiography reveals gaps, and not only gaps in time and space or between the individual and the social, but also a widening divergence between the manner and matter of its discourse. That is, autobiography reveals the impossibility of its own dream: what begins on the presumption of self-knowledge ends in the creation of a fiction that covers over the premises of its construction. (11)

That the presentation of a realized "self" and "truth" in autobiography might cause additional problems for women has also been suggested by a number of contemporary scholars. Autobiography—the writing of one's life experiences—presupposes at least the illusion of individualism, and individuality is the property of the privileged. As Susan

Friedman writes, "It is also the privilege of power. A white man has the luxury of forgetting his skin color and sex. He can think of himself as an 'individual.' Women and minorities, reminded at every turn in the great cultural hall of mirrors of their sex or color, have no such luxury" (39).

Ellen Glasgow lived in a place and time in which what Friedman calls "the great cultural hall of mirrors" reflected a particularly fragmented set of images. She came to maturity as a southern woman in the era of the "New Woman." While the ideal for members of her social class was the "lady," with all of its accompanying baggage—a baggage that was itself highly conflicted—of purity and condescension, social responsibility and inherent racism, Glasgow was, as Elizabeth Ammons has recently argued, one of a group of turn-of-the-century women writers who regarded themselves not as "writers," as had the women of the nineteenth century, but as "artists." And to be artists meant that these women had somehow "to claim for themselves the territory of Art—powerful, difficult to negotiate—that in western culture had been defined and staked out by white privileged men as their own" (Ammons 10). To claim to be an artist therefore required an act of self-creation, and it should not surprise us that the outlines of a fictive self are evident in such ostensibly revelatory autobiographical works as Glasgow's *The Woman Within.*

In his 1972 biography, *Ellen Glasgow: The Woman Within,* E. Stanly Godbold, Jr., perhaps unwittingly reveals his own ambivalence about the "truth" of *The Woman Within.* While Godbold calls the autobiography "extraordinarily frank and accurate," and speaks of the "candor" with which Glasgow presents "the whole truth of her own life," he also points out that in preparation for writing what she began in 1934 with the working title "The Autobiography of an Exile," Glasgow read James Joyce's *Portrait of the Artist as a Young Man* and "set out to prove that her own suffering had been greater than that of any other artist" (208–9). This suggests the creation of a *persona* large enough to at once carry the burden of the classic suffering artist in the masculine tradition and reinforce the traditionally feminine notion of suffering as metaphor for womanhood itself. Godbold finally concedes that "the reader cannot help suspecting that she did not suffer quite so much as she pretended and must have found her extraordinary success in her own lifetime to be at least some consolation for the agonies of her inner conflicts" (210). The memoir, he concludes, presents a double image of Glasgow: "the woman who is shrieking but cannot be heard" and the "Great Lady of Richmond" (210; Godbold quoting Alfred Kazin and John Cook Wyllie). Both images are potentially susceptible to public judgment, and as

Sidonie Smith points out in *A Poetics of Women's Autobiography*, women who place themselves in public view by recording their lives may run particular risks of which they are on some level aware:

> Attuned to the ways women have been dressed up for public exposure, attuned also to the price women pay for public self-disclosure, the autobiographer reveals in her speaking posture and narrative structure her understanding of the possible readings she will receive from a public that has the power of her reputation in its hands. (49)

From the time she began writing *The Woman Within* in 1934, Glasgow seemed to have in mind a potential readership. As early as 1935, she signed a contract with Harcourt, Brace for posthumous publication of the manuscript, and as chapters were completed they were carefully sealed in envelopes that were subsequently placed in a briefcase in a bank vault to await the action of her literary executors. *The Woman Within* was completed in 1944, less than two years before her death, and was published in 1954.

Yet at several points in *The Woman Within*, Glasgow expresses doubts about the eventual publication of her memoir. Writing about her first adult acquaintance with James Branch Cabell, for example, she seems to fear that she is revealing too much:

> What I am writing now of that spring in Williamsburg, when he was graduated from the College of William and Mary, may never be published. But, then, as I go on, trying to write the simple truth of things, without vanity or evasion, I begin to wonder whether I should wish any of this autobiography to be given to strangers—or even to friends who are still strangers. So I am recording these episodes chiefly in the endeavor to attain a clearer understanding of my own dubious identity and of the confused external world in which I have lived. (130)

Later, just before writing about her meeting with the man she calls "Harold S—," Glasgow again expresses reservations about her autobiographical enterprise. In this instance, she seems reluctant to retrieve the memory of the relationship. Chapter 18 of *The Woman Within*, titled "Fata Morgana," begins, "If a note of hesitation or reluctance has crept into these memoirs, it can mean only that I have come to the one episode I dread most to live over again" (213). But a page or so later, she concludes that "fidelity to life is the sole merit I can attribute to these more or less incoherent memoirs" and that "[t]heir value as psychology depends upon their unqualified truth as autobiography." "From the beginning," she continues, "I resolved that the appeal of this book, whether or not it was ever published, should rest upon intellectual and emotional veracity, and upon that basis alone" (214).

What these two sets of comments reveal, in addition to understandable reservations about the response of unknown future readers, is that Glasgow wrote *The Woman Within* at least in part as a way of coming to understand herself. During the years that she wrote her memoir, she was seeing a psychiatrist periodically, a fact that seems mirrored in the language of *The Woman Within* when she speaks of her "dubious identity" and of the value of her memoirs as "psychology." Indeed, the conflicts revealed in the autobiography are fundamental ones that could well prompt an effort at self-discovery. The first of these she identifies as the effect of the differences between her kind, unselfish mother, whose natural gaiety was worn away by the birth of ten children, and her stern, Calvinistic father, who, in Glasgow's words, "never committed a pleasure" (15). Her description of her father recalls Emily Dickinson's comment that her father's heart was "pure and terrible," and, like Dickinson, she rebelled in part by refusing to embrace the religious tradition she had inherited. Her claim that she "inherited nothing from him, except the color of my eyes and a share in a trust fund" (16) seems contradicted by her description of refusing to attend church, when she meets his stubbornness with one of equal force.

A conflict less openly acknowledged by Glasgow is her ambivalence about her native Richmond, Virginia, which is related to her anger at the fact that her fiction was not awarded the honors she felt it deserved. The term *exile* in her working title refers more to a psychic than to a geographical condition; despite long trips to England and Europe, extended visits to New York, and, in later years, summers spent in Maine, she always returned to Richmond—returned, in fact, to the house in which she and her brothers and sisters had grown up, and in which she lived for fifty-seven of her seventy-two years. In part, such a return to her native South was necessary for her art—for her ambitious and finely realized project of charting in her fiction the changes in southern sensibility from the period of the Civil War to the 1930s. The characters in her novels, she writes, "needed their own place and soil and atmosphere" (195), and she speaks of coming back to Richmond as a return "from a long exile" (216). Yet the real exile that comes through the pages of *The Woman Within* is a sense of personal, individual alienation—a self-imposed detachment from place, from emotional ties, and from a world that she increasingly perceived as inhumane and lacking in intellectual substance. This sense of isolation begins early in

Glasgow's narrative. She recalls that when she was seven, she was devastated when her beloved "Mammy" left to work for another family:

> It was the beginning of that sense of loss, of exile in solitude, which I
> was to bear with me to the end. . . . I knew suddenly that I was alone. I
> had always been alone. *Nobody could come near enough to shut out the loneli-*
> *ness.* (30–31; emphasis added)

The last sentence in this passage suggests not that other people fail to
give her affection and companionship, but rather that she holds the
world at arm's length.

The South whose history nurtured her fiction offered Glasgow little
intellectual stimulation. "I had always done both my reading and my
thinking alone," she writes, because "I have known intimately, in the
South at least, few persons really interested in books more profound
than 'sweet stories'" (216). She describes Richmond social life as frivolous and superficial:

> When I went out to parties in Richmond, I talked of Tom, Dick, and
> Harry. Even if I had never heard of them before, I still talked of them.
> I talked of whether they were engaged or were not engaged, of whether
> they were to be married or to be divorced, of how much they had paid
> for their curtains, and whether marquisette was really more fashionable
> than the Brussels lace our grandmothers favored. (217)

New York was little better, "scarcely less flat and stale than the familiar climate of Richmond" (139). Glasgow's sense of herself as an outsider to the American literary establishment comes through clearly in
her description of "the various authors who would soon become, by
self-election, the Forty Immortals of the American Academy" (139).
Of these authors—all male, and including William Dean Howells,
Hamlin Garland, and Richard Watson Gilder—she writes bitterly,
"When they were not, as Charles Lamb once remarked of a similar
coterie, 'encouraging one another in mediocrity,' they were gravely pre-
paring work for one another to praise" (139–40). In sharp contrast to
these comments are Glasgow's warm and richly detailed memories of
her meetings in England with that country's literary establishment, including Thomas Hardy, Joseph Conrad, John Galsworthy, and Arnold
Bennett. She seems to have felt herself to be in less direct competition
with these luminaries. (Interestingly, only two of Britain's female writ-

ers are referred to admiringly in *The Woman Within:* Vita Sackville-West, whom Glasgow met, and Virginia Woolf, whom she did not.)

Glasgow's sense that she has not been accorded the attention she deserves is one of several similarities between her autobiography and that of Margaret Halsey, *No Laughing Matter: The Autobiography of a WASP*, published in 1977. Halsey, a social critic and humorist best known for her 1938 best-seller, *With Malice toward Some*, records in her autobiography her bitter disappointment that her analyses of several of America's social problems, including *Color Blind* (1946) and *The Pseudo-Ethic* (1963), were not widely embraced as the important statements she believed them to be. "I thought I had written a Deathless Message," she writes, "which would eventually take its place in people's minds and hearts a little below the Gettysburg Address" (118). Halsey's books addressing race relations, materialism, and ethics in government were each published at least a decade prior to widespread public concern about these issues, so that, unlike Glasgow, she did not attract a large readership for her work. Held in tension in *No Laughing Matter* are her dual and contradictory motives for writing her autobiography: to confess her lifelong sense of moral superiority, and simultaneously to vindicate herself by pointing out how right she had been about the problems of American society. The first of these motives allows Halsey to take a mocking, ironic look at herself. For example, recalling her reaction when her book *The Folks at Home* was virtually ignored by the press, Halsey writes, "Confronted with such a rejection, what was the happy Protestant—the self-appointed guide to the Good, the True, and the Beautiful—going to do next? That was the problem" (167). The irony that Halsey thus directs at herself, Glasgow reserves for the "Forty Immortals of the American Academy," from whose charmed circle she feels excluded.

A further similarity between *The Woman Within* and Halsey's *No Laughing Matter* is the way in which the authors connect isolation and rejection—real or imagined—with illness. Frequent illness clouds Glasgow's childhood, and increasing deafness marks her adult years. In Halsey's case the illness is emotional: agoraphobia and dependence on alcohol. Both deafness and agoraphobia are, in their different ways, extreme forms of isolation, forcing their victims to inhabit a largely private world rather than the public arena they sought with their writing, and reinforcing the traditional split between the woman writer's private and public selves—the former suffering at least in part because of the latter. That one of the purposes of autobiography is to explore this private, isolated self is articulated by Halsey in *No Laughing Matter* in a way that seems to comment directly upon *The Woman Within:* "Every self-respecting autobiography—and this one is no exception—has intermittent, fully orchestrated crescendos about How I Suffered! But the corollary—How I Made Others Suffer (no exclamation point)—is usually rendered in the softest of pianissimos" (171). And, Halsey continues, "[O]ne is balanced on a knife edge all the time between being cursory and/or evasive on the one hand or long-windedly self-important on the other" (222). One of Halsey's goals in her autobiography is to describe the suffering she inflicted on others; she sees herself as a synecdoche for the entire WASP establishment and its ills. Glasgow's autobiography, on the other hand, features the crescendos and the evasion that Halsey describes so graphically.

When it comes to Glasgow's intimate relationships, *The Woman Within* becomes a web of silences—veiled allusions rather than revelations—for which Glasgow's own increasing deafness becomes a metaphor. The death of her favorite sister Cary's husband, Walter, is one instance of this tendency. The circumstances of his death are never stated, and only the clause "he had chosen the one way of escape" suggests suicide (101). When Cary herself becomes terminally ill, Glasgow devotes a number of pages to her own grief, but Cary's illness is identified only as "this particular malady" (190). About Glasgow's first engagement to be married there is no detail, even though, despite what Glasgow terms "my sound conviction that I was not made for marriage" (178), the engagement lasted three years before it "was broken" (179), the passive voice obscuring the agency of the breaking. The other two men with whom Glasgow acknowledges being romantically involved are given pseudonyms, though one of these, "Harold S—," is a thin disguise for Henry Anderson, with whom she had an off-and-on relationship for many years. The two chapters she devotes to Anderson comprise Part 5 of *The Woman Within:* "The Years of the Locust." The barely controlled anger at Anderson contained in these two chapters in turn contains her anger at herself for becoming emotionally involved with "the kind of person I had always avoided" (223).

Glasgow's relationship with the man she calls "Gerald B—," apparently the most intense of her life, had more intrinsic reason for being described enigmatically: he was married and thus unavailable in any permanent sense to the woman who "was not made for marriage." Similarly, as she reminds her reader—or herself—several times, she had no desire to be a mother. At times she merely states this as one of her characteristics, as when she writes, "I have never suffered, sentimentally, from the maternal instinct, and I have cared little for children" (147). But when she writes of falling in love with "Gerald B—," she adds her fear of passing along her deafness to a child: "I felt that my increasing deafness might be inherited, and that it would be a sin against life to pass on an affliction which, even while it was scarcely noticeable, had caused such intense suffering" (153).

Glasgow's "scarcely noticeable affliction" becomes a very noticeable theme in *The Woman Within.* The accumulated force of her many references to her deafness makes it a shield against intimacy and strangers alike. In the early years, she depended on her sister Cary as interpreter:

> I would never see strangers, and not even my former friends, except in the presence of Cary, who would know by intuition the words that I missed and would hasten to snatch up the broken thread. . . . I stopped seeing my friends. I would go out of my way to avoid those I had loved rather than ask them to raise their voices. (137–38)

Later she writes, "For years, now, . . . I had felt as if I were waiting for an impenetrable wall to close round me. Meeting strangers had become torture, and I would go blocks out of my way to avoid a person I knew" (181). And even at the point of noting her engagement to "Harold S—," she also states that she knew the marriage would not take place: "We were looking ahead to a future together—though, because of my terror of deafness, I knew then, as I had always known in my rational mind, that marriage was not for me" (230).

The struggle that Glasgow goes through to create her *persona* in *The Woman Within* is evident in her ambivalence about whether she wants finally to be seen as victim or heroine of her own story. As the former, she feels pursued and tortured by tragedy: the deaths of her mother, Walter, and Cary, while her father stubbornly lived on to the age of eighty-six; the loss of "Gerald B—"; her own frail physical and emotional health. But doing battle with this set-upon, feminized portrait is the image of the isolated, masculinized exile: a lone intellectual in a shallow, nonthinking culture; a person shut off by deafness from ordinary social intercourse; a writer who can announce that five of her novels comprise "some of the best work that has been done in American fiction" (270).

The battle between these two forms of self-representation is encapsulated in Glasgow's autobiographical account of what E. Stanly Godbold and Linda W. Wagner understand to be a suicide attempt in July of 1918. Anguished by the suffering caused by World War I, and more specifically by "Harold's" infatuation with the Queen of Rumania, which was making his Red Cross work there a pleasure, Glasgow vacillates between the voice of the rootless exile, who finds "no help in religion[,] . . . philosophy[, or] . . . human relationships" (237), and that of the victim, haunted by the past, which "followed me, step by step" (238). She claims that her overdose of sleeping pills was not an attempt at suicide—"Sleep, not death, was in my mind as I undressed and put out the lights" (238)—yet when she awakens, she notes that "life would not release me" (240). Remembering this event years later, Glasgow must try to find a language that will convey sufficiently her despair and at the same time present her to future readers in the way she wishes to be known to them. This dual task of the autobiographer creates a constant tension between revelation and concealment, complicated by the vagaries of memory.

Thus, what Ellen Glasgow's autobiography presents to us is not so much "the woman within," but rather the process of fashioning a self capable of standing as the artist, as the figure of the artist was traditionally and somewhat romantically conceived. Writing her fiction in a period in which American literature was just beginning to be accorded stature, and when the South in particular was regarded as a cultural wasteland, Glasgow portrays herself as a romantic exile, alienated from the expectations of conventional womanhood, isolated by actual and symbolic deafness, and activated by a pattern of leaving and returning. While *The Woman Within* does not provide us with the objective "truth" about Glasgow, it may provide us with something more valuable: an understanding of the value and the necessity of self-creation in a world that did not readily bestow selfhood on women writers.

Works Cited

Ammons, Elizabeth. *Conflicting Stories: American Women Writers at the Turn into the Twentieth Century.* New York: Oxford UP, 1991.

Benstock, Shari. "Authorizing the Autobiographical." *The Private Self: Theory and Practice of Women's Autobiographical Writings.* Ed. Shari Benstock. Chapel Hill: U of North Carolina P, 1988. 10–33.

Friedman, Susan Stanford. "Women's Autobiographical Selves: Theory and Practice." *The Private Self,* 34–62.

Glasgow, Ellen. *The Woman Within.* New York: Harcourt, 1954.

Godbold, E. Stanly, Jr. *Ellen Glasgow and the Woman Within.* Baton Rouge: Louisiana State UP, 1972.

Halsey, Margaret. *No Laughing Matter: The Autobiography of a WASP.* Philadelphia: Lippincott, 1977.

Smith, Sidonie. *A Poetics of Women's Autobiography: Marginality and the Fictions of Self-Representation.* Bloomington: Indiana UP, 1987.

Wagner, Linda W. *Ellen Glasgow: Beyond Convention.* Austin: U of Texas P, 1982.

Composed Selves
Ellen Glasgow's *The Woman Within*
and Edith Wharton's *A Backward Glance*

Susan Goodman

Ellen Glasgow (1873–1945) and Edith Wharton (1862–1937), two of the most prolific, successful, and critically acclaimed women writers after the turn of the century, never met. Nor did they acknowledge the similarities of their vision. While Glasgow's fictional territory is primarily her native South and Wharton's is the old New York of her youth, in the novels of both, one encounters the decline of a culture and the passing of tradition, an ironic analysis of morals and manners, a scathing study of the destructive double standard for male and female behavior, and what Glasgow described as the "spectacle of an innocent soul suffering an undeserved tragedy" (*WW* 64).

Glasgow may have dismissed Wharton as a lesser Henry James, but after reading her autobiography, *A Backward Glance* (1934), she felt one of her "rare reflective pangs of envy" (*ACM* 52). Where was her Walter Berry, she asks in *A Certain Measure* (1943), that friendly critic who had taught Wharton whatever she knew about the writing of clear, concise English? "My only critic," Glasgow tells us, "was within" (*ACM* 52). Despite her tribute to Berry, Wharton felt the same. The novelist's best safeguard, she advised, "is to put out of his mind the quality of the praise or blame bestowed on him by reviewers and readers, and to write only for that dispassionate and ironic critic who dwells within the breast" (*ABG* 212). When writing an autobiography, however, the question of audience becomes more complex. If one writes for the critic within, or, as Glasgow states, for the "release of mind and heart" (*WW* v), one also writes for future readers, who might include critics. More than other genres perhaps, autobiography highlights the fictionalizing of history, the composing and mythologizing of self. "How can one tell where memory ends," Glasgow asks, "and imagination begins?" (*WW* 281).

On the surface, Glasgow and Wharton wrote very different memoirs, yet both live on their quality of myth, that is, on what Bernard
Berenson called "an assimilable and inspiring ideated personality" (*BBT*
138). Aside from style and tone, the stories themselves are not unalike.
Wharton lived under the shadow of her mother's icy disapproval and
Glasgow in the half-light of her mother's disappointing marriage. Early
childhood days were filled by the comforting presence of a surrogate
mother, Glasgow's Mammy Lizzie and Wharton's Nurse Doyley. Both
felt that they were—as Glasgow phrases it—"born with an appreciation
of the best, and an equal aversion from the second best" (*WW* 42). After
their first efforts were ridiculed, they wrote in secret, and perhaps this partial silencing led them to develop an enduring empathy for inarticulate
creatures, especially dogs. They shared an antagonism toward romantic
love, misgivings about marriage, a belief that "the primary influence of
woman" would remain "indirect" (*WW* 187), a distaste for sentimentality,
and a hatred of the senseless cruelty that Wharton termed "sterile pain"
(*Mother's Recompense* 266). Each suffered from and revolted against convention in an age they felt to be declining. Eventually, they found it "easier
to break with tradition than to endure it" (*WW* 280). Feeling lonely, different, and besieged, they bore physical and psychic ailments as they
struggled to fashion authorial identities compatible with their social roles.

The Woman Within (1954) and *A Backward Glance* dramatize the division between "writer" and "woman" in the sense that they house two
sometimes competing voices. One asserts the uniqueness of the author's
artistic vision and her importance to letters; the other disarms. As
Glasgow strips away each layer of self, we must either avert our eyes or
extend a protective hand. Her intimacy forces us to collude. Always
the gracious hostess, Wharton invites us into her drawing room, a place
our snobbery, ambition, or sensibility has led us to feel a natural birth-
right. The differences are partly strategic. Glasgow's comments about
the collaborative nature of Wharton's work, for example, underscore
the originality of her own. "[A]t the turn of the century," she tells us,
"I owed less than nothing to these creators" (*WW* 142)—Robert Louis
Stevenson, William Dean Howells, and Hamlin Garland. Referring to
Barren Ground (1925), *The Romantic Comedians* (1926), *They Stooped to
Folly* (1929), *The Sheltered Life* (1932), and *Vein of Iron* (1935), she stresses:
"As a whole, these five novels represent, I feel, not only the best that
was in me, but some of the best work that has been done in American
fiction" (*WW* 270). Similarly, Wharton testifies that she never let her
"inward conviction as to the rightness of anything . . . be affected by
outside opinion" (*ABG* 114)—including Berry's or, more to the point,
Henry James's.

Discussing their artistic contributions, Glasgow and Wharton struggle within and finally undermine the ladylike conventions they despised. To a degree, they disguise their voices and their purposes. Each analyzes the characters, rather than the art, of the friends whose influence or vision they wanted to dispute, Henry James and James Branch Cabell. Wharton's accounts of her "literary rough-and-tumbles" with James illustrate the double game they played. She wants her readers to know that he accepted her as an equal; with her, he could speak truthfully or "hit straight from the shoulder" (*ABG* 184). Both writers would have denied their own competitiveness, but Wharton in particular makes sure that we are left with her version of the past, that we see her scoring the final hit: "'What was your idea in suspending the four principal characters in 'The Golden Bowl' in the void?'" she recalls having asked its author in all innocence. "'Why have you stripped them of all the *human fringes* we necessarily trail after us through life?'" Her questions focus James's "startled attention on a peculiarity of which he had been completely unconscious," and he can only answer "in a disturbed voice: 'My dear—I didn't know that I had!'" (*ABG* 191). Glasgow is perhaps more subtly cruel when she defends Cabell against the charges of homosexuality that haunted him just before his graduation from the College of William and Mary or describes him, even then, as possessing "that air of legendary remoteness, as if he lived in a perpetual escape from actuality" (*WW* 133), the very quality she most values.

Both women feel the need to make modest disclaimers about the lasting merits of or interest in their work and then argue the opposite. According to Wharton, readers want to discover "heroes and heroines of the 'society column'" (*ABG* 212), and critics, "the man with the dinner pail" (206). "Drab persons living drab lives" (*WW* 276) is how Glasgow puts it. Art, which depends upon "human significance," should be judged "almost wholly on what the author sees in it, and how deeply he is able to see *into* it" (*ABG* 206). Glasgow sees no reason to believe that "the literary judgment of the future will be superior to the literary judgment of the present," despite admitting:

> so paradoxical is human vanity, that I, who have avoided contemporaneous notoriety, would exchange immediate recognition for the sake of becoming a name to generations which I could never know, and to which, no doubt, I should be supremely indifferent if I ever encountered them in the flesh. (*WW* 278–79)

The Woman Within pleads her case; because intellect is such a "difficult master," all "the bold young men from the Middle West" have courted unbridled sensation and called it truth (*WW* 267). In *Hudson River Bracketed* (1929) and *The Gods Arrive* (1932), Wharton gives us one of these bold young men, Vance Weston. He is her critique of the male artist and of a tradition that she saw privileging him. And he is incomplete without his female half, Halo Spear, the embodiment of the novel's dominant spiritual image—taken from Faust—of "the Mothers," the mysterious source of life and art.

The structure of *The Woman Within* and *A Backward Glance* reflects their authors' different, though related, visions of the self. Wharton saw the self, described in "The Fullness of Life" (1893), as "a great house full of rooms":

> there is the hall, through which everyone passes in going in and out; the drawing room, where one receives formal visits; the sitting room, where the members of the family come and go as they list; but beyond that, far beyond, are other rooms, the handles of whose doors perhaps are never turned; no one knows the way to them, no one knows whither they lead; and in the innermost room, the holy of holies, the soul sits alone and waits for a footstep that never comes. (14)

This self is contained, inviolate, and fixed. It reigns in a space much like the one that Wharton created for herself immediately after the armistice ending World War I in St. Brice sous Fôret. Here she exteriorized an interior domain, that innermost room. Today Pavillon Colombe sits relatively undisturbed, surrounded by acres of immaculate grounds. Both the house, with its corridor of rooms that appear to march in step, and the gardens, ringed by hedgerows to form an outdoors equivalent, reflect the novelist's need for order and control.

Not surprisingly, Wharton, who characterized herself as a "priestess of the Life of Reason" (*Letters of EW* 483), found Freud's theory of the unconscious, which undermined the idea of free will, fundamentally repugnant. At any time that unexplored, untapped domain could threaten to wrest control from the conscious mind and engulf the "I." Writing to Bernard Berenson in 1922 about a mutual female friend, she begged him to ask his wife "not to befuddle her with Freudianism & all its jargon. She'd take to it like a duck to—sewerage." Wharton advised that "what she wants is to develop the *conscious*, & not grub after the sub-conscious. She wants to be taught first to see, to attend, to reflect" (*Letters of EW* 450–51). In her autobiography, Wharton resisted Freud's construct of a "self," whose parameters are only tenuously fixed and—as the title *A Backward Glance* suggests—she chose to emphasize social realism over psychological truth.

Glasgow shared many of Wharton's misgivings about Freud, claiming that she was never a disciple and that she disliked the "current pattern of Freudian theory" (*WW* 227). Nevertheless, she ranked herself "among the first, in the South, to perceive the invigorating effect of this fresh approach to experience" (*WW* 269).[1] Believing that a work's "fidelity to life" was tied to its "value as psychology" (*WW* 214), Glasgow offers herself as a case study in both psychology and literary history. The attempt to record impressions as they occur and without revision as she tracks the elusive figure of her memoir's title underscores Freud's influence on the book's structure and content.

While Wharton's memoir is limited almost entirely to what Georges Gusdorf defines as "the public sector of existence," *The Woman Within* reveals its "private face" (36–37). "I am speaking the truth, as I know it," Glasgow writes, "because the truth alone, without vanity or evasion, can justify an intimate memoir" (*WW* 8). Shari Benstock suggests that female autobiographers are less successful than their male counterparts at keeping the ego intact (12). They find it more difficult to present a consonant and consistent self. If this is the case, Wharton, who warns her readers that they must not expect a memorialist who spares no one or who sets "down in detail every defect and absurdity in others, and every resentment in the writer," is a notable exception (*ABG* xx). Not wanting to acknowledge a gulf between "self" and "consciousness," she uses language as a defense against unconscious material surfacing. Glasgow, on the other hand, stretches, tests, and disrupts language as a way of unveiling "the woman within." In her purpose and her uses of language, she resembles Virginia Woolf, an author whom she (and Wharton very grudgingly) admired: "I have tried to make a completely honest portrayal of an interior world," Glasgow explained to her literary executors, "and of that one world alone" (*WW* v).

The Woman Within and *A Backward Glance* seek to isolate the irreducible core of self that made each woman unique. They open with their authors waking to consciousness. In Glasgow's memoir, *ta onta*—a state James Olney describes as a "seamless fabric woven of perception, consciousness, memories, and the surrounding universe"—dominates *bios*, the historical course of life (*Olney* 244). The reverse is true in *A Backward Glance*. *Bios* rules, although emerging memories threaten to disform the text.

Glasgow begins by showing how language gives birth to self:

> Beyond the top windowpanes, in the midst of a red glow, I see a face
> without a body staring in at me, a vacant face, round, pallid, grotesque,
> malevolent. Terror—or was it merely sensation?—stabbed me into con-
> sciousness. Terror of the sinking sun? Or terror of the formless, the un-

known, the mystery, terror of life, of the world, of nothing or everything? Convulsions seized me, a spasm of dumb agony. One minute, I
was not; the next minute, I was. I felt. I was separate. I could be hurt. I
had discovered myself. And I had discovered, too, the universe apart
from myself. (*WW* 3–4)

Before this experience, Glasgow describes herself as drifting in a state
of preconsciousness, "[m]oving forward and backward, as contented
and as mindless as an amoeba, submerged in that vast fog of existence"
(*WW* 3). Her terror arises from the split second between being and
nonbeing, from the feeling that she was a face without features, a soul
without a body, an intelligence without a voice. The qualified questions, the short disjointed sentences, the emphasis on sensation, and
the intruding "I's" mix memoir and fantasy. Glasgow realizes that the
language which allows her to articulate her "earliest remembered sensation" and which she attaches to it "long afterwards" (*WW* 3) also
transforms that sensation's essence.

The face that marks Glasgow "as a victim" before she learns to put
"fear into words" (*WW* 112) mirrors both her own and an "other." The
same is true for Wharton when her moment of waking separates her
forever from her adored father. Speaking of herself in the third person,
she writes:

It was always an event in the little girl's life to take a walk with her father, and more particularly so today, because she had on her new winter bonnet, which was so beautiful (and so becoming) that for the first
time she woke to the importance of dress, and of herself as a subject for
adornment—so that I may date from that hour the birth of the conscious
and feminine *me* in the little girl's vague soul. (*ABG* 2)

The memory appears more straightforward than Glasgow's stylized
form of what seems like Freudian free association, but it is Wharton's
tone rather than her narrative technique that most distinguishes the
two. Wharton's anecdote reads as if the twin birthing of "femininity"
and "consciousness" were indeed known to the little girl, yet it is the
adult "I" who critically examines and marks the date. When the Glasgow
passage shifts from present to past tense, the same change in view occurs: the older self envisions the younger, and from the process a third
character emerges. In Wharton's account, the intrusion of the "I" con-
trols the child, whose vague soul recalls Glasgow's image of the form-
less face. By placing the little girl in perspective, the analytical "I" less-
ens the threat of "vagueness" or chaos while asserting itself as a coherent,

stable identity. Glasgow is not as self-controlled (or controlling), and her lifelong feeling of victimization is partly linked to the discovery of herself in relation to that horrifying "other."

In a sense, Wharton internalized the horrifying "other"; the woman, who characterized herself as the least attractive member of her family, had a lifelong antipathy toward ugly people. Her mirror was not, however, always displeasing, for in her father's eyes, she saw a positive reflection of her own femaleness, and it led to a second and sexual awakening. On the walk already described, the author met her cousin, Daniel, "and suddenly he put out a chubby hand, lifted the little girl's veil, and boldly planted a kiss on her cheek. It was the first time—and the little girl found it very pleasant" (*ABG* 3). Glasgow experiences a comparable sensation when, as a little girl, her cousin embraces her in her pretty pink coat, exclaiming, "'Why, she looks like an angel!'" (*WW* 13). Years later, the love of Gerald B. makes it possible for her to overcome what she regarded as an insurmountable impediment, her growing deafness: "The great discovery that my own identity, that I, myself, could triumph over brute circumstances, had destroyed and then re-created the entire inner world of my consciousness. 'I will make myself well,' I resolved. 'I will make myself happy. I will make myself beautiful'" (*WW* 160).

Like Glasgow, an autobiographer has the power to "make" him or herself. A woman, perhaps more than a man, must come to terms with her individual identity within a larger cultural context that has already categorized her sex: as Susan Stanford Friedman argues, a woman's sense of her unique "self" exists in tension with her sense of a generically female one (38, 44). Wharton illustrates this point in her simultaneous recognition of her own separateness (consciousness) and her connection to a group identity (femininity).

Glasgow obviously fits the pattern of female autobiographers when she defines her life in relation to the lives of her mother, Anne Jane Gholson Glasgow, her sisters, Cary and Rebe, and women friends, such as Caroline Duke, Elizabeth Patterson, Marjorie Rawlings, and Anne Virginia Bennett. Wharton also fits the pattern, but in reverse, defining herself in opposition to her mother, Lucretia Jones, a prosaically unsympathetic character. In Wharton's version of the Freudian drama, her father would have been a far different man, less "lonely," less "haunted by something always unexpressed and unattained" (*ABG* 39), if he had married someone less like his wife and more like his daughter. Although Wharton clearly aligns herself with him, she refuses to grant Lucretia the power of having circumscribed her own development. Describing her mother's prohibitions on her reading, for example, she writes: "By denying me the opportunity of wasting my time over ephemeral rubbish my mother threw me back on the great classics, and thereby helped to give my mind a temper which my too-easy studies could not have produced" (*ABG* 65–66). Wharton implies that as a great consumer of "ephemeral rubbish" her mother was not so lucky. By criticizing the societal definitions of womanhood that her mother represented, the "memorialist" establishes her own. The identities of mother and daughter are nevertheless interdependent; the daughter constitutes her mother's image and concurrently fashions her own.

The novelists' female identification does not, however, preclude their having and affirming qualities—a love of solitude and the "sharp realities" (*WW* 97), for example—that make them different from other members of their sex. "I stood alone," writes Glasgow. "I stood outside. I wanted only to learn. I wanted only to write better" (*WW* 144). "What I wanted above all," remembers Wharton, "was to get to know other writers, to be welcomed among people who lived for the things I had always secretly lived for" (*ABG* 123). If we accept the popular contention that the assertion of a unique identity is a predominant pattern in lives written by men, then Glasgow and Wharton seem to bridge male and female forms of autobiography.[2]

Neither Glasgow nor Wharton can repair the rent that separates them from "the universe apart," but each uses her memoir to create in a Lacanian sense a "self" in language. To quote Glasgow's mammy, both were "born without a skin" (*WW* 5) into a world that they perceived as cold and indifferent. As a result, Glasgow felt that a "sensitive mind would always remain an exile on earth" (*WW* 271), and Wharton believed, as she writes in "A Little Girl's New York," that "the creative mind thrives best on a reduced diet" (357). Words were their armor; for Wharton they were also weapons. She used them in particular to control her mother, who (as she wrote in the first, more candid draft of her autobiography, "Life and I") helped to "falsify & misdirect my whole life" (35). When the young author told her, "'Mamma, you must go and entertain that little girl for me. *I've got to make up*'" (*ABG* 35), she was neatly reversing their roles. Tellingly, the room in which she "made up" stories was her mother's bedroom ("Life" 12), and she kept parents and nurse enthralled as she strode the floor reciting with Washington Irving's *Alhambra* upside down in her outstretched arms.[3] Early on Wharton coupled the manipulation of language with the manipulation of people and events. "Making up" served three purposes: it corrected, as Freud argues in "Creative Writers and Daydreaming" (1908), an unsatisfying reality; it gave her an identity distinct from the other members of her family; and it gave her an instrument for keeping them—like *The Alhambra*—at arm's length. By giving her the means to see, to attend, and to reflect, storytelling allowed the novelist to keep at bay all the vagueness associated with that distant little girl. The format of her autobiography does the same. Readers learn about her genealogy, the old New York of her childhood, her travels and friendships, but they learn little of her feelings. In fact, Wharton makes a point of denying any equation between "psychology" and "autobiography" when she writes of her younger self, "I might have suffered from an inferiority complex had such ailments been known" (*ABG* 88–89).

Glasgow's version of self—a "continual becoming" (*ACM* 111)—allows her to define herself as a "modern" as early as 1897 (*ACM* 114). Initially, storytelling kept veiled that terrifying face which marked her coming to consciousness. It made her separateness bearable by helping her "to escape from the particular into the general, from the provincial into the universal" (*WW* 128). Glasgow's step into consciousness and the "universal" foreshadows her miss[ed]-steps into death, her failed suicide attempt and her bouts with illness. At first afraid of the loss of self that death represents, Glasgow eventually associates it with "a sense of infinite reunion with the Unknown Everything or with Nothing . . . or with God" (*WW* 289). Instead of a surrender or an extinction of identity, she experiences an "enlargement and complete illumination of being" (*WW* 290) of the kind that "universal" art provides. In a sense, Glasgow's memoir goes full circle, from fearing the face at the window to embracing it. Proving that there is "no permanent escape from the past" (*WW* 209), she does what she hoped: "to leave the permanent record of an adventure into the far unknown" (*WW* 56).

While *The Woman Within* and *A Backward Glance* present visions of the self, they also present versions, separate portraits or compositions of the "women" and the "authors." Like many of their contemporaries, male and female, they defined their writing selves as androgynous; however, the autobiographical form would not allow them to ignore gender. Despite her many friendships with women, such as Sara Norton, Daisy Chanler, Mary Cadwalader Jones, and Elisina Tyler, Wharton chose to present her life in a male context. Choosing her own sex as a mirror might have necessitated a restructuring of the self she had fought so hard to win. Any absences in her life as a woman, such as children, disappear when viewed from a masculine perspective. The unwomanly woman is transformed—to use Virginia Woolf's phrase—into an extraordinary one. Glasgow's descriptions of her long relationships with "Gerald B—" and "Harold S—," which emphasize the woman over the artist, suggest that the former thrived at the expense of the latter. "If falling in love could be bliss. . . ," she writes, "falling out of love could be blissful tranquillity" (*WW* 244)—all "my best work was ahead of me" (*WW* 243). In a sense, Glasgow grew to see herself as a character in one of her own books: "Years before, when I began *Barren Ground,* I knew that I had found a code of living that was sufficient for life or for death" (*WW* 271). To some extent, the same held true for Wharton: Robert Norton recalls that "the habit of transposing everything into terms of her art extended to herself" (49).

The separation between the "womanly" self and its "writerly" counterpart occurred for Wharton when Scribner's accepted her first collection of short stories, *The Greater Inclination* (1899):

> *I* had written short stories that were thought worthy of preservation! Was it the same insignificant *I* that I had always known? Any one walking along the streets might go into any bookshop, and say: "Please give me Edith Wharton's book," and the clerk, without bursting into incredulous laughter, would produce it, and be paid for it, and the purchaser would walk home with it and read it, and talk of it, and pass it on to other people to read! (*ABG* 113)

"Significant," public, and capable of economic independence, the authorial self has come into being through the act of writing. Wharton's two selves recall Mary Austin's distinctions between her powerful creative self, "I-Mary," and her lonely social self, "Mary-by-herself" (*Earth Horizon* 47). Glasgow's self is far less compartmentalized than Wharton's, although the image of her unable to write except "behind a locked door, alone in a room" (*ACM* 262) intriguingly echoes the other's metaphor of the innermost room.

Wharton visualizes her interior creative space as a "secret garden," a place where plants grow and unfold "from the seed to the shrub-top," but she cautions her readers, "I have no intention of magnifying my vegetation into trees!" (*ABG* 198). The statement functions as a playfully modest disclaimer and a prohibition. Unlike Glasgow, she does not invite her readers to wade in an underground "stream-of-consciousness," perhaps because she now associates her "making up" with a loss of control:

> What I mean to try for is the observation of that strange moment when the vaguely adumbrated characters whose adventures one is preparing to record are suddenly *there*, themselves, in the flesh, in possession of one, and in command of one's voice and hand. It is there that the central mystery lies, and perhaps it is as impossible to fix in words as that other mystery of what happens in the brain at the precise moment when one falls over the edge of consciousness into sleep. (*ABG* 198)

In becoming "a recording instrument" (203), Wharton duplicates Alice's experience in Wonderland: she enters a realm of seeming, where the "appearance of reality" (205) has a darker side (reminiscent of Glasgow's face at the window): the disappearance of tangible substance. Possibly for this reason, "making up" is less empowering in the adult's than in the child's world. She lives Glasgow's two "twisted" lives, yet sees them as "totally unrelated worlds . . . side by side, equally absorbing, but wholly isolated from each other" (*ABG* 205). Wharton is afraid that if she does not wall off her "secret garden," its tendrils will choke the entire landscape. In contrast, Glasgow welcomes "the unconscious worker," for after she has "withdrawn from the task, or taken a brief holiday," the "actual drudgery" of writing begins (*ACM* 199). The fictive settings, which become the native country of her mind during composing, are more vivid, more vital, than any landscape found in the external world.

Glasgow's hyperconscious experiments with form in *The Woman Within* are an attempt to replicate an interior domain. The memoir's interrupted chronology, its repetitions that unveil and advance plot, create the sense that she has indeed not molded "both causes and effects into a fixed psychological pattern" but has left "the inward and the outward streams of experience free to flow in their own channels, and free, too, to construct their own special designs" (*WW* 227). "Analysis," she contends, "if it comes at all, must come later" (*WW* 227). The unfolding story of her brother Frank's suicide exemplifies this method. Glasgow has previously hinted at the cause of his death without disclosing it until the end of an anecdote about his departure for school: "In a last effort to spare us as far as it was possible, he went, alone, from the house, and, alone, into a future where we could not follow him" (*WW* 67). The sentence applies equally well to either his temporary or permanent exile, though, as Glasgow reminds us, the latter "was years afterwards" (*WW* 67). Instead of continuing her narrative in a chronological fashion, she then retraces similar ground by recounting his return home for the school holidays. Pages earlier Glasgow has asserted that he was "the only one of my mother's children who never failed her" (*WW* 17). Introducing the revelation of his suicide, she restates it: "I repeat that he was the only one of Mother's children who never failed her in word, or in act, or in sympathetic understanding" (*WW* 66). Retrospectively, the statement becomes his epitaph.

The Woman Within and *A Backward Glance* are in form and approach representative of each author's fiction. Glasgow's willingness to experiment with prose style grows from her search for one "so pure and flexible that it could bend without breaking" (*WW* 123). Unlike Wharton she recognized the profound effect that psychology was to have on the nature of narrative, noting that "it is true that the novel, as a living force, if not as a work of art, owes an incalculable debt to what we call, mistakenly, the new psychology, to Freud, in his earlier inter-pretations, and more truly, I think, to Jung" (*WW* 269). *The Sheltered Life* (1932) is such a work. In it she aimed to "[a]lways, and as far as it is possible, endeavor to touch life on every side; but keep the central vision of the mind, the inmost light, untouched and untouchable" while preserving, "within a wild sanctuary, an inaccessible valley of rev-eries" (*SL* xxii). The novel's section entitled "The Deep Past" moves back and forth through time as it is perceived in the unfolding con-sciousness of the elderly General Archbald. Although Archbald muses that "[w]ithin time, and within time alone, there was life—the gleam, the quiver, the heart-beat, the immeasurable joy and anguish of being" (*SL* 109), the section's synchronic structure belies his conclusion.

Uncomfortable with literary techniques that broke down the barri-ers between life and fiction, Wharton did not (as her autobiography demonstrates) subscribe as fully as Glasgow to the belief that the emo-tional and the intellectual life "formed a single strand, and could not be divided" (*WW* 56). Nevertheless, these two lives often became tangled in her fiction; for example, *The Reef,* with or without Wharton's conscious intent, "takes up the same [autobiographical] material in complete free-dom and under the protection of a hidden identity" (Gusdorf 46). The story of Anna Leath's and Sophy Viner's love of the same man, George Darrow, closely parallels its author's history with Morton Fullerton, a journalist who conducted his affair with Wharton during his engage-ment to his cousin, Katherine Fullerton. A believer in the supremacy of reason, Wharton persistently sought the dividing line between illu-sion and truth, despite insisting that literature is—as she writes in "The Criticism of Fiction"—a "contemplation of life that goes below its sur-face" (230). Her heroines, from Lily Bart in *The House of Mirth* (1905) to Nan St. George in *The Buccaneers* (1937), strain to remove the veil of illusion that separates them from reality.

Glasgow's aesthetics align her with Wharton, another admirer of Tolstoy. She may have more willingly admitted the arbitrary distinc-tions between substance and illusion, but she too felt that her "best books" had "all been written when emotion was over" (*WW* 214). Agreeing with Wharton's essentially pessimistic view that civilization helps people to adjust their relations and protects them against their own natures, she predicted: "After both world wars are over, we shall still be fighting an eternal conflict between human beings and human nature" (*WW* 285). Explaining *The Sheltered Life* to Allen Tate, she criticized the society that she, like Wharton, thought necessary: "I was dealing with the fate of the civilized mind in a world where even the civilizations we make are uncivilized" (*Letters of EG* 124). Wharton could make the same claim for *The Age of Innocence* (1920). In both Glasgow's and Wharton's fiction, the individual does not escape, redefine, or recreate the existing world; rather, he or she struggles within the confines of "civilization." The two women shared the same quarrel, which Glasgow described as being "less with the world than with the scheme of things in general"; she was, she tells us, "in arms against the universe" (*WW* 279).

One of the stories hinted at, but not fully told, in either *The Woman Within* or *A Backward Glance*, is how much these authors enjoyed their quarrel with a universe that taught them the full extent of their own worth. It allowed them to justify the sole occupancy of their innermost rooms or what both called the Republic of the Spirit, a place Wharton defined in *The House of Mirth* (1905) as "beyond the ugliness, the pettiness, the attrition and corrosion of the soul" (90), a place where Glasgow said she "ranged, free and wild, and a rebel" (*WW* 40); it unravels forever perhaps the twisted strands of self, which Wharton saw as often incompatible: "the dissecting intellect" and "the accepting soul" (*ABG* 159). It gives one the tools to compose a "self" that can claim, as does Wharton: "In spite of illness, in spite even of the arch-enemy sorrow, one *can* remain alive long past the usual date of disintegration if one is unafraid of change, insatiable in intellectual curiosity, interested in big things, and happy in small ways" (*ABG* xix). Glasgow more than concurs: "I have done the work I wished to do for the sake of that work alone. And I have come, at last, from the fleeting rebellion of youth into the steadfast—or is it merely the seasonable—accord without surrender of the unreconciled heart" (*WW* 296). Glasgow tells the story of a soul achieving peace, Wharton, the story of a soul at peace. One might add that the art, which provided them with a means for coping with the world, for shaping the self that in turn shapes it, led to this final composure.

Notes

1. For Glasgow's ambivalent references to Freud, see *The Woman Within*, 54, 173, 227–28, 267 esp.; *A Certain Measure*, 168, 209, 228, 240 esp.
2. See Mary Mason, "Autobiographies of Woman Writers," *Autobiography: Essays Theoretical and Critical*, 210; Germaine Bree, "Autogynography," in *Studies in Autobiography*, Ed. James Olney (New York: Oxford UP, 1988) 171–79; Julia Watson, "Shadowed Presence: Modern Women Writers' Autobiographies and the Other," in *Studies in Autobiography*, 180–89; and Sheila Rowbotham, *Woman's Consciousness, Man's World* (London: Penguin, 1973) 27.

3. For a detailed analysis of Wharton's "making up," see Judith Fryer, *Felicitous Spaces: The Imaginative Structures of Edith Wharton and Willa Cather* (Chapel Hill: U of Carolina P, 1986) 148–69.

Works Cited

Austin, Mary. *Earth Horizon.* New York: Literary Guild, 1932.

Benstock, Shari. "Authorizing the Autobiographical." *The Private Self: Theory and Practice of Women's Autobiographical Writings.* Ed. Shari Benstock. Chapel Hill: U of North Carolina P, 1988. 10–33.

Berenson, Bernard. *The Bernard Berenson Treasury.* Ed. Hanna Kiel. New York: Simon, 1962.

Friedman, Susan Stanford. "Women's Autobiographical Selves: Theory and Practice." *The Private Self,* 34–62.

Glasgow, Ellen. *A Certain Measure: An Interpretation of Prose Fiction.* New York: Harcourt, 1943.

———. *Letters of Ellen Glasgow.* Ed. Blair Rouse. New York: Harcourt, 1958.

———. *The Sheltered Life.* 1932. New York: Hill, 1979.

———. *The Woman Within.* New York: Harcourt, 1954.

Gusdorf, Georges. "Conditions and Limits of Autobiography." *Autobiography: Essays Theoretical and Critical.* Ed. James Olney. Princeton: Princeton UP, 1980. 28–48.

Norton, Robert. "Memoir of Edith Wharton." The Beinecke Rare Book and Manuscript Library. Yale University.

Olney, James. "The Ontology of Autobiography." *Autobiography: Essays Theoretical and Critical,* 236–67.

Wharton, Edith. *A Backward Glance.* 1934. New York: Scribner's, 1964.

———. "The Criticism of Fiction." *The Times Literary Supplement* 14 May 1914: 229–30.

———. "The Fullness of Life." *The Collected Short Stories of Edith Wharton.* Ed. R. W. B. Lewis. Vol. 1. New York: Scribner's, 1968. 12–20.

———. *The House of Mirth.* 1905. New York: Bantam, 1986.

———. *The Letters of Edith Wharton.* Ed. R. W. B. Lewis and Nancy Lewis. New York: Scribner's, 1988.

———. "Life and I." The Beinecke Rare Book and Manuscript Library. Yale University.

———. "A Little Girl's New York." *Harper's Magazine* 176 (March 1938): 356–64.

———. *The Mother's Recompense.* New York: Appleton, 1925.

PART III

Poetry and Short Stories

The Poetry of Ellen Glasgow
The Freeman and Other Poems

Terence Allan Hoagwood

In 1902, Ellen Glasgow published *The Freeman and Other Poems,* her only book of poetry and an important volume for several reasons. First, Glasgow's poetry *is* "good verse," as she said in a letter to Walter Page, who had proposed publishing a volume of her poetry in January of 1902 (see *Letters* 36–39; Raper 174). Her poems develop interesting relationships in the context of contemporaneous poetry,[1] but *The Freeman and Other Poems* is also conceptually coherent with Glasgow's fiction. Her novels and her poetry share themes and also strategies, including the use of ironized voices and mutually undermining points of view. By way of these strategies she presents a socially critical vision that is at once profound, bitter, submerged, and subversive.

My argument in the present essay can therefore be stated simply: an ironized point of view, elaborated with considerable poetic artifice, produces here an impressively unified poetic volume. The machinery of duplicitously ironized voices is an important vehicle for a social vision: the poems treat substantive issues including sexual politics and religion, and always they are treated skeptically. Glasgow's techniques include the art of the dramatic monologue and the presentation of contradictory voices left in irresolution; consistently and evocatively, these techniques thematize Glasgow's precisely social contentions. As J. R. Raper has aptly said, "The central drama of Ellen Glasgow's early career is the struggle to unmask an ideology within which her contemporaries took shelter" (ix).

An example of ideological constructs that are under critique in the poetic volume involves the falsehoods of the merely conventional fictions of true love, popularized as compensatory fantasies for the consumption of oppressed people, chiefly women. In these poems as in

Glasgow's novels, these fantasies exact the price of submission and even slavery. Another set of examples of ideological fictions that the poems unmask involves the figments of her father's traditional religion, likewise a set of compensatory fictions for the consolation of the oppressed. In *The Woman Within*, Glasgow indicates repeatedly that patriarchal religion has been especially powerful in the lives of southern women. She also explains the social and political power of that religion: "Nothing else could have made them accept with meekness the wing of the chicken and the double standard of morals." Nothing else, likewise, could have induced women's quietly accepting the role in life of "waiting beside the beds of the sick and dying" during the male-organized ritual of war.[2] The satire of the *Freeman* poems attacks the fictitiousness of these compensatory illusions ("evasive idealism" is a phrase with which she names such figments—see *The Woman Within* 97, 104). The poems also exhibit the brutal exercises of power that these evasive illusions mask. The artistry of the poems includes strategies of skeptical distantiation that help to treat ideological fictions critically. It is this structure—strategies of skeptical distantiation, used in a project of ideological unmasking—which is in my view the single most important achievement of the book.

The early reviews of *The Freeman and Other Poems* point out, though briefly, some of the distinctive characteristics of Glasgow's poetry whose meanings I shall explicate in greater detail. For example, the *Boston Evening Transcript* (10 Sept. 1902: 12) praises the poems' "imagination and vigor of thought" and calls attention to "her satiric powers and a grim humor." The skeptical, socially critical, and evolutionary forms of thought embodied in the volume are noticed in "Some Recent Verse," *New York Times Saturday Review of Books and Art* (20 Sept. 1902: 639): these are "thoughts plain spoken and daring, making a truly vigorous 'criticism of life.'" Glasgow's poetry exhibits "fine philosophic courage"; "there is freedom from the commonplace and an original power" ("Miss Glasgow's Novels and Poems," *World's Work* 5 [Nov. 1902]: 2791–92).[3]

The skepticism expressed in the poetry is noticed more specifically in a later article, "Poems by Ellen Glasgow," also appearing in the *Boston Evening Transcript* (22 Dec. 1902: 10), which mentions Nietzsche in comparison. Further (and "Oddly enough," the reviewer says), "though the volume is a woman's and a very young woman's, the theme of love may be said to have been not touched upon at all." The reviewer quotes a line which specifies an evolutionary sequence: "weed and flower and worm and man." The same review notices the book's sociocultural themes, its "revolt from the dire and futile worry of the Western nations." The review observes justly that the "whole volume is . . . a powerful and fine expression of a widely spread and markedly modern trend of thought."

The specifically feminist implications of Glasgow's theme of unmasking form a central concept in Linda W. Wagner's important book: "The contrast between the expected female role and the life Glasgow chose to lead" is, as Wagner shows, a recurrent theme of her art (4). This theme forms much of the point of Glasgow's retrospective statement, "I began my literary work as a rebel against conventions."[4] The poetic volume treats critically "the masculine drama of action," to apply a phrase that Glasgow used subsequently to describe one of the critical and innovative ambitions of her novel *They Stooped to Folly* (Glasgow, *ACM* 245). But this ambition and achievement *also* appear as early as 1902 and in the considerable formal artistry of the poetic volume.

Dorothy M. Scura has shown how Glasgow's feminism is expressed in her poetry, specifically in "The Call," a poem first published in 1912, ten years later than *The Freeman and Other Poems*. Scura documents with precision Glasgow's active participation in the women's movement, from 1908 onward, and she observes justly that Glasgow's "ideas on feminism were always philosophical rather than political" ("Knowledge" 30). Long before the first record of feminist activism on Glasgow's part, her life and art had incorporated feminist thought and feeling in important ways, and the poems of the *Freeman* volume are an impressive (and remarkably early) case in point.

The book's themes include the fictitiousness of social codes (including sexual roles and traditional religion), but my own argument involves a single but complex feature which these thematic treatments share: the unmasking of ideological illusion by way of the strategies of skeptical distantiation. Poems' speakers unwittingly betray their folly and the deadliness of its consequences, sometimes in the manner of dramatic monologues like Robert Browning's, one of which Glasgow cites specifically, by title, in her own book ("The Master Hand" mentions Andrea del Sarto). Poems contradict each other; images are sometimes grotesquely juxtaposed; and this structure of doubleness, opposites, contrasts, and duplicity amounts to a formal strategy, coherently joined throughout the volume to a critical and conceptual project.

In *The Woman Within* Glasgow writes, "Only on the surface of things have I ever trod the beaten path" (296). In *A Certain Measure* she writes:

> I have led, for as many years as I can remember, a dual existence. The natural writer must, of necessity, live on the surface the life of accepted facts, which is the life of action and shadows, while with his deeper consciousness he continues to live that strangely valid life of the mind. (vii)

In Glasgow's deceptively simple poems, her subversiveness is submerged; her critique generates a dual form of a surface illusion and a depth that undermines it.

Glasgow's poems, which expose and attack conventional illusions underlying the politics of sex, religion, and war, were offered to a world that still wanted to consume and to credit those illusions. "I was," Glasgow writes, "in my humble place and way, beginning a solitary revolt against the formal, the false, and affected, the sentimental, and the pretentious, in Southern writing" (*ACM* 8),[5] and "I hated—I had always hated—the inherent falseness in much Southern tradition" (*WW* 97). Her literary rebellion has thus a specifically political content, and the vehicle of that rebellion was a subversive exhibit of critical duplicity: "I would write, I resolved, as no Southerner had ever written, of the universal human chords beneath the superficial variations of scene and character. I would write of all the harsher realities beneath manners, beneath social customs, beneath the poetry of the past" (*WW* 98).

One of the more comprehensive conceptual structures of her rebellion was the "all-embracing philosophy of organic evolution" (92), a conceptual scheme that made social customs and hierarchies intelligible as historical developments.[6] Unfortunately (from the viewpoint of the religiously orthodox), such a conceptual scheme also exhibited the merely temporary and historically relative status of cherished beliefs. In her autobiography, Glasgow narrates the punitive treatment she received from her family and, more largely, from her entire social community for her interest in and advocacy of evolutionary forms of thought. But, determined to *be* rebellious, she sustained and developed that evolutionary outlook for many years before and after 1902, when that outlook helps to organize her book of verse (Glasgow, *ACM* 8; see Wagner, *Ellen Glasgow* 13). Unwelcome as her critical treatment might have been in 1902—that is, her treatment of religion, of conventional sex roles, of traditional hierarchies of power, chiefly patriarchal—the compression and artistry with which her poems present that critical vision warrant some sustained analysis now.

The epigraph for the volume is a single sentence: "Hope is a slave, / Despair a freeman." This epigraph points out the psychological subject of the book. As Glasgow says in *The Woman Within*, "My soul was a battleground" (16), but here as in her novel *The Battle-Ground* those metaphors produce statements whose meanings encompass other forms of oppression. In the later poem, "The Call," Glasgow writes of the struggle of feminists: "Queen or slave or bond or free, we battled." In "The Freeman," the governing metaphors are "battle-field," "chains," "slave," "prison."

The book's conceptual structure is embodied with considerable art-istry at the level of prosodic detail. "The Freeman" uses a pattern of rhyme as of the ballad stanza, *abcb,* but each line has five feet, which is the elegiac number, rather than the traditional ballad stanza's four. An exception appears once within each stanza, as the fourth and final line of each stanza is truncated to two feet.[7] The effect is to add an empha-sis to the bite of the satire. The speaker reports that he feels no terror and then (in the truncated final line) "Nor any God."

This technique of truncation returns with some frequency in the vol-ume: in "Justice," the woman speaker of the poem is subjected to dis-tinctly patriarchal cruelty—of men, God, and society at large—and there the final line of each balladlike stanza is also reduced to two feet, as it is in the title poem. In "Justice," a woman (loved only by her dog) is cursed, beaten, and branded in the name of the community's reli-gion; the especially effective shortened line (of two feet) ends the final stanza by summarizing what the religious community (in the "name of God") did after the woman's death: "The dog they stoned." In "Cow-ard Memory," the poem's speaker expresses anxiety about an unspoken horror in an upstairs room, and the last line of the third (final) stanza, which is about the failure of memory, is short by a foot.[8]

In the only substantial commentary on "The Freeman" or *The Free-man* to appear since the reviews that greeted its publication, Raper makes this important point about the title poem: "Cosmic irony often seems the only posture for the freeman vis-à-vis the injustice of the uni-verse" (177). As the term *injustice* might suggest, together with Raper's own apt emphasis on southern ideology, Glasgow's poems present social criticism as well as cosmic generalization. For example, the Civil War is in part a trope of masculine violence, with the pleasant accompani-ment of women "waiting beside the beds of the sick and dying."

"A Battle Cry," the fifth poem in *The Freeman and Other Poems,* rep-resents in its first stanza a condition of war as a hopeless, total, and futile struggle in which the speaker is surrounded. In the second stanza the speaker is treated critically with the poet's tongue in her cheek: the speaker "measured hate with hate"—not a moral norm that Glasgow celebrates. Stanza three ridicules the male ethos of companionless and selfish aggression, by having the belligerent speaker rejoice in that ethos. It is with grim humor that the poem has the speaker say (but not think much about) the fact that his "guerdon" is only a solitary death.

The verse form of "A Battle Cry" is a tetrameter version of the bal-lad stanza, rhyming *abcb,* like "The Freeman." This is likewise the rhyme scheme of a subsequent poem in the collection, "Aridity," in which, as in "Justice," the speaker is very clearly a woman. "Aridity" is rich in duplicities: in the first stanza, to the east is a sickly sea, to the west the "land's aridity." In the second stanza, the rising sun is not the image of optimism that it usually is in nineteenth-century poetry (as in Swinburne's political sequence, *Songs before Sunrise*): instead, like the curses of the religious populace in "Justice" it smites the woman. And then it crawls like a slimy thing, recalling Coleridge's *Rime of the Ancient Mariner* (a favorite of Glasgow's) in which the rising sun brings suffering rather than relief and in which the crawling of slimy reptiles becomes an important symbol. The structure wherein dichotomies become contradictions appears in the third stanza of "Aridity": the woman's hand takes up the weary round of quotidian activity, and her "stillborn hopes" are "buried" in the "desert of her heart."

Of course, the theme of the buried life is also important in *The Woman Within:* like the unspoken horror in the upstairs room in the poem "Coward Memory," which the woman cannot even bring herself to remember, the buried life is not sentimentalized, not an inner Eden of fancied bliss, but a site of pain—in her mother's case, "the constant pain hidden under her sparkling vivacity" (62). Generalized among her family (especially the women in her family), "the glow would fade from life, and the air of melancholy wash over us. This was our actual life, beneath the smooth conventional surface" (63). In both books, *The Freeman* and *The Woman Within,* the buried life is *not* a matter of inward desire for a man, as per the perennial fictions of true love; it is rather a matter of her identification with her mother who died, as Glasgow perceived the case, under the cruelty of her father. She refers thus to the time of her mother's death: "A part of me, buried but alive, was held there, imprisoned" (83).

Submergence (burial) is not only a matter of her poetry's tropes; it is a large part of the substance of Glasgow's social critique, which the poems embody so recurrently. Under the language of piety, the unthinking mob perpetrates brutality in "Justice"; unable to endure a confrontation with her own past, the victim of an unspoken horror represses that past in "Coward Memory"; and (according to *The Woman Within*) under the dictatorial regime of her father, with his Old Testament religion, the life of the mother is smothered. Reproducing this sequence of repressions, the poetry of *The Freeman* submerges its critical exhibits beneath a surface in which a nation sounds its thanks to God, as piously (it would appear) as need be.

Sometimes the context of the volume as a whole is necessary to reveal the satirical dimensions of single poems within it. For example, "A Creed" seems conventional enough on its surface, affirming "Lord, I believe" repetitiously, in fact ending every stanza with that little line of two feet. But as Glasgow and her early reviewers agreed, her work is conventional *only* on its surface; it is wise to look further.

"A Creed" refers to a "fellowship of living things, / In kindred claims of Man and Beast." But this animal kinship takes on some other implications when the poem starts drawing analogies among weed and flower and worm and man: that sequence suggests evolution. The poem's speaker asserts that weed, flower, worm, man, and the sequence they represent result from a supernal cause; this supplementary hypothesis attempts to retrieve a religious outlook from a naturalistic admission. But that assertion is arbitrary and entirely questionable, though the speaker does not question it. Certainly in *The Woman Within* Glasgow exhibits a great deal of skepticism about such assertions as this one, that a supernal cause dependably arranges developments in the natural world. She calls such optimism "evasive idealism," as I have said, and she is writing of her cast of mind during the years in which *The Freeman* was written when she says, "I had never known a person, certainly not in the Solid South, who believed as little as I did, for I doubted the words of man as well as the works of God" (141); "All religion, for me, was a more or less glorified mythology, and, too often, a cruel mythology" (167). She says that she had an almost constitutional skepticism that "warned me to doubt everything I wished to believe" (173). The speaker of "A Creed" has no such doubts: "man" is assimilated with the mortal worm, and the bare assertion of supernal protection satisfies the speaker, who chants mechanically, "Lord, I believe."

"A Creed" mentions Buddha and Christ, claiming to believe in them, too, and in the efficacy of spiritual love wherever it appears. This sentence in the poem is not manifestly ironized, in itself, but the contexts of the poetic volume and of Glasgow's other books do ironize it. For example, one page after her assertion about doubting everything she wished to believe, Glasgow writes at some length about the appealing but futile illusions of hope offered by Buddha and Christ:

> a Divine teacher came, and spoke and was misunderstood, and changed his world, and passed on; and the world that he had changed closed again in the old pattern. Then the Christ came, and spoke, and was misunderstood, and passed on; and Christianity settled back again into the old human pattern. (*WW* 174)

Glasgow emphasizes the temporary character of each of these religious solutions. The old pattern of merely mortal cruelty returns inevitably, and history erodes the hopeful systems of idealism, successively. "I could not believe," she says, plainly enough. In contrast, however, the speaker of "A Creed" says, over and over again (without considering any of the problems that troubled Glasgow), "Lord, I believe."

By the end of the volume, those critical ironies become apparent. The poem "To a Strange God: In the British Museum, August 1896" produces the same reflections on the historicity (rather than eternity) of "gods" and the fabrication (rather than truth) of religious formulations. The evolutionary theme is expressed: all night "men and beasts go down / Into the struggle of the street"; here, the evolutionary theory of life-forms in perpetual struggle recalls Herbert Spencer's extension of evolutionary thought into social, industrial, and economic terms. (Glasgow read Spencer several times, claiming a "profound acquaintance" with his *Synthetic Philosophy*.)[9] The speaker in "To a Strange God" finds in the British Museum a statue of an ancient deity, described in the poem as an overthrown god in a case of glass; a myth is here reduced to an exhibit of a defunct and alien culture, amid "gods of other creeds than ours." Gods, too, are subjected to evolutionary change. Further, divinely ordained rewards and punishments are not relevant: the favors of this god "Know not belief from unbelief." The deity is unperturbed by damning doubt (stanza six), being merely insensate stone. In stanza five, the god who had sovereignty over a whole civilization is seen to have bowed to the rod of mutability—which is what Buddha and Christ are seen to have done, in *The Woman Within*.

In stanza eight, "we" (not ancients, but "we") have been "blind with carnage." In stanza nine, "Our right hath been the right of steel"— "our" religion has been propaganda for bloodshed; the poem "War" has already said so (though ironically rather than directly, as here). "Our litany" has been "the battle-cry." "A Battle Cry" and "War," more and more evidently, *ridicule* the voices of patriotism and the march of Christian progress. In "To a Strange God," "Our proud hosannas rend the air" where the children of this god's culture "came in prayer": their worship was futile to resist the onslaught of *our* inspired conquest.

The following stanza emphasizes the merely temporary viability of "our" religious system, too: "Our fortresses and faiths decay." The speaker of "A Creed" is happy to keep repeating, "I believe," but this poem indicates very clearly that his belief is quite as mortal as he is. "A Creed" is (by this point in the volume) very explicitly treated as one among a deplorable number of "canker creeds." Historicity is the governing principle: the evolutionary form of thought appears without the unearned optimism about a supernal plan assuring the goodness of all this decay. In stanza eleven, "Our future is a people's past"—i.e., our entire civilization is (like all others) doomed to mutability and decay. It is not the strange stone deity in the museum only who suffers historical change;

such "blows . . . smite the God of all." This poem's speaker is confident that *all* religion is a temporary social form.

"To a Strange God" is followed immediately by "The Vision of Hell," which provides a cosmic vantage on the earth, perceiving human beings as "mortal shadows" and "blind atoms" moving briefly from birth to death. The coherence of "The Vision of Hell" with the preceding poem, "To a Strange God," is obvious, but the poem is linked with earlier poems in the book as well. Its rhyme is the pattern of a ballad, *abcb,* like the rhyme of "The Freeman," "A Suppliant," "Justice," and "Aridity." The meter is the elegiac five (which is the meter of "The Freeman"), except that the fourth line of each stanza is truncated to two feet (exactly as it is in "The Freeman"). There is a single exception to that rule, which is the elongation of one line (in the whole poem) to three feet (which is exactly what appears in "The Freeman"). This much exact repetition of the (unusual) versification of the title poem invites a comparison of these two poems in *other* ways, and as in the rereading of "A Creed," which is prompted by "To a Strange God," this rereading of "The Freeman" ironizes its apparent bombast.

"The Vision of Hell" portrays "the earth in tragic irony" plunging to death. This vision casts an altogether different light on the freeman's speech in the title poem: the freeman is a "vagabond between the East and West," treading "where arrows press upon my path." Proudly he says, "I face the thunder and I face the rain . . . I face the autumn as / I face the spring." The prospect of "tragic irony" raised in the later poem, however, suggests that these cycles may be meaningless. And then one wonders how one could have missed the moral darkness of the title poem's concluding stanza:

> Around me, on the battle-fields of life,
> I see men fight and fail and crouch in prayer;
> Aloft I stand unfettered, for I know
> The freedom of despair.

That final line, "The freedom of despair," voices just the same vision as "The Vision of Hell." We have seen the alliance of religion and war frequently enough in the volume to recognize the bitter tone of the phrase "fight and fail and crouch in prayer," and (as in "To a Strange God") we may well be suspicious of the religiosity of "prayer." If (as even "A Creed" admits) the supernal protector has divinely ordained these cycles of destruction, then asking Him to intervene at this point would be blasphemous; in the terms of "To a Strange God" it is simply futile.

The speaker of "The Vision of Hell" speaks directly to Jehovah: "the life you gave / Is but a lying travesty, whose lie / Ends in the grave." This passage raises the theme of parody ("travesty"), which is important elsewhere in the volume, too, as I shall be showing in a moment. It also recalls the defiant speech addressed to Jehovah by the speaker in "Resurrection," earlier in the volume: the first stanza of that poem generalizes dust becoming flesh and refers to the sea giving up the dead. In the second stanza, one person is singled out, as a voice, from the multitude or universe of souls. This single voice complains beneath Jehovah: "Couldst Thou not leave me death?"

The Jehovah theme is important in Glasgow's work: "Father gathered us about him, and read aloud his favorite belligerent passages from the Old Testament. What comfort he could have found in the slaughter of Moabites or Amalekites, or even of Philistines, it is hard to imagine"; Father (and the conventionally religious community generally) worshipped "a God of terror, savoring the strong smoke of blood sacrifice" (*WW* 85). The article *a* in the phrase "a God" recalls the plurality of time-bound and historically relative deities in "To a Strange God," and so does the pluralism of deity in the following sentence: "Father had offered me, not Christ, but Jehovah" (*WW* 93); and the life given by this God (in the perspective of "The Vision of Hell") is but a lying travesty, ending in the grave. In her autobiography Glasgow is explicit about God's being a psychological projection of His believers, and this fact is perhaps the basis of her suspicion of any belief that she *wishes* to believe: "Oh, Thou who dost take the shapes imagined by Thy worshipers!" (*WW* 93).

Of course, "The Vision of Hell" is only one among many perspectives produced in the *Freeman* volume. I would not suggest that this grim vision of bloody slaughter cloaked by lying travesties and terminated in mute but absolute mortality is the only (or final) moral vision of the book. There is positive ethical vision in the book, but before examining it, it will be useful to look at one more enormously important fiction of which the book is harshly and recurrently critical: the cultural fictions surrounding sexual love. In the poem "Reunion," the speaker cares not of sun, moon, stars, world, blood, tears, or the flames of hell—only romantic love.

This is satire. "[T]he illusion of romantic love was an ancient antagonist," quite the opposite of a comfort and consolation according to Glasgow's feminist perspective (*WW* 56). In fact, when Glasgow does treat the theme of sexual love directly, as in "Reunion," she does so precisely to ridicule the ethos of sentimental and womanly love. In "Love Has Passed Along the Way," for example, Glasgow again uses the increasingly ironic repetition (apart from its use as a title, the phrase

"Love has passed along the way" is used three times in twelve lines). "Hearts have fluttered" in the first stanza of Glasgow's poem, but this lovely fluttering is succeeded by "ashes," "gloom," and a "corpse upon the bed." The poem has found a disaster even more serious than "loving overmuch." In the face of the tragic irony of earth—a merely mortal plunge for a moment among blind atoms, with decay the only discernible "law" of life—it does not much matter how much one's private heart might have fluttered among its evasive idealisms: "Break my heart as best it may, / Love has passed along the way." That last application of the tenacious refrain has at least two edges. What "love" does in Glasgow's book is the same thing that deity and civilization do: it passes.

What the social themes of the volume (including its feminism) share with the cosmic themes (its use of the theory of evolution) is clearly the critique of conventional fictions. The common lot of women is perceived and treated as a temporary and wholly artificial kind of prison in which women are kept; the creeds that are mumbled in selfish prayer (in "A Suppliant") or chanted to accompany mob violence (in "Justice") are likewise temporary constructs and thus fictions (Latin *fictus* = made, shaped). The operation of Glasgow's verbal and dramatic ironies is an unmasking of duplicities, the false surface of life being contradicted by the buried but inevitable life (or death) forever turbulent below that surface.

The Freeman and Other Poems is not all critique. As I have said, the book does include positive moral vision, and it does so in one of the poems that is specifically dated: "England's Greatness: At the Grave of Charles Darwin, 1896." Darwin had died in 1882; the point of the date, 1896, is to locate the poem temporally with the other poem that bears that date in its title—"To a Strange God," which also originated in Glasgow's 1896 visit to England. Both are about evolutionary thinking. The poem has obvious thematic coherence with "The Vision of Hell" and "To a Strange God," and it has formal coherence with other poems in the book—for example, the poem is written in elegiac stanzas (like the preceding poem in the book, which is "To My Dog") except that the fourth line in each quatrain is truncated to two feet, as likewise in "The Vision of Hell," "The Freeman," "A Creed," "Justice," and "The Master Hand." ("The Master Hand," like one of Robert Browning's great dramatic monologues, is about Andrea del Sarto.) As always in this book, the formal repetition marks a conceptual coherence as well.

In the first stanza, England's greatness is said *not* to be a matter of the sword—not the bloody history that we have heard about in so many previous poems, not the slaughter of conquered nations as in "War" or "To a Strange God," and not the cross of blood: those things are "ghosts of old barbaric splendours / Rotting where Imperial Rome lies low." The archaeological relics of Roman legions now cause the conquering armies, under the symbol of the "Imperial Eagle," to look ephemeral and even meaningless—"All, with the lapse of Time, have passed away."

England's greatness, instead, "shall last when her superb oppressions / All are done." There is, of course, plain sarcasm here, calling oppressions superb, but there is a positive moral claim as well. After soldiers, and wars, have perished, scientific achievements (her example is Darwin's) remain. Despite (and after) the wars and the cultural fictions that propagandize wars ("tales of slaughter," like the stories in her father's Bible), "Truth" remains.

Some problems in *knowing* truth, however, also remain. The book's penultimate poem, "Mary," begins very skeptically: the Blessed Virgin is called "Daughter of dreams and visions." The offspring (daughter) of dream is obviously an illusion, a projection of desire or fear—the sort of thing that Glasgow says she avoids believing. But again the prosody is artfully designed to generate conceptual tension: each sixteen-line stanza (*ababcdcd*, etc.) consists of eight lines describing Mary in terms of a psychological projection: she is a projection of human desire in the first part of stanza one and a projection of despair in the first part of stanza two; each stanza ends with eight lines of invocation: "By . . . , By . . . ," ending "We hail thee 'Blessed,' now." "We" may be prompted by our own emotions (desire and fear); the mother of God, consolingly enough, takes "the shapes imagined by . . . worshipers" (*WW* 93). The line "We hail thee 'Blessed,' now" is situated in an ironic tension. The phrase about blessedness is juxtaposed with despair, gloom, ravage, tears, pangs, and broken hearts (lines 2, 4, 6, 7, and 15 of stanza two). In this context, "blessed" looks like an evasive illusion. And while Mary is the *daughter* of dreams (at the beginning of stanza one), she is the *mother* of sorrows at the beginning of stanza two. The formal and even mechanical parity of halves within each stanza and the parity of the two equal stanzas constitute a doubleness (duplicity) reinforced by the emotional opposites—the desire of stanza one and the despair of stanza two. The poem arrives at a suspension of contradictory alternatives.

That conflict is, of course, homologous with the unending oppositions portrayed in poem after poem, replicating the oppositional stance between ironized speaker and implicit critique with oppositional relationships between poems (as between "A Creed" and "The Vision of Hell") and, in "Mary," in a poetic portrait of what the heart's desire and fear can project. What one cannot do, knowing that one's objects of worship are projections of one's own emotions, is believe them. And, to quote Glasgow's blunt disavowal again, in contrast to several of the speakers of the poems, she "could not believe." The artistry of the poems is not, I emphasize, a mere versification of a negative answer to a question of religious belief. The poems' ironies treat thematically the larger process of cultural and conceptual fictions, of which her father's religion (like the propaganda of war, or the sentimental fictions of true love) is only one example. Glasgow's poems, including "Mary," are portrayals in dramatic and metaphoric forms of the drama of desire and fear that underlies such projections. "Mary" and other poems in the volume amount to a satirical critique of those tales of slaughter and prayer which are among the results of the ideological conventions that (in her poems as in her novels) Glasgow attacks.

The volume's last poem, "The Hunter," finds "the Truth" not in icons of Christian worship but in "the secrets of the night," which are in "skeletons." The eternal Mysteries are read where the spider makes his web. The secrets of the dust are found in graves. And the volume closes with a poem returning to the imagery of its early poems: "In living men and worms I trace / Old allegories of the race"—evolution enables a *reading* of the book of the world, as present species (and customs, and institutions) bear in their present forms meaningful signs of their preexistence, their past. The "kindred claims of Man and Beast" look very different now, after the poem in praise of Darwin.

Again, feminism, criticism of the ideology of war, criticism of traditional religion, satire of the conventions of true love, and a positive presentation of the theory of evolution (chiefly social evolution) alike exhibit a principle much larger than the mere topicality of any one of these issues. The poems' larger theme involves the exhibit of beliefs, customs, social codes, and traditions as fictions. The operation of unmasking is ubiquitous in the book, but Glasgow's irony removes several kinds of masks.

The movement of the poetic volume is a progress from the apparent piety of mechanical repetition, through a vision of hell, to a celebration of the historicizing and evolutionary model of thought. The affirmations made in the closing poems leave doubt and inquiry (Greek *skepsis* = "inquiry") as active forces in the life of the mind. Doctrine and denials aside, the artistry of the poems is considerable—in their prosody, in the orchestration of their imagery and tones, and in the complex set of relationships established among the poems. It always was, and doubtless will be, Glasgow's novels that earned widespread recognition. Their dialogical form, their greater capacity for large social vision, and their popularity helped to ensure that it would be so. But the artful poetry of *The Freeman* volume is coherent with the novels' skeptical strategies and with the large project of ideological unmasking that Glasgow made her life's work.

Notes

1. Though the present essay deals with the integrity of Glasgow's book itself, her work is related in important ways to poetry by her contemporaries, including Thomas Hardy and Ella Wheeler Wilcox. Those relationships form matter for other studies.

2. These quoted phrases appear in an Associated Press Sketch, now located among the archives at the University of Virginia Library; the passage is quoted by Wagner (4).

3. I am grateful to Dorothy M. Scura for pointing out to me these early reviews of *The Freeman and Other Poems* and for providing me with the text of several of them, from the page proofs of Scura's important new book, *Ellen Glasgow: The Contemporary Reviews*.

4. Glasgow, "Relation of the Scholar to the Creative Arts," an unpublished essay located among the archives at the University of Virginia Library and quoted in Wagner (16).

5. See Wagner (5–6) for an account of this statement and theme in Glasgow's work.

6. Raper's central concern in *Without Shelter* is "to follow Ellen Glasgow's use of the complex realism associated with Darwin as a critical tool to strip away the veneers of southern ideology" (ix). Those who felt that the life of their social structure depended on the maintenance of that veneer did not, of course, wish to see it stripped away; this fact may, I am suggesting, have contributed to the impercipience with which her social world responded (rather, did not respond) to her book of verse.

7. In the final stanza of "The Freeman," however, the last line is lengthened to three feet and thus distinguished by amplification: that line, "The freedom of despair," recalls the volume's epigraph and (as the epigraph does) generalizes the poem's reference beyond the literal and historical facts of slavery.

8. For an analysis of truncation as a technique in the versification of feminist poetry, using as an example a poem by Elinor Wylie, of whom Glasgow writes flatteringly in *The Woman Within*, see Anna Shannon Elfenbein and Terence Allan Hoagwood, "'Wild Peaches': Landscapes of Desire and Deprivation," *Women's Studies* 15 (1988): 387–97. Wylie shortens the octave of a sonnet for satirical effect.

9. *WW* (102). Spencer was on Glasgow's mind and in her conversation while she was working on the poems of *The Freeman* volume: in October 1898 Hamlin Garland visited Glasgow in Richmond; as Raper has pointed out, "He talked with her about Spencer and Darwin and was encouraged by her 'alarming candor of statement': . . . . She showed him a collection of her poems," obviously *this* collection (see Raper 123).

Works Cited

Elfenbein, Anna Shannon, and Terence Allan Hoagwood. "'Wild Peaches': Landscapes of Desire and Deprivation." *Women's Studies* 15 (1988): 387–97.

Glasgow, Ellen. *A Certain Measure: An Interpretation of Prose Fiction.* New York: Harcourt, 1943.

———. *The Freeman and Other Poems.* New York: Doubleday, 1902.

———. *Letters of Ellen Glasgow.* Ed. Blair Rouse. New York: Harcourt, 1958.

———. *The Woman Within.* New York: Harcourt, 1954.

Raper, Julius Rowan. *Without Shelter: The Early Career of Ellen Glasgow.* Baton Rouge: Louisiana State UP, 1971.

Scura, Dorothy M. *Ellen Glasgow: The Contemporary Reviews.* Cambridge: Cambridge UP, 1992.

———. "A Knowledge in the Heart: Ellen Glasgow, the Women's Movement, and *Virginia.*" *American Literary Realism* 22.2 (Winter 1990): 30–43.

Wagner, Linda W. *Ellen Glasgow: Beyond Convention.* Austin: U of Texas P, 1982.

"Experience Illuminated"
Veristic Representation in Glasgow's Short Stories

Stephanie R. Branson

> The true realists, I felt, must illuminate experience,
> not merely transcribe it; and so, for my own purpose,
> I defined the art of fiction as experience illuminated.
> —Glasgow, *A Certain Measure* 14

Ellen Glasgow published a short story entitled "A Woman of To-Morrow" in *Short Stories* (Vol. 19 [1895]: 415–27) when she was twenty-two. Throughout her long literary career, Glasgow continued to write short stories, despite her own feeling that she was a novelist by nature and against the specific advice of editors such as Walter Hines Page who suggested that she shouldn't waste her time on such a minor genre. She persisted in writing what was considered at the time to be "minor" fiction, minor generically and philosophically—fantastic short stories produced over decades dominated by realistic and modernist novels.

Glasgow's fantastic short stories have not received the attention they deserve because of this minor status and because they are also feminist fictions. As Nina Baym points out in an essay on American literary history, women have generally been excluded from the American canon (63). She specifically mentions the exclusion of Ellen Glasgow and attributes this to Glasgow's invention of female protagonists who did not fit the roles apparently preferred for female characters by male authors and male critics. This predisposition may be what motivates Warner Berthoff, for example, to remark, "The buried vein of authenticity in Ellen Glasgow's work is almost entirely subjective and emotional, referring to nothing else so surely as to the pathos of her own undeliverance" (254). Although in a brief discussion of the short stories Linda Wagner asserts that the portraits of women in the stories were among Glasgow's most feminist,

Wagner's book-length study of Glasgow reflects the general trend in Glasgow criticism to offer biographical interpretations of her novels (66–67).

Glasgow's fantastic short stories deserve serious attention because they represent a special form of social commentary running contrary to what can be seen as the dominant discourses of realistic and modernist fiction. Glasgow counters the dominant modes of writing—what she called "the pale realism of New England and the florid romance of the South and West" (*ACM* 75)—with a different kind of writing:

> But I was never a pure romancer any more than I was a pure realist. Rather I should have called myself a verist had such a term come my way. The whole truth must embrace the interior world as well as external appearances. Behaviour alone is only the outer envelope of personality; and this is why documentary realism, the notebook style, has produced merely surface impressions. (*ACM* 27–28)

The formal verist movement at the turn of the century identified itself more with "documentary realism" than with the mix of realism and romanticism adopted by Glasgow. That the term had not "come her way" suggests that the author was not familiar with the verist movement. In her use of the term, as Monique Parent carefully writes: "Ellen Glasgow élabore un romantisme constructif et un réalisme positif qui se rejoignent dans le vrai" (394–95)—"Ellen Glasgow expresses a constructive romanticism and a positive realism that together ring true" (my translation). These feminist fantastic fictions ask the reader to consider especially female experience in the context of a fully imagined world.

The term *verism* suggests its counterpart, *verity*, or a kind of transcendent or universal truth (i.e., the eternal verities). A *nisus formativus* of Glasgow's stories is the pursuit of this kind of truth. But as her contemporary William James says, "Absolute existence is absolute mystery, for its relations with the nothing remain unmediated to our understanding" (9). Glasgow believed in the absolute mystery of life, and if, like the formal verists, she relies only on her senses to discover truth, a "sixth sense," that of the imagination, is of vital importance in its pursuit. Glasgow called the realm of absolute mystery the "fourth dimension." In *A Certain Measure* she states: "[I]t is true even with a novelist of philosophy rather than life that there must be a fourth dimension in every fiction that attempts to interpret reality. There must be a downward seeking into the stillness of vision, as well as an upward springing into the animation of the external world" (142). Veristic representation, then, fluctuates from the material to the numinous, using methods of distancing—either of retrospective or historical distance, or of rhetorical distance (irony), or both—and methods of unification—through a search for identity, and/or through the expression of inner vision.

Glasgow's verism, at least as it is applied in her fantastic short stories, thus approximates Tzvetan Todorov's definition of the fantastic. Todorov states that the fantastic "occupies the duration" of uncertainty in assigning causes to apparently supernatural events in stories or novels: "Either total faith or total incredulity would lead us beyond the fantastic: it is hesitation which sustains its life" (25, 31). Glasgow's stories contain numinous or marvelous elements such as pathetic fallacy and ghosts. Linda Wagner cites this treatment of the supernatural as "the ostensible reason" for Glasgow's move into short fiction (67). These elements differentiate the stories from conventional realist texts, even from Glasgow's own novels, which are less experimental both in feminist and Todorovian terms.

In "Dare's Gift," in "The Past," and in "The Shadowy Third," it is possible to identify a suspension between fact and fantasy, between historical realities and present concerns, between the actual and the ironic ideal. The tension resulting from such conflicting motivations invigorates these stories; it is also what causes them to elude easy generic or representational categorization.

Realistic elements in the stories abound. Georg Lukacs defines realistic fiction in this way: "The literature of realism, aiming at a truthful reflection of reality," "implies a description of actual persons inhabiting a palpable, identifiable world" (23–24). He allies realistic fiction with other forms of "traditional art" that assume "an immanent meaning to human existence" (40). For Lukacs, "In realistic literature each descriptive detail is both *individual* and *typical*" (43; Lukacs's emphasis). In these three stories, all the living human characters are plausible, and they inhabit an identifiable world—the American South. Glasgow provides minute detail regarding their environment, naming each flower whose path they cross, describing in detail the houses they inhabit. In addition, she offers more than a glimpse at their inner world, their ideas and emotions.

In "Dare's Gift," for example, a corporation lawyer from Washington becomes the eminently rational narrator of an extraordinary—but not unnatural—event. Another main character, his wife, is also typical. Mildred is a high-strung but normally passive and acquiescent woman who has always supported her husband. The fact that she reveals his guilty professional secret, thereby turning from submissive partner in marriage to independent actor on the national scene but betraying the complete confidence her husband has placed in her, is not entirely without justification or rational cause, despite Harold Beckwith's utter astonishment and despite the fact that he considers the act to stem entirely from her recurrent depression.

The setting is realistically defined also. Dare's Gift is an Old World estate not far from Richmond, Virginia, with a doorway of "pure Colonial lines," with "crude modern additions to the wings," with cedars in front and a luxurious garden in back (*CS* 91). Its gardens open onto the sleepy James River. The realistic description of place is complemented by details of time. We know from one of the narrators, Dr. Lakeby, that the present of "Dare's Gift" occurs fifty years or so after the Civil War, and we know from various references that the story takes place in spring. That part of the story which is related by Dr. Lakeby takes place on the same estate, fifty years earlier, at the end of the war. Colonel Dare and his daughter, Lucy Dare, are described as characteristic Southerners of the Civil War era, as genteel patriots starving for the cause.

Other touches of realism include brief references to the case that Harold Beckwith is working on. Its questionable moral nature provides the impetus for his wife's betrayal. Beckwith describes it in this way: "Some philanthropic busybody, employed to nose out corruption, had scented legal game in the affairs of the Atlantic & Eastern Railroad" (97). This seems a plausible problem for a corporation lawyer to be working on, and the fact that Beckwith finds "a mass of damaging records" that undermine his defense of the railroad represents a commonplace development (98).

Glasgow suggests in the story, however, that Dare's Gift is "haunted by treachery"—that Mildred wasn't acting out of either depression or moral outrage alone, but that she was inspired to betray her husband by the act of betrayal/heroism of a kindred spirit—Lucy Dare—who had acted in a similar fashion half a century earlier (104). It is in this connection that both women, Mildred and Lucy, acquire legendary (romantic) proportions, and it is with the introduction of a *genius loci* that fantasy enters the story.

As Alastair Fowler points out in *Kinds of Literature,* setting "is a highly developed feature with romance, science fiction, the gothic short story, and the psychological novel" (68). In verisimilar works of all kinds, a multiplicity of straightforward detail is sufficient to the purpose of setting the fictional, but representationally transparent, scene; in fantastic or veristic fiction, supernatural detail is introduced in concert with realistic detail. In "Dare's Gift," Glasgow animates the house that the Beckwiths and others inhabit, using a form of the pathetic fallacy, or what Josephine Miles calls the "attribution of feeling to things" (1).

Mildred Beckwith and Lucy Dare also leave the realm of realism because the (male) society in which they live judges their extraordinary actions to be acts of madness prompted by this supernatural environment. Mildred is acting out of depression, invisibly compelled by the "mental atmosphere" of Dare's Gift (*CS* 104). Lucy Dare acted out of starvation and isolation from the reality of an already defeated Confederate army.

The romantic dimension of the two women is demonstrated both by the interpretations provided by rational male narrators and by the inclusion of other traitorous actions joining the cycle of betrayal. The first act of betrayal that is recounted is offered by an anonymous woman who is inhabiting Dare's Gift before the Beckwiths acquire it. She tells Harold Beckwith that her husband has run off with her sister—even though she is the prettier of the two (*CS* 92). The owner of Dare's Gift, Mr. Duncan, has also been betrayed by a man whom he "had picked up starving in London, and had trusted absolutely for years" (94). These traitorous actions are, like the actions of Lucy and Mildred, unexpected though not unrealistic; the suggestion is that they are supernaturally motivated.

If either of the heroines, Mildred or Lucy, had narrated her own tale, she would possibly have stated the cause of her actions unequivocally. According to Harold Beckwith, an "invincible spirit of darkness" residing in Dare's Gift creates an impenetrable mystery and causes unexpected misery to him (90). To his wife, her action might have stemmed from her dissatisfaction with the marriage (as evidenced by her nervous breakdown and subsequent periods of depression), from her belief that her lawyer-husband was acting immorally in concealing the damaging evidence, from influences felt or imagined from the house itself, or from all or none of these things. By narrating the story indirectly, through the men in the story who merely observe and attempt to interpret the women's actions, Glasgow allows the reader to formulate his/her own interpretation of the actions and of their causes. She also effects that quality of hesitation between the seen and the unseen that Todorov describes in fantastic fiction which is part of veristic representation in the story. Lastly, Glasgow asks us to "seek downward into the stillness of [her] vision" (*ACM* 142)—moral dilemmas such as those confronting Mildred and Lucy may (must?) be resolved through intuition or with reference to influences other than conventional ones.

Glasgow has said, "Knowledge, like experience, is valid in fiction only after it has dissolved and filtered down through the imagination into reality" (*Letters* 14). Her four ghost stories, along with the ghostly "Jordan's End," are related retrospectively (generally a year after the event). Even with that perspective, her narrators do not always completely understand. In defining veristic perspective in "Dare's Gift," it is interesting to note that the experiences of Mildred and Lucy are interpreted only after, not during, their occurrence. But Harold Beckwith begins the story with an expression of doubt and confusion:

> A year has passed, and I am beginning to ask myself if the thing actually happened? The whole episode, seen in clear perspective, is obviously incredible. . . . Yet, while I assure myself that the supernatural has been banished, in the evil company of devils, black plagues, and witches, from this sanitary century, a vision of Dare's Gift . . . rises before me, and my feeble scepticism surrenders to that invincible spirit of darkness. (*CS* 90)

While Harold Beckwith senses that invisible forces are at play, the corporate lawyer lacks sufficient imagination to solve the mystery of Dare's Gift, despite a period of reflection following the episode he recounts.

In "The Past," retrospection is itself the subject. As in "Dare's Gift," the house inhabited by the major characters is haunted. However, this house is haunted not by an idea but by a woman whose guilt regarding her marital infidelity, coupled with Mr. Vanderbridge's misplaced guilt at her untimely death, holds her spirit unnaturally in suspension between life and death.

The story is related retrospectively by Miss Wrenn, the secretary of the current Mrs. Vanderbridge, mistress of the house. She is "looking back after a year" following the successful exorcism of the ghost of the first Mrs. Vanderbridge (*CS* 119). The present is infected or haunted by events in Mr. Vanderbridge's past—some which he is not even aware of. His first wife's infidelity and her subsequent guilty haunting of the house cause the "secret disturbance" of which Miss Wrenn is immediately aware (119). By burning letters written to the first Mrs. Vanderbridge by her illicit lover, the current Mrs. Vanderbridge releases the house and its inhabitants (living and dead) from the unnatural domination of the past over the present caused mainly by Mr. Vanderbridge's obsession with and misinterpretation of past events. He is unaware of his wife's infidelity and believes he is responsible for her early death. Miss Wrenn discovers the truth regarding this unusual love triangle only upon reflection:

Not until afterwards did I realize that it was the victory of good over evil. Not until afterwards did I discover that Mrs. Vanderbridge had triumphed over the past in the only way that she could triumph. . . . Oh, long, long afterwards, I knew that she had robbed the phantom of power over her by robbing it of hatred. She had changed the thought of the past. (*CS* 138–39)

Past events do not themselves change, but our interpretations of them are perhaps constantly changing. As we gain experience, our perspective toward those events is shaped and rearranged, and our memory selects pieces of our past to fit present needs. Glasgow's narrator selects those events she wishes to relate in telling the Vanderbridges' story, and she interprets those events based upon her retrospective understanding of them. This is the formula Glasgow demonstrates in veristic representation.

Present concerns in "The Past" can also be defined as eternal verities—friendship and support among women, love between man and woman. Glasgow describes human nature in this way: "it is a law of our nature, as of all nature, that change only endures, and the perfect mould must be broken" (*ACM* 91). In "The Past," the seemingly unsolvable dilemma that faces Mr. and Mrs. Vanderbridge is solved by an agent of change, Miss Wrenn, who enters the haunted house and exorcises it by finding at its heart the letters that Mrs. Vanderbridge then burns. The fatal static condition of the Vanderbridge marriage, which appears perfect from the outside, is broken and the natural order—change—is reinstated through the unselfish actions of the women in the house.

Temporal distance from the event recounted is required for understanding in Glasgow's stories. According to the author: "literary creation demands a foreground, a middle distance, and a perspective. When one is too near, or too much involved in the subject, values are displaced, and the fluid contours are apt to solidify freezingly" (*ACM* 55). Another kind of distance is afforded in the stories by a rhetorical device, irony. Glasgow is quoted as saying that she has always "looked through a veil of irony" at life (Rouse 35). But as Henry Seidel Canby suggests, "Miss Glasgow's irony is always tender" (4); rather than looking down with contempt upon her characters and their foibles as representations of the ills of society, and without surrendering to existential despair, Glasgow satirized the conventions of her society, especially as they affected women, but always with a degree of self-reflection. In this way, she maintained the proper distance from her subject.

As Linda Wagner points out, Glasgow was "amused by the differences between the traditional concepts of woman and her own personal concepts" (4). In the introduction to Glasgow's letters, Blair Rouse asserts: "Into her novels, even the darker and prevailingly tragic stories, she brought the balance and relief of high comedy" (17). In *Ellen Glasgow and the Ironic Art of Fiction,* Frederick P. W. McDowell states that "it was ironic laughter, rather than philosophy, which best permitted her, she said, to escape the insistent self within. A lightly sardonic view of her own frustrations and of the larger tragedy of the world gave her spirit release" (29). Glasgow's moderate use of irony in her short stories suspends the reader between the actual and the ideal, the tragic and the comic.

"The Shadowy Third" is a case in point. Mrs. Maradick is a woman thoroughly wronged by life. Having inherited a fortune, she becomes the prey of a talented surgeon who is so much in love with someone else that he is willing to marry the heiress, murder her daughter, drive his wife crazy, and send her to an asylum to die, all so that he might inherit the fortune which he believes will endear him to his former mistress. The female narrator, who eventually sides with Mrs. Maradick and her daughter, is nevertheless early drawn into Dr. Maradick's spell, and her admiring description of him offers an ironic twist to the story:

> Like the patients and the other nurses, I also had come by delightful, if imperceptible, degrees to hang on the daily visits of Doctor Maradick. He was, I suppose, born to be a hero to women. . . . If I had been ignorant of his spell—of the charm he exercised over his hospital—I should have felt it in the waiting hush, like a dawn breath, which followed his ring at the door and preceded his imperious footstep on the stairs. (*CS* 53)

Nurse Randolph introduces a conventional ideal in this passage—that Dr. Maradick, as a talented surgeon and a handsome and favored man, would protect and enchant the women who came in contact with him, that he would perform heroic services for them, that he would be their Prince Charming. Glasgow then ironically explodes that myth—in actuality Dr. Maradick is a cold-blooded villain who destroys the woman who loves him by killing (although it is not made clear how he does it) her daughter, Dorothea, a "gift of God" (62). The story ends with this gift from God becoming an angel of death for Dr. Maradick, who trips on the immaterial skipping rope she leaves on the stair. But Mrs. Maradick, who is innocent of all but poor judgment of character, also dies. In "The Shadowy Third," Glasgow demonstrates the danger of believing in Prince Charming.

Margaret Randolph is the agent for irony in other circumstances as well. After she has seen the apparition of the little girl, but before she has been told that Dorothea died two months before, Nurse Randolph thinks that she has discovered the secret of Mrs. Maradick's illness, and she expresses her discovery in the following way:

> Then it was that light burst on me in a blaze. So this was Mrs. Maradick's hallucination! She believed that her child was dead—the little girl I had seen with my own eyes leaving her room; and she believed that her husband—the great surgeon we worshipped in the hospital—had murdered her. (*CS* 60)

As Glasgow has said in previously quoted passages, it is difficult (if not impossible) to understand experience without the distance of retrospection. Nurse Randolph believes that she understands why Mrs. Maradick is kept a virtual prisoner in her room and why her illness is veiled in secrecy. And because the reader comes to know, as Nurse Randolph does, that the little girl is dead, that Dr. Maradick sends his wife away to die, that he inherits the money and plans to marry his former mistress—in short, that everything Mrs. Maradick says is true—this passage regarding Nurse Randolph's immediate insight into the mystery becomes ironic.

One of the consistent ironies of the story is that medical men (Drs. Maradick and Brandon) whose job it is to heal harm instead. Dr. Maradick somehow causes the death of Dorothea and hastens his wife's death, due to greed. Dr. Brandon is an "alienist," or psychologist, called in to help Mrs. Maradick. Brandon "lacked red blood in his brain," regarded "all life as a disease," "analyzed away everything except the bare structure"—he lacked imagination and thus lacked the ability to understand or to heal his patient (62). According to Nurse Randolph, the night nurse to Mrs. Maradick, Miss Peterson, is "stupid, so armoured and encased in her professional manner" that she also lacks the ability to heal (66). Nurse Randolph, who in the beginning of the story is lightly admonished by her superior for being too sympathetic to her patients, is the only medical professional in the story who is able to help Mrs. Maradick. She is also the only person in the house, other than the black butler, who sees the little girl's ghost.

Thus, Glasgow treats the tragedy of a woman and her child in an ironic fashion, placing the proper distance between author and subject, and suspending the reader between the actual and the ideal. Mrs. Maradick's terrible fate is softened by the sympathy she receives from Margaret Randolph before she dies, and justice is served by supernatural agency. In a balance of realism and romanticism, the "fluid contours" of life are preserved.

Retrospective and irony in Glasgow's stories provide the proper distance from the actual that is required in order to infuse the narratives with the numinous, evidenced in the form of ghosts and living houses. This numinous element also constitutes a subtle criticism of patriarchal convention and consensus reality. Both feminism as a sociopolitical project and verism as a literary mode require imaginative departures from convention, and as Linda Wagner remarks regarding Glasgow's three short stories that are the subject of my discussion, "her four stories billed as 'ghost tales'. . . are as much character studies of female protagonists as they are suspense stories" (67).

"Dare's Gift," "The Past," and "The Shadowy Third" can be seen as feminist fantastic fictions because in them, strong women struggle cooperatively against the male-defined society in which they live. They are aided in this struggle by supernatural agents—ghosts and living houses—that balance the perhaps cruel rational forces that are attempting to limit or even end their lives. In this way, Glasgow suggests that misogyny can be overcome through imaginative living in an organic cosmos.

In "Dare's Gift," the actions of Mildred Beckwith and Lucy Dare take on a different meaning than that ascribed to them by the male narrators who interpret them. In "The Daring Gift in Ellen Glasgow's 'Dare's Gift,'" Lynette Carpenter states: "Lucy Dare's legacy [to Mildred] is one of impersonal responsibility, of female commitment to something beyond personal loyalty. It is also one of individuality, of independence from stereotypes and other constraints on personal expression" (101). Thus, the actions of the two women in the story can be defined as heroic and feminist. According to Dr. Lakeby, however, Lucy acting in accord with the dominant idea of the South—the Confederacy—"was alien to the temperament of the people among whom she lived," for "though Lucy Dare was sublime, according to the moral code of the Romans, she was a stranger to the racial soul of the South," which ordinarily placed personal loyalties over impersonal ones (105–6). But Dr. Lakeby's interpretation of Lucy's act is contradictory because it is based on gender, not "racial" difference. Because Lucy (and by extension, all women) was "ordinary, submissive, feminine, domestic" before and after her heroic act, Dr. Lakeby considers the action to be "strange" and unheroic (107). Glasgow provides two unreliable narrators in "Dare's Gift" in order to provide an ironic twist to the telling of the tales and in order to inspire Todorovian hesitation on the part of the reader.

In fact, in their capacity as traitors to love but as loyal servants of other ideals, Lucy and Mildred create themselves. The last line of the story comes from Dr. Lakeby: "'After all,' he added slowly, 'it is the high moments that make a life, and the flat ones that fill the years'" (118). Both women live otherwise "flat" lives, as almost invisible helpmates to the men in their lives; in acting "out of character" they become hero- ines and people. Lucy Dare and Mildred Beckwith are modern-day Antigones, but this time the author of the story is female.

Both "The Past" and "The Shadowy Third" demonstrate yet another important feminist concept—sisterhood. Glasgow has said the follow- ing regarding friendship among women:

> It is seldom in modern fiction that a friendship between two women, especially a pure and unselfish friendship, with both women loving the same man, has assumed a prominent place. Although such an associa- tion appears to be not uncommon in life, the novelist, since he is usually a man, has found the relationship to be deficient alike in the excitement of sex and the masculine drama of action. But more and more, in the mod- ern world, women are coming to understand their interdependence as human beings; and without an example of this, a picture of our time that denied the place and the permanence of any such friendship would be wanting in complete veracity. (*ACM* 245)

"The Past" and "The Shadowy Third" both provide demonstrations of the principle of interdependence mentioned above, and in this way they become feminist fictions.

Ellen Glasgow provides a demonstration of unselfish friendship among all the women in "The Past"—Miss Wrenn and the maid Hopkins both work unselfishly to help Mrs. Vanderbridge, and Mrs. Vanderbridge un- selfishly aids her ghostly predecessor. Hopkins asks Miss Wrenn to help Mrs. Vanderbridge, saying, "If she was my own sister, I couldn't be any fonder of her, and yet I have to see her suffer day after day, and not say a word—not even to her" (*CS* 123). Miss Wrenn becomes the agent for change when she finds letters that incriminate the ghost she sees through the superior force of her imagination. Without this aid, it is likely that the first Mrs. Vanderbridge would have haunted the house indefinitely and that as a consequence of her unnatural influence the second Mrs. Vanderbridge would have died. Three living women and one dead woman find a way to resolve the mystery/misery that haunts the house.

In "The Shadowy Third," even though Nurse Randolph greatly ad- mires and even desires Dr. Maradick, she is led by sympathy and in- stinct to side with Mrs. Maradick instead. She says,

While he watched me I was conscious of an inner struggle, as if opposing angels warred somewhere in the depths of my being. When at last I
made my decision, I was acting less from reason, I knew, than in obedi-
ence to the pressure of some secret current of thought. Heaven knows,
even then, the man held me captive while I defied him. (*CS* 64)

Glasgow demonstrates through Margaret Randolph that contrary to
popular male depictions of jealousy and "women's scorn," many women
do unselfishly and instinctively help one another, despite the attraction
of the opposite sex.

These short stories perform several functions, then. As feminist fictions, they reflect Glasgow's version of female experience. As veristic
fictions, they combine realistic and romantic elements in an attempt to
capture "the whole truth" of human existence. If, as Glasgow states in
her definition of verism, "[t]he whole truth must embrace the interior
world as well as external appearances" (*ACM* 28), Glasgow's interior
world included a belief in the invisible, and the external world was meta-
physical as well as physical. As feminist fantastic fictions, Glasgow's short
stories deserve to be moved from the critical category of *Trivialliteratur*
to the category of "literature of vision"—Kathryn Hume's term for fantastic stories that "make us feel the limitations of our notions of reality,
often by presenting one that seems more rich, more intense, more coherent (or incoherent), or somehow more significant" (82). These fantastic fictions provide a rich, intense, coherent, and feminist view of
reality that does more (and less) than offer an avenue of escape from
quotidian difficulties. Glasgow's stories illuminate female experience
through veristic distancing and unity, as a blueprint for the processing
of human experience at large.

Works Cited

Baym, Nina. "Melodramas of Beset Manhood: How Theories of American Fiction
    Exclude Women Authors." *The New Feminist Criticism*. Ed. Elaine Showalter.
    New York: Pantheon, 1985. 63–80.
Berthoff, Warner. *The Ferment of Realism: American Literature, 1884–1919*. New York:
    Free Press, 1965.
Canby, Henry Seidel. "Ellen Glasgow: Ironic Tragedian." *Saturday Review of Litera-
    ture* 10 Sept. 1938: 3–4, 14.
Carpenter, Lynette. "The Daring Gift in Ellen Glasgow's 'Dare's Gift.'" *Studies in
    Short Fiction* 21.2 (Spring 1984): 95–102.

Fowler, Alastair. *Kinds of Literature: An Introduction to the Theory of Genres and Modes.* Cambridge: Harvard UP, 1982.

Glasgow, Ellen. *A Certain Measure: An Interpretation of Prose Fiction.* New York: Harcourt, 1943.

———. "A Woman of Tomorrow." *Short Stories* 19 (1895): 415–27.

———. *The Collected Stories of Ellen Glasgow.* Ed. Richard K. Meeker. Baton Rouge: Louisiana State UP, 1963.

———. *Letters of Ellen Glasgow.* Ed. Blair H. Rouse. New York: Harcourt, 1958.

Hume, Kathryn. *Fantasy and Mimesis: Responses to Reality in Western Literature.* New York: Methuen, 1984.

James, William. *Essays in Pragmatism.* Ed. Alburey Castell. New York: Hafner, 1948.

Lukacs, Georg. *The Meaning of Contemporary Realism.* Trans. John and Necke Mander. London: Merlin, 1963.

McDowell, Frederick P. W. *Ellen Glasgow and the Ironic Art of Fiction.* Madison: U of Wisconsin P, 1960.

Miles, Josephine. *Pathetic Fallacy in the Nineteenth Century: A Study of a Changing Relation between Object and Emotion.* 1942. New York: Octagon, 1976.

Parent, Monique. *Ellen Glasgow: Romancière.* Paris, Nizet, 1962.

Rouse, Blair. *Ellen Glasgow.* New York: Twayne, 1962.

Todorov, Tzvetan. *The Fantastic: A Structural Approach to a Literary Genre.* Trans. Richard Howard. Cleveland: Case Western Reserve UP, 1973.

Wagner, Linda W. *Ellen Glasgow: Beyond Convention.* Austin: U of Texas P, 1982.

PART IV

Novels

Restoring Order
Matriarchal Design in
The Battle-Ground and *Vein of Iron*

Lucinda H. MacKethan

Ellen Glasgow's eighteenth novel, *Vein of Iron* (1935), represents a remarkable breaking of new ground. For this late work, she turns for the first time to a setting in the Virginia mountains, where her father's Scotch-Irish forebears had settled and where he himself had been born. Yet the story that she embeds with close fidelity in the world of her paternal ancestors is one in which she manages, more successfully than in any of her other works, to exorcise her father's ghost and the ghost of southern patriarchy that he embodies. She does this largely through the creation of a grandmother/father/daughter relationship grounded in values that challenge and finally nullify the assumptions of power that she associated with her father's South. Although *Vein of Iron* takes root in a new setting and illustrates a new perception of identity as maternally and generationally empowered, it also looks back to the novel that Glasgow named as her first work to treat Virginia social history, *The Battle-Ground,* published in 1902.

While it has often been dismissed as a purely conventional Civil War romance, *The Battle-Ground* is really much more; in it a very young southern woman novelist, well-schooled in her culture's denial of freedom to women, realistically and intelligently dramatizes the flaws of the patriarchal system. In Betty Ambler, Glasgow creates a prototype for the strong individualism united with commitment to family that we see in *Vein of Iron*'s Ada Fincastle.

Between *The Battle-Ground* and *Vein of Iron* are novels often considered Glasgow's most important works, such as *Virginia* (1913) and *The Sheltered Life* (1932), which show the damaging effects of patriarchy on women's lives, or *Barren Ground* (1925), which creates a portrait of an empowered but radically isolated woman. *The Battle-Ground* and

Vein of Iron both envision a design that can be called matriarchal: it connects family and community, with women operating successfully in primary sustaining roles which they share with men without sacrificing their individuality. A matriarchal design can be defined as a structure of relationships based on sharing rather than competitiveness, on negotiation rather than self-assertion, and on integration rather than exclusion.

To examine the imaginative process by which Glasgow shaped her version of this design, we will look first at her autobiographical portrait of her father, in which he becomes the symbol of all the patriarchally promoted restrictions that she encountered in her life. Then we will look at *The Battle-Ground* to examine her earliest treatment of patriarchal order vs. matriarchal possibility in a South of the past that cast a long shadow over the world that Glasgow chose both to live in and to struggle against. Finally, we will assess her achievement in *Vein of Iron*, which is, as she herself said, "different from anything I have done" and a book of "quiet power" (*Letters* 179). That quiet power rests in large part on her ability to transcend her bitter fight against her father's values through her most direct but also most imaginative construction of the sources of his identity, which she could finally accept as one source of her own vein of iron.

In *The Woman Within* (1954), the autobiography published nine years after her death, Glasgow's opening chapters define the opposing values that her parents represented in scenes that mark her position as that of a battleground on which the struggle between them would be decided. Of her mother she says, "Her whole nature was interwoven with sympathy. She would divide her last crust with a suffering stranger" (14). Describing her father's "Calvinistic" virtues, she says caustically, "With complete integrity, and an abiding sense of responsibility, he gave his wife and children everything but the one thing they needed most, and that was love" (15). Glasgow believed that her father regarded her not as a human being with a mind and needs of her own but as a possession, an object existing to showcase his successful set of values. Although he took care of her when she was sick as a child, she distrusted him, "I must have felt, instinctively, that his attention was more patriarchal than paternal, and that I was not myself to him, but merely one of his ten children" (87).

In *The Woman Within* Glasgow constructs a series of scenes in which her father is consistently presented as an authoritarian committed to advancing his own interests at the expense of others'. With what amounted for her to criminal insensitivity, he sold the farm where she had been healthy and happy, he sent away the dogs who provided her with companionship, and most importantly, he separated her from the mother who was "the center of my childhood's world, the sun in my universe" (13). In the chapter entitled "Early Sorrow," Glasgow describes how her mother was emotionally removed from her by an incapacitating mental illness that only by inference, yet very strong inference, she associates with her father. Julius Rowan Raper points to convincing evidence that Mrs. Glasgow suffered a nervous breakdown after discovering that her husband had enjoyed sexual liaisons with black women in Richmond (29–30). Her autobiography makes no explicit charge of this nature, but it convicts Francis Glasgow of more general tendencies that would easily accompany this kind of betrayal: his lack of love, his coldness, his inability to appreciate his wife's gentle beauty, his treatment of his family as objects. He was, in short, not paternal but patriarchal in relation to both wife and children.

Francis Glasgow, seen through his daughter's eyes, exemplified the patriarchal ordering of relations that had shaped his region in slavery times and continued to exert its force throughout most of Glasgow's life in the South. The southern system of patriarchy granted the father absolute authority and defined mothers, wives, and daughters as obedient, silent ornaments reflecting his power and accomplishments. Glasgow made her autobiography into an indictment not only of her authoritarian father but of the system with which he identified, one that sanctioned the victimization of women, blacks, and indeed all those not empowered by white male privilege. Defined by her love of her sacrificial mother, Glasgow's relationship with her father, as well as with her own culture, was a power struggle. In the autobiography the unequal war, with the father always tyrant and the mother always victim, raged in the soul of a child who came, as Glasgow says, to regard life as "divided between the stronger and the weaker, the fortunate and the unfortunate." Her own stake in the battle is clear: "Either by fate or by choice, I had found myself on the side of the weaker" (59). Her rejection of her father seems very clear when she describes her open rebellion against his church: "I refused to attend divine service—and there was nothing left that they could do about it. My will, which was as strong as Father's, plunged its claws into the earth" (72). Yet there is irony in this confrontation because when she claimed for herself her father's "strong will," Glasgow was in some respects not so much rejecting him as she was turning away from her mother's seemingly hopeless position. She might find herself on the side of the weaker, but she portrays herself always as a fighter who would never succumb as her mother had to the father's rule.

All of Glasgow's sympathy went to her beautiful, good, gentle, but also weak and inarticulate mother. Her father, she says, "had estranged me, without thinking a child could be estranged" (92). Yet he was a man of power, action, authority, and accomplishment. Again tying his personality to his religious views, Glasgow notes that he regarded love and mercy as virtues "belonging by right to a weaker gender," preferring for himself "a God of terror, savoring the strong smoke of blood sacrifice" (85). Whatever consequences Francis Glasgow's failings entailed, weakness was not one of them. Herein is one major source of tension in Ellen Glasgow's search for a system of values to use both in her life and in her fiction.

She was determined to be strong, to fight for what she wanted—in other words, to be like her father, the man from whom she felt completely estranged precisely because he had no love or mercy in him. In her fiction Glasgow associates many characteristics with success, including endurance and strength of mind and will. But the quality she repeatedly calls "fortitude" dominates. The central dramatic question of most of her fiction concerns her female characters' strength, their capacity for endurance, their ability to overcome the weakness that is their allotment in a culture that offers only protection, and protection at the expense of freedom and selfhood. Yet how could women achieve strength without betraying the virtues that Glasgow loved in her mother or without endorsing the lack of simple humanity that she despised in her father? As a writer who felt that her art came directly out of her own emotional life, Glasgow inherited, as one major artistic/emotional dilemma, the problem of endowing her female characters with successful survival mechanisms when survival seemed dependent on the kind of strength that she had witnessed actively only in her father. His belief in the strong, Calvinistic God kept him from being a victim, while his wife's and his daughter's natural love of beauty and sympathy with others offered them only lives of suffering.

Elizabeth Ammons has defined the conflict that Glasgow faced in these terms: "She would have to write unpretty, complicated, fierce fiction—not the delicate imaginings of a Lady, which she as the daughter of solid upper-middle-class Virginia parents had been raised to epitomize" (169). Yet Ammons feels that Glasgow's divided loyalties made her task impossible. The South was a place in which "overt rebellion against the authority of white men of one's own or a higher class was strictly forbidden," and Ammons asserts, "Enmeshed, Glasgow both lived within and despised this Southern ethos" (169). Glasgow could not finally deal directly with her own hatred of the traditions that enclosed her life in the South, according to Ammons. Anger was not allowed by the culture to which she felt deeply attached, while "anger against white men, beginning with her father, was the primary, driving force of Ellen Glasgow's life as a woman" (169). Ammons concludes that this "tortuous, buried anger at the feminine ideal assigned her by her region, class, and race compromised almost all of Glasgow's work" with the partial exception of *Barren Ground,* because it kept her from dealing openly with "her own experience as a woman" (169). This judgment, however, ignores the need to account for and assess strategies for dealing with her anger that Glasgow began developing very early in her career. These strategies, I would argue, are first significantly in evidence in *The Battle-Ground,* and they find their fullest expression in *Vein of Iron.*

The word *compromise* as Ammons uses it bears a decidedly negative connotation, yet it is possible that for Glasgow, compromise represented a positive alternative for gaining strength precisely because it differed from the patriarchal mode of achievement. By concentrating on Betty Ambler and Ada Fincastle, we can see that Glasgow was always interested in designing ways for strong, free women to earn fulfilling identities that allowed them to operate creatively within their culture and allowed them, even more, to revise the patriarchally ordered traditions of their culture so that matriarchal values could be affirmed.

The Battle-Ground was Glasgow's only novel to explore the world of the South before the Civil War. In *A Certain Measure,* she wrote, "In *The Battle-Ground,* I have tried to portray the last stand in Virginia of the aristocratic tradition" (13). The novel "was designed to begin a history of the social transition [of the South] by imaginatively restoring the old order" (13). Much of the second half of the novel realistically dramatizes the Civil War itself through the eyes of Dan Montjoy, the grandson of an aristocrat who joins the Confederate army as a common foot soldier. Yet Glasgow's imaginative restoration of the old order is accomplished largely by forcefully rendering the lives of the women who symbolized its ideals at the same time that they were powerless to shape them.

The Battle-Ground opens with a revelatory scene in which ten-year-old Betty Ambler races to meet her male cousin and announces that she has outrun her sister, Virginia. Directly contradicting the evidence standing before him, he replies, "You can't run. . . . I'd like to see a girl run, anyway" (2). Challenged by Betty, who flashes "a clear defiance," he changes the subject and begins to taunt her about her bright red hair (2). The little girl is immediately subdued and ashamed; red hair is unfeminine and unrefined. When Virginia arrives, she is presented as a complete contrast. She, indeed, cannot run, and so fits her cousin's and her culture's definition of a girl. Virginia is "a fragile little creature, coloured like a flower, and her smooth brown hair hung in silken braids to her sash" (4). The flower of southern womanhood is represented in the fair, ladylike, totally unassertive, and docile Virginia. Yet the race and the novel belong to Betty.

As a young girl, Betty might try to dye her hair and wash away her freckles with buttermilk in order to remake herself into the image that her sister effortlessly embodies. We learn that "[o]n cloudy days she would sometimes have her ambitions to be ladylike," and that she is upset when she watches all the boys dance with Virginia while she sits "against the wall" (70). Yet it is as an unconventional, active, compassionate but sensible woman that she wins the love of Dan Montjoy and becomes the mainstay of two plantation families during the war. Her sister dies in childbirth in war-ravaged Richmond, a tragic but appropriate and unavoidable death for a southern lady bred and trained to act out her culture's fate in her very body.

Like Virginia and unlike Betty, the other women of *The Battle-Ground* live to serve and to decorate the world that clearly belongs to white upper-class men. The sheer irrelevance of the southern lady to the pulse of real life is illustrated comically by Betty's two maiden aunts, Aunt Lydia and Aunt Pussy, who live with her family and spend their time gardening and making jams. At dinner their roses and their quince preserves are admired while they blush "and cast down their eyes, as they did every evening at the same kindly by-play" (20). When Aunt Lydia mourns her uselessness, Governor Ambler protests, "My dear Miss Lydia, your mere existence is a blessing to mankind" (21). The patriarchal code decrees that southern womanhood fulfills itself as an ideal simply in existing, although existence in the case of most women, and certainly unmarried ones, is limited to frivolous adornment. Glasgow's sketches of these women are not without barbs. Aunt Lydia, we are told, could never forgive a woman who painted her face, yet "[f]or the purely masculine improprieties, her charity was as boundless as her innocence," for she has read Shakespeare and Sir Walter Scott and has their bold heroes "enshrined in her pious heart" (52).

Glasgow's portrayal of Betty's mother is more complex. She is not only an ornamental figure who participates in her own relegation to second-class status but also an active force in sustaining the plantation both physically and morally. "Of all the souls on the great plantation, the mistress alone had never rested from her labours" (25). She has persuaded her husband to free "the servants" after her death, and she only consents to buy more when the slave in question would otherwise be separated from family in the neighborhood. Yet while Mrs. Ambler embodies all womanly virtue, Glasgow does not present her sacrificing nature as an unmixed good. Governor Ambler notes what her sense of duty has cost, as well as the difference between the husband's and wife's roles in this idyllic world:

> The cares she met with such serenity had been too heavy for her strength; they had driven the bloom from her cheeks and the lustre from her eyes; and, though she had not faltered at her task, she had drooped daily and grown older than her years. The master might live with a lavish disregard of the morrow, not the master's wife. (48)

As saintly as Mrs. Ambler is, Glasgow makes it clear that her acceptance of a sense of ordained gender-based inferiority is a form of blindness. Its effects are most damaging when she tries to teach her daughters to accept inferiority as divine decree. At one point, while sewing "dainty stitches" on her husband's shirtfront, she tells Betty, "Women do not need as much sense as men, my dear." She goes on to proclaim, "If the Lord had wanted you to be clever, He would have made you a man" (49). Glasgow condemns Mrs. Ambler's unquestioning loyalty and service to a male-dominated order that asks not only that women and slaves (and there is not much difference in Glasgow's scale) sacrifice mind and body but that they make such sacrifice their only measure of self-worth. Mrs. Ambler succeeds in passing on this system of values to Virginia, with the inevitable result that this beautiful, helpless daughter cannot survive the threat that the Civil War represents to the flawed basis of her identity.

Glasgow created two patriarchal figures for this novel, the masters of adjoining plantations. Governor Ambler and Major Lightfoot are types who divide between them the somewhat contradictory qualities associated with the figure of the Virginia gentleman. Governor Ambler is described as "beneficent," "comely," "a bland and generous gentleman, whose heart was as open as his wine cellar" (45). He bows to his wife's insistence that their slaves be freed eventually, yet he also finds it easy to be remote from their cares, even their identities. When he finds his wife in the quarters, where she has gone to nurse a dying slave, he realizes that he knows nothing of his chattels' lives: "He should hardly have known her had he met her last week in the corn field" (250). Through such understated perceptions, Glasgow conveys the heart of slavery's reality and proves what is wrong with even the best Virginia gentleman. Betty's father served as governor of his state and in the novel ardently opposes secession; yet like Robert E. Lee, an obvious model for his character, he puts the honor of Virginia above all and goes off to fight when his state secedes. He dies from battle wounds, which is perhaps Glasgow's way of passing judgment on his way of life, for he becomes a casualty to what he has allowed himself to stand for—graciousness, kindness to family and friends, love of home and state, but finally, too, a limited humanity that puts duty to an inherently, irredeemably tyrannical order ahead of better instincts.

Major Lightfoot represents a more insidious aspect of patriarchal dominance in the Old South. "In his day," we learn, Major Lightfoot "had matched any man in Virginia at cards or wine or women—to say nothing of horseflesh" (16). His reckless pursuit of self-gratification is allowed, even expected, within the conception of a southern gentleman. Tall and spare in his old age, he has "an odd resemblance to a bird of prey" (15), a detail which suggests a menacing appetite that his deference to ladies and his generosity to those who please him cannot completely mask. When angry he victimizes everyone within reach, including his long-suffering wife, a daughter who eloped to escape his disapproval, and a grandson who is banished for exhibiting some of the major's own hotheadedness. Through Major Lightfoot, Glasgow places the roots of the South's doomed aristocratic order in an irrational adherence to a romantic conception of manliness. The major enshrines chivalry as his chief social value, but hot blood, even violence, is a sanctioned component of his chivalric ideal. His lust for action, a kind of blood lust, can only be satisfied by the holocaust of war, which he ardently supports as proof of his culture's manly courage. Unlike Governor Ambler, Major Lightfoot is not killed in the war. Like the South itself, he lives to see all that he cherished in ruins. His home is burnt and he must live in the overseer's cabin, dependent on none other than tactful, resourceful Betty.

In his recent reading of *The Battle-Ground*, R. H. W. Dillard notes, "The future . . . seems to belong to (and to depend heavily on) Betty" (68). Throughout the novel she has rejected the passivity, the romantic posturing, and the artificial helplessness that characterize the other women, and she exhibits a compassion for others that becomes a better source of strength than bravery provides the men of the novel. Holding both plantations together after months of ravaging by both armies, she readily excels at both male and female forms of labor. "Her sunny humour had made play of a man's work as of a woman's anxiety" (*Battle-Ground* 435), and she thrives on purposeful action, the kind denied to her by the customs of her society. When her lover, Dan Montjoy, returns from the war, she can comfort him "as a mother soothes a tired child" (511). At the same time she refuses to allow him to treat her as someone who needs his protection. In the closing pages *her* "protecting arms" and *her* "strong courage" are emphasized as the source of *his* renewed strength, and she pronounces the unsentimental terms on which they will live in a new world: "'We will begin again,' she said, 'and this time, my dear, we will begin together'" (512).

As Dillard notes, "Betty and Dan are able to establish a relationship that is not based upon dependency—either of willingly weak wife on strong husband or of wounded soldier/child on surrogate mother" (77). Yet Betty's successful emergence as a capable, free woman is not seen as a sure sign that the South will change to recognize her kind of strength as a force to embrace. Glasgow employed a powerful image, the portrait of Aunt Emmeline that hangs in the hall at Chericoke, as a reminder throughout the novel of the standard for women that ensured their imprisonment as an ideal. Aunt Emmeline within her picture frame symbolized perfect femininity controlled as a motivating illusion for the culture in which she functioned as icon; she was imprisoned as symbol, "the abiding presence of the place" (31). With a realistic understanding of how durable the belle's illusory presence would be, even following the demise of the old order, Glasgow arranges for her portrait to be as Dillard has noted, the only object saved when Chericoke is burned by the Yankees (76–77). Both Betty and Aunt Emmeline survive, then, to represent the South's continuing dilemma in relation to its valuing of women.

In a preface to *The Battle-Ground*, Glasgow identified it as "the first of a series of novels which composes, in the more freely interpretive form of fiction, a social history of Virginia from the decade before the Confederacy" (*ACM* 3). Perhaps the most important aspect of the social history for which *The Battle-Ground* provides the cornerstone is its exploration of how southern women fare in their own private battles within the larger economic and political clashes involving their region. Speaking in *A Certain Measure* of Betty Ambler's popularity among readers, she writes that Betty seems to personify the spirit "that in defeat remained undefeated" (5). This theme related *The Battle-Ground* to other novels dealing with the struggle to survive that is a human quest, but one conceived in Glasgow's work largely through a dramatization of women's limited position in society.

Glasgow remained intrigued by the concept of the undefeated spirit throughout her life as an artist. Writing of *Vein of Iron* to Stark Young, she said, "The theme of my book, which I should like brought out, is easiest put in a question. What is it that has enabled human beings to endure life on the earth?" (*Letters* 190). While *The Battle-Ground* answers this question somewhat differently from *Vein of Iron*, both novels embody the fighting spirit for survival in women who must struggle against a dying but still powerful patriarchal southern ethos.

Betty and her sister, Virginia, are prototypes for women characters that Glasgow developed in two separate but related novels written several years later. Virginia is an early version of one of Glasgow's most important figures, the Virginia Pendleton whom we meet in *Virginia*, who, like her earlier namesake, sacrifices herself to cultural expectations that grant her no identity of her own. *Life and Gabriella*, Glasgow noted, was "a companion study" to *Virginia*, "which had portrayed woman as an ideal conforming to Victorian tradition" (*ACM* 97). She goes on to speak of Gabriella in terms that relate her to Betty: *Life and Gabriella*, she says, "is concerned with woman as a reality," and Gabriella is "a character of native energy and independence, blessed with a dynamic philosophy and a quick relish for the immediate" (*ACM* 97).

Gabriella, the first character fully to inherit Betty's spirit, was created to show a contrasting option to what Glasgow calls Virginia Pendleton's "martyrdom" (*ACM* 83). Betrayed by a weak, philandering husband, Gabriella responds by taking back her maiden name, becoming a successful career woman in New York, providing for her two children, and discovering, in her struggle, a "vein of iron" that allows her to be refreshed and exhilarated by conditions that caused her exile from the traditional role of dependent wife and mother. Dorinda Oakley, whose character and story Glasgow began to consider about the time she published *Life and Gabriella*, also exhibits this "vein of iron," surviving a similar betrayal by a feckless, petty lover to go on to transform her family's unproductive, rundown farm into a thriving dairy. Betty, Gabriella, and Dorinda are freed by potentially devastating adverse circumstances from participation in traditional woman's roles mandated by a patriarchal society. Exclusion frees them to find fulfillment in challenging labor; this allows them to make what Glasgow called a "vital affirmation of life" (*ACM* 160), to create possibilities that are matriarchal in design.

Betty differs, however, from both Gabriella and Dorinda, whose success as matriarchal figures is limited by the ultimate solutions they devise to solve the problem of their identities as women. As Anne Goodwyn Jones has pointed out, Gabriella works in an establishment "entirely run by women, whose business is to fabricate identities for women," and in this business she has been successful: "she reshapes the definition of womanhood, giving it more integrity" (260). But when she meets Ben O'Hara, the energetic, honest, self-made man, she is at first repulsed but then intrigued and finally attracted to his masculinity. When she hears of Ben O'Hara's active, dramatic life, she both admires and envies what he has accomplished and immediately belittles her successes, thinking she has "been living a little life, with little standards, little creeds, little compromises" (Glasgow, *L&G* 421). After establishing Gabriella's freedom on very firm ground, Glasgow seems to decide that she deserves more, and that, for a woman, "more" is best guaranteed by participation in a dynamic man's life, not as an equal but as the adored object of his energy and protection. In spite of Glasgow's insistence that Gabriella is making a choice "between action and inaction, between endeavor and relinquishment" (529), in marrying O'Hara, she is clearly also choosing to relinquish just that way of life that she has been able to direct for herself, in order to enjoy the excitement of her man's life on his terms.

Dorinda Oakley takes a very different course from Gabriella, rejecting all forms of love that would take her out of herself or compromise her hard-won triumph over dependency of any kind. Yet the cost, which Glasgow seems to have felt was inevitable, is that she must live joylessly. Dorinda exists, Glasgow wrote in 1933, "wherever a human being has learned to live without joy, wherever the spirit of fortitude has triumphed over the sense of futility" (*BG* viii). The cost of fortitude is joy and also full companionship with others. Dorinda survives the deaths of parents and friends, including that of the husband who was a helpmate but never a sexual partner; she has the satisfaction of seeing the man who betrayed her lose everything and, like Gabriella's husband, find himself dependent upon her for a final shelter where he can go to die. Yet she is at heart untouched by all these human abandonments, for in order to find a way to accept life, she has had to design a world in which she can, indeed must, live alone. What joy she has will depend always on her creative, largely antagonistic, relationship to the land she has coerced into productivity, and this, for her, is triumph enough.

Gabriella and Dorinda do not so much forge compromises that allow them satisfactory relationships as they abandon certain parts of themselves to attain power of one kind or another. This makes them different from Betty Ambler, who at the end of *The Battle-Ground* exhibits the potential for designing a life with others—a husband, mother, neighbors, even the arrogant, unyielding Major Lightfoot—in which she is yet independent and self-fulfilled. Glasgow does not take Betty beyond the Civil War, which, when it destroyed the economic foundations of southern patriarchy, gave her a foothold on which to build a new kind of life. Certainly novels like *Virginia, Life and Gabriella, Barren Ground,* and *The Sheltered Life* indicate Glasgow's understanding that women in her society would continue to struggle, as she did, for recognition, freedom, and self-direction. Yet Betty Ambler as a character type and her situation as an affirming member of a family and a community suggest a vision of matriarchal success that Glasgow did not relay again in her fiction until her creation of the Fincastles, a family that allowed her to re-envision her own.

In her preface to *Vein of Iron*, Glasgow remarked on how the novel's locale differed from her other fiction: before this work, set in the Valley of Virginia, she had "written only of the Tidewater and Richmond," home of "my mother's people" (*ACM* 165). The valley was home to her father's forebears, and it is significant that in the novel that she felt would be her last, she turned finally to examine a background steeped in associations with the man whom she personally rejected so vehemently. In the novel, the image of the father is transformed and essentially restored. Glasgow used the properties of fiction to accomplish what she never satisfactorily managed in her personal relationship with Francis Glasgow: an imaginative reclaiming of the part of her identity that she owed, through blood and training, to him. The reclaiming is accomplished by the unique affirmation that *Vein of Iron* makes of the idea of family as intergenerational community, matriarchally centered and inherited.

Vein of Iron shows four different generations interacting in order to trace an ideal of what Glasgow called "fortitude" and to show its transmission as a force transcending specific manifestations in particular characters. As she explained in her preface, "From the beginning, I had known that I was engaged upon a family chronicle, that I was studying, not a single character or group of characters alone, but the vital principle of survival" (*ACM* 169). At the end of the novel, Ada Fincastle follows her father back to their home in the mountain community of Ironside, and she articulates to herself her understanding of that principle of survival as a matriarchally charged force: remembering all her ancestors, but especially her grandmother Fincastle and great-great-grandmother Tod, she "had a sense, more a feeling than a vision, of the dead generations behind her. . . . [T]hey were lending her their fortitude; they were reaching out to her in adversity. . . . She could lean back on their strength; she could recover that lost certainty of a continuing tradition" (461). Ada's long journey to this discovery makes *Vein of Iron* one of Glasgow's most compelling studies of women's experience, one that had particular relevance to her need to claim her whole past as daughter and writer.

In the first chapter, young Ada tells her minister that she is going out to watch for her father, who is bringing her a doll "with real hair" (13). She has earned the money for the doll herself and eagerly dreams of naming and dressing her. When at last her father arrives, Ada finds that he has not saved out enough money to buy her the doll with real hair; upon opening the package he gives her and seeing only a doll with painted china hair, she cries, "Oh Mother, Mother, she isn't real!" (30). Ada's terrible disappointment is, as her grandmother notes, indicative of her "single heart" (32), her tendency to passionate, unwavering attachment to objects of her desire, and this single-heartedness characterizes all of the choices that she is shown making from early girlhood through middle age in Glasgow's chronicle. The episode with the doll also reveals much about Ada's father, John Fincastle. He is a kindly but ineffectual man who has been driven from his post as Presbyterian minister because of his scholarly heresies. For many years he has worked on books of philosophy which only a few European intellects appreciate. His family struggles to secure the basic necessities while he dreamily responds to each crisis as he does to Ada's disappointment over her doll, with the gentle excuse, "I did the best I could" (33). At this early point in the novel it is difficult to know how to judge John Fincastle. He has rejected what Glasgow clearly sees as a repressive Calvinism, he is a gentle and loving father, yet he is also curiously detached from his role of protector and provider for his family. His complacency in the face of challenges from the real world represents, as he himself later admits, a retreat from life.

The doll scene, which Glasgow uses in *Vein of Iron* as a kind of early touchstone to define her two main characters' personalities, can be scrutinized as well for its relation to her memory of her father's power and insensitivity. In *A Certain Measure* (1938), Glasgow wrote, "I could well remember the hungry 'eighties; and I could remember, too, that when I wanted a doll with 'real hair,' I was told I could not have it because we had 'lost everything in the war'" (12). Raper is probably correct in assuming that it was Glasgow's father who denied her the doll. Such an act would be of a piece with several other recollections of Francis Glasgow that we have cited earlier. Raper remarks, concerning her memory of being refused the doll with real hair, that Francis Glasgow could probably at the time have afforded such a gift "if he had had the sympathy and imagination to see the world through eyes other than his own" (22).

In the doll scene, Glasgow replays through Ada and John Fincastle the deprivation and disappointment that she experienced in her own childhood relationship with her father. Yet beyond this one seemingly similar action, John Fincastle and Francis Glasgow are almost complete opposites. Ada's father is passively comfortable within a maternally anchored family, he takes a firm stand against the religion that Francis Glasgow wholeheartedly supported, and he makes a journey to full engagement in a community's struggle for elemental survival. Ada's grandmother in some ways more closely resembles Francis Glasgow, for she is an unshakable adherent to his rigid brand of Presbyterianism. However, like her son, she is able to change; in old age she meets the challenge to offer charity and sustenance to her wayward granddaughter. The Fincastle family is thus dramatically different from Glasgow's own or from those we see in her other fiction.

The five figures of Ada's childhood family—grandmother, father, mother Mary Evelyn, Aunt Meggie, and Ada—are set consistently in relation to one another in terms of both their motivations and the consequences of their actions. Early in the novel, Glasgow arranges these five around the fireplace in their small, cozy home in a scene that has no model in her earlier fiction. Glasgow called this section an innovation in which she was attempting "to enter completely into the mental processes of these five different human beings" (*ACM* 181). Each character is rendered through an interior monologue, suited in rhythm, imagery, and content to his or her mood and vision. Thus the monologues provide a way to introduce the characters as individuals, but they function more importantly to show that each is primarily a component of a larger whole, a family. All five, dreaming by the fire, weave a tapestry of thoughts concerning goals, events, and feelings that the others' monologues echo. Grandmother, for instance, takes the family history far back in time, seeking, in memories of earlier Fincastles, to understand her rebellious son and her present circumstances. Through her memories she is knit "into the past as she knitted life into stockings" (46), and she knits her family into her vision of "the changeless past and the slow accretion of time" as it has brought them all to their present configuration (46). John Fincastle remembers his grandmother, Margaret Graham, as he seeks to know whether his own "endless seeking" was "an inheritance from the past" (51). Mary Evelyn measures all of her thoughts against her sense of how her mother-in-law would respond to them: "Mother Fincastle said all that was mere silliness" (54). All of them think of what John's church trial for heresy has cost them, of Mary Evelyn's failing health, of some aspect of their struggle with poverty. Ada herself, who is ten years old at the time, brings her family into different focus through perceptions untempered by adult understanding. The effect of the section is to mark each character's identity with something of all the others, so that neither time, nor distance, nor death can separate them. They endure in one another.

The two family members whose interwoven lives are explored most thoroughly are Ada and her father, each of whom commits an act of individual nonconformity that reshapes the family as a whole. By publishing his heretical views, John Fincastle makes himself an outcast and places his family in uncomfortable circumstances, all for his private quest. He thinks wryly, "No man who has to provide for a family . . . has a right to search after truth" (48). He agonizes over the price his dependents have had to pay for his attention to his "inner life" (50), and the novel records his journey from his early, necessary self-absorption to his equally necessary recognition of how his life is bound up in the welfare of others. Living in Queenborough during the Depression, he becomes a father figure to the entire struggling neighborhood of Mulberry Street. His final act is to make a physically agonizing journey back to Ironside to die, ostensibly to save the money it would take to send his body there for burial. He also knows that his daughter and her family will follow him home, and so he becomes the agent of their rejuvenating decision to stay in Ironside where the ancestral land and family heritage will sustain them. In his return he is guided by memories of his mother, and at the end, when he is dying, he sees her face last: "the dark face—dark and stern and bright—watching beyond the panes was the face of his mother" (457).

Ada, like her father, asserts her own will over the needs and expectations of her family; she agrees to accompany Ralph McBride, who earlier was forced to marry someone else, to a mountain cabin for a weekend tryst before he goes off to war. Ada's act is necessary for her self-completion, yet it repeats the father's defiance with the similar result of creating an outcast for the family to bear. Her grandmother's religion will not allow her to forgive Ada when she confesses that she is pregnant, yet when her labor begins, Grandmother comes to her aid, and Ada feels that the "steadfast life of the house, the strong fibers, the closely knit generations, had gathered above, around, underneath" (260). Thus family sustains and restores one of its own again.

While Ada's father will lead her back finally to her strong maternal ancestors as a source of strength, it is Ada who first leads her father away from that home for a kind of descent that provides a necessary testing and transformation for them both. Josephine Donovan has commented on the enactment of the Demeter-Persephone myth that Ada's journey to the city represents; the years in Queenborough are "cast as a period of exile and a time of the fall" (154). In the city, Ralph is able to prosper for a time by selling automobiles, symbolic of this cold, mechanical environment. He is mysteriously paralyzed in a car accident, however, and soon the Depression comes to throw the family back into a raw struggle for food and shelter. At the same time, the Fincastle circle of family expands to include neighbors suffering far more than they, and their acts of reaching out affirm the idea of community over competition. Ada is the head of her family, and although Queenborough is usually portrayed as wintry and dark, Glasgow uses the firelight and window lamps of Ada's home to project her as a kind of matriarchal goddess.

In their return to Ironside, the father and daughter of *Vein of Iron* ensure the restoration of a matriarchal order. Neither father nor daughter has dominated, and together they have worked to mitigate the disastrous effects of a modern, competitive, male-dominated economic system. Their religion has been one of love and respect for all living beings. The novel opened with Ada and her friends chasing an idiot boy, one of God's hunted creatures, until Ada recognizes her kinship with the miserable, grotesque child. At the end, John Fincastle remembers visiting mountain people with his mother and being chased by idiot children of this primitive family. Ada and John's identification with victims unable to survive alone gives them a kind of power that is understood as maternal, nurturing, and renewing. Dying, John Fincastle leads his daughter home and bequeaths to her the means to save her own child from the wasteland of the barren city. She envisions rebuilding the ruined homestead, planting a garden, finding work with her husband, in ways that bind her to "the first Fincastle" (460). She has become "a rock to lean on" still capable of desire, hunger, and satisfaction (461). In *Vein of Iron* Glasgow created an interdependent daughter and father who—as dreamers, workers, and bearers of a continuing tradition—allowed her to reach back into and beyond her father's strength to restore her own creative and inherited order.

Works Cited

Ammons, Elizabeth. *Conflicting Stories: American Women Writers at the Turn into the Twentieth Century.* New York: Oxford UP, 1991.

Dillard, R. H. W. "On Ellen Glasgow's *The Battle-Ground.*" *Classics of Civil War Fiction.* Ed. David Madden and Peggy Bach. Jackson: UP of Mississippi, 1991. 63–82.

Donovan, Josephine. *After the Fall: The Demeter-Persephone Myth in Wharton, Cather, and Glasgow.* University Park: Pennsylvania State UP, 1989.

Glasgow, Ellen. *Barren Ground.* 1925. Old Dominion Edition. Garden City: Doubleday, 1933.

———. *The Battle-Ground.* New York: Doubleday, 1902.

———. *A Certain Measure: An Interpretation of Prose Fiction.* New York: Harcourt, 1943.

———. *Letters of Ellen Glasgow.* Ed. Blair Rouse. New York: Harcourt, 1958.

———. *Life and Gabriella.* Garden City: Doubleday, 1916.

———. *Vein of Iron.* New York: Harcourt, 1935.

———. *The Woman Within.* New York: Harcourt, 1954.

Jones, Anne Goodwyn. *Tomorrow Is Another Day: The Woman Writer in the South, 1859–1936.* Baton Rouge: Louisiana State UP, 1981.

Raper, Julius Rowan. *Without Shelter: The Early Career of Ellen Glasgow.* Baton Rouge: Louisiana State UP, 1971.

Between Ellen and Louise
Female Friendship, Glasgow's Letters to
Louise Chandler Moulton, and *The Wheel of Life*

Pamela R. Matthews

By the time Ellen Glasgow met the older writer Louise Chandler Moulton (1835–1908) in Paris in October 1905, Moulton had long occupied a prominent position in literary circles. A published poet at fifteen, Moulton later associated with the New York literary circle surrounding Richard Henry Stoddard and Elizabeth Drew Stoddard (Edgerly 108; Spiller 811). After marrying in 1855, Moulton and her husband, editor-publisher William U. Moulton, established their Boston home as a locus of literary activity. Their intellectual "Friday evenings" attracted much the same well-known crowd that also gathered at the home of Annie Adams and James T. Fields (Roman 108). Perhaps best known for her poetry, Moulton also wrote fiction (including stories for children), journalism, and travel books. A central figure in the London literary scene beginning in the late 1870s, Moulton had what Sherman terms a "genius for friendship" that caused her to be especially highly regarded as a mentor (Edgerly 108; Sherman, "Louise Chandler Moulton" 521–22).

Appropriate in the atmosphere of friendship and professional advice fostered by Moulton, Glasgow met her through their mutual close friend, Virginia writer Amélie Rives Troubetzkoy, who sent a letter in 1905 to Moulton in Paris by way of Glasgow. After forwarding the letter, Glasgow called on Moulton, and the two women began corresponding. The eight unpublished letters from Glasgow to Moulton date from 1905 and 1906; in the absence of additional information, there is no way to tell whether they corresponded more frequently or for a longer time. The letters reveal that Glasgow felt for Moulton an immediate and warm friendship, and their tone suggests that Moulton reciprocated.

In the two sections that follow the letters printed below, I will consider in detail the letters themselves and their significance in Glasgow's life and art, their theoretical implications for reading correspondence between women, and their importance for understanding Glasgow's long-overlooked sixth novel, *The Wheel of Life* (1906). For now, let me suggest that the letters support my sense that female friendship provided Glasgow greater emotional fulfillment than did heterosexual relationships. Further, the letters and the emotions they bespeak, juxtaposed with *The Wheel of Life*, show Glasgow exploring the narrative implications of women's friendships: nontraditional relationships—anything other than romantic, heterosexual ones—carry with them unconventional narrative requirements (DuPlessis; Miller; Todd). Together, the letters and *The Wheel of Life* illuminate Glasgow's burgeoning awareness of the possibility in "writing beyond the ending," as DuPlessis terms the narrative strategy that imagines life beyond the traditional plots of marriage or death for the female protagonist. For Glasgow, learning to do so becomes both an experiential and a narrative necessity.

Ellen Glasgow's Letters to
Louise Chandler Moulton, *1905–6*

I.

> Thursday night
> [4 October? 1905]
> Hotel de la Tremoille, Paris

My dear Mrs. Moulton,
 My Amélie has sent me the enclosed little letter to you which I forward at once. It will make me very happy to know you, but she tells me that you have not been well of late, so if for any reason you find that you would rather not see me just now, I shall understand how it is from my very heart. Don't let me be a burden, dear Mrs. Moulton, but if you do really feel that you would care to have me come to you for a little talk, send me word and I will run to meet you. The Deutschland, my boat, sails on Friday, so you can understand what a busy time we [are] now having—not too busy, though, to drop trifles light as ours for the sake of something really worth [remainder of letter missing][1]

2.

October 5th 1905
Hotel de la Tremoille, Paris

[no salutation]

My thoughts have been so full of you since this morning that
before going to bed I must send you this little message of love and
farewell. It was so beautiful to *me* the way we came together not as
strangers but as dear friends who meet again after a long absence
and the sweet familiar recognition was the loveliest thing I have felt
for a long time. You brought the spirit very close to me and because
of this I know—I feel, oh, my dear friend, with a sense that is above
and beyond knowledge that we have come together—as Amélie
and I have come—for some wonderful and lovely end. Somewhere—
someday the soul that I saw and loved in you I must have known
and loved before, and when one believes this the whole universe
becomes not a wilderness but a home. Dear, dear friend, may that
same light which has shone on dark waters for me shine for you,
too, and lead us always [along] the same path into that peace which
is the one enduring happiness of life. There was so much—oh, so
much I wanted to say to you today, but I was not only pressed for
minutes, I was also a little shy, for you seemed so much wiser than
I and I felt that it was an impertinence to offer you my joy of soul.
But you will understand, I know, that it is not I but the wonderful
rest that I want you to share and to take as I want you to share and
to take my love. It is the liberation and the reconciliation of the
spirit that I would make the joy that we hold and feel together,
Amélie and you and I. What a poor attempt at expressing my
thoughts this is, but it is late and my sister tells me that we must be
up early. Don't think me too great a mystic and yet where one
meets constantly with wonderful ways of the spirit what else can
one be but a believer in and a lover of the [wiser?].[2] My love was
with you before we met, it is with you now and it will be with
you always but mine is so little compared to that love which is
both light and knowledge, the love in which we live and move
and have our being. The first thrill of joy with which I came to
know it returned to me after seeing you today, and this is the
surest sign that the spirit of love was with us when we met.
Goodbye, dear newly *found* but not new friend,

Yours always,
Ellen Glasgow
1 West Main Street
Richmond, Virginia

3.

November 10, 1905
Richmond, Virginia

Dear friend:

Welcome—thrice welcome back to America and to Boston!
It seems only yesterday since I left you in Paris—our beautiful
coming together is as fresh in my mind as it was that evening
when I wrote to you and you—dear you—have filled so many of
my thoughts since then? [*sic*] How is the rheumatism? and how
are you? Just now I am working very, very hard, but the day that
my book³ is finished I shall flit into the world again—first to the
country for two weeks with a friend who is not well,⁴ then to New
York and in February, I hope, to Boston. You will be there, then,
will you not? If not I will change my plans for I want to see you and
to have some long, long talks. Life has opened so much to me of
peace and beauty in these last months that the moments pass in
a wonderful swiftness. I am content now since I feel that I have
had no beginning in time and shall have no end in eternity, but
there are hours when I fairly burn with eagerness to pass on to
other worlds—to seek [also?] a new and a less earthly body—the
eternal self that is in me longs for eternity. Oh, I *do* want to see
you! Amélie writes that she has been ill, but is well again by now.
With much love and with my thoughts always.

Yours,
Ellen Glasgow

4.

Sunday
[envelope postmarked
December 10, 1905]

Dear friend:

This is a little note to say that in a few days I shall write you a
letter. You have been so much in my thoughts today that I feel that
I can't wait—that I must let you hear of my love. I have been working eight hours a day, and it has broken my health down, so I'm
going to run away as soon as my book is finished. There is so
much—oh, so much I want to say to you.

Yours always,
Ellen Glasgow

5.

> Hotel Seville, NY
> [envelope postmarked
> January 28, 1906]

Dear friend:

I hope now—unless I fall ill again to be in Boston the 10th, or perhaps a little earlier. It will be a great joy to see you again—though, of course, I realize that you may have to go away because of the rheumatism. How I hope that it is better! Oh, there is so much to say when we meet!

> Affectionately
> Ellen Glasgow

6.

> March 18, 1906

Dear friend:

The last few days in Boston were very dismal. Our tickets were bought and we were all prepared to leave Sunday when I was taken ill and had to go to bed for several days. On Tuesday I paid a few feeble calls in the neighborhood, but after reaching home I had to give myself a thorough rest. What I regretted most was that the days flew by without my having those long, dear talks with you. The Friday afternoons[5] were charming, but, somehow, I never seemed quite to "get at" you on those occasions. Never mind next time will come someday and then we'll leave out the other people once in a while. This is just a word before I run in to see some friends who are waiting. Tomorrow I expect to go up to Castle Hill[6] and, indeed, I'll give our Amélie your messages. It *was* good and lovely to see you even in the midst of a crowd. I am so sorry that you are still ailing. May the spring bring you health and peace! Rebe,[7] I know, would send love.

> Most affectionately yours,
> Ellen G.

7.

> April 18, 1906

Dear friend:

So many things have kept me from writing since your sweet letter came to me while I sat with Amélie in her room. First of all, I have been very far from well—merely run down and nervously exhausted—so that even the writing to those I love has seemed a burden. Then I've been away from home almost constantly, and now I've run back for a few days before going off again to Atlantic City. But I've thought of you so much this beautiful Easter—a time which has for me a beautiful symbolism, too. Not as a suggestion of a resurrection of the mere personal life, but as expressive of that endless chain of births and deaths and rebirths through which the soul [moves?] to its freedom and its final [word illegible] with God. I wish I could talk to you about this—I wish you could feel it in every fibre of your heart as I do today. Of course, one can't always feel so exquisitely alive to the unfolding spirit, but when one does—ah, when one does, the whole universe is but a home in which one cannot lose one's way because of the friendly faces of the stars. There is a verse in the Wisdom of Solomon which I love to repeat in the silence at night: "For to know Thee is perfect righteousness; yea, to know Thy power is the root of immortality."[8]

Lovingly yours,
Ellen Glasgow

8.

December 13th 1906

[no salutation]

It was very sweet and good of you to write me, dear, true friend. All summer I had you in mind, but there were many worries, and I worked so hard to get well again that there was little time left for any pleasure—even for writing to those I love. Now in the midst of the excitement of my sister's wedding[9] I have been reading your beautiful book.[10] How dear it was of you to send it! She [?] has, of course, told you this [word illegible] by now. I am so sorry you are no better for your "cure." Is the rheumatism still so painful? And what are your plans and prospects for the winter? Oh, I only wish that I could come to Boston within the next few months—but it doesn't look tonight as if that would be possible. When I *do* come I shall probably bring another sister. She is an invalid now, but when she is well, we hope to go North together and I am sure you will find her as delightful as I do.[11] I can hardly write about my missing Rebe—it cuts too deep. Yet she has promised to go to New York with me in May and to spend next summer in Virginia. Would I might say Europe! Amélie is at "Castle Hill"—or will be within a week. I haven't seen her since she landed, so, of course, I am eager to be with her as soon as possible. It seems an age since I last saw her dear, lovely face. And now, dear, I must stop and go down to my sick sister. You have always been so sweet and kind to me that it touches my heart when I think of it. I do hope that I may see you before many months.

Most affectionately yours,
Ellen Glasgow

Women in Correspondence

For me, three features of the letters stand out: an emphasis on the importance of talk or conversation; the sense of a community of women inhabited by Glasgow, Rives Troubetzkoy, and now Moulton (and, at times, Glasgow's two sisters, Rebe and Cary); and the mysticism, or spirituality, that other scholars have noticed as characteristic of Glasgow's philosophical leanings around this time (Raper, "Ambivalence"; *Without Shelter* 177–79, 205–13). These three features of the letters characterize not just the Glasgow-Moulton correspondence but, more generally, Glasgow's relationships with women in her life and among women in her fiction. All three are linked by a thematics of female connection that implicitly rejects patriarchal traditions for women and, in doing so, suggests personal and narratological resistance to accepted female conventions. I do not wish to overread Glasgow's letters to Moulton, which are, in some ways, typical of women's correspondence especially in the nineteenth century (see Cott; Sahli; Smith-Rosenberg, *Disorderly Conduct;* Vicinus, "Distance and Desire"). The Moulton letters also resemble others from Glasgow during the same time period, such as those to her childhood friend Elizabeth "Lizzie" Patterson (later Crutchfield) and to novelist Mary Johnston. But I do not want to underread them, either. Glasgow's early twentieth-century letters to Moulton show a willingness, usually missing in her letters to male correspondents, to reveal innermost thoughts and to establish intimacy (see *Letters* for comparisons).

Letters between women can in themselves challenge male-dominated discourse, as Susan S. Lanser's fascinating study of a nineteenth-century "secret correspondence" demonstrates (esp. 615–25). Perhaps in part because of the familiar nineteenth-century public-private dichotomy, women wrote differently to their close women friends in writings not intended for publication, as Glasgow's correspondence often reveals.[12] Not needing the mask required for acceptable public self-representation—a mask that would require de-emphasizing emotionally charged relationships between women and emphasizing heterosexuality, for example—women letter-writers, like Glasgow in her letters to Moulton, resisted conventional (male-defined) expectations and emphases by a simple epistolary exclusion, ignoring for the moment men and the man's world that women in public had no choice but to negotiate.

Such resistance often revolves around language, as many feminist theorists have suggested (among them Cixous, de Lauretis, DuPlessis, Meese, Ostriker, and Yaeger). Also at issue here is the related capacity to find a female voice appropriate for expressing a reordered world of connection among women. These letters reveal an awareness of the importance of women's *shared* language. In this context, Glasgow's repeated desire for "talk" with Moulton and her expressed concern about the inadequacy of her language to convey meaning invite us to think about the search for female utterance generally and about the gendered language implied in female correspondence.

Examining private letters between women can provide promising opportunities for hearing female voices relatively unconcerned about pleasing a male public. Such letters potentially yield fruitful consideration of the implied female dialogic voices that Dale Bauer examines, as distinct from the unidirectional search for *a* female voice. When the issue is women's language, the intended audience in women's private correspondence often is a woman absorbed in a like-minded quest for a female voice. Women's letters to other women, I think, might help us in understanding the relationships forged between women through their shared search for not just their individual voices but a *mutual* voice. Even a statement that on the surface seems simple, such as one in Glasgow's seventh letter—Easter is "a time which has for me a beautiful symbolism, *too*"—implies a dialogue that can help us "read" one-sided correspondence through interpolation. In other words, in this letter the thoughts and emotions expressed about Easter are not just Glasgow's; rather, they are Glasgow's in response to, or in combination with, Moulton's.

Language—especially as spoken in conversation (or imagined in actual conversation) and therefore reciprocal—clearly forms a bond in the Glasgow-Moulton correspondence. In her first letter, Glasgow seeks Moulton's acquaintance by suggesting "a little talk." In the second, obviously written the evening of the day the women first met, Glasgow regrets that she did not "say" more and expresses frustration that she cannot put her deeply felt emotions clearly into written words: "There was so much—oh, so much I wanted to say to you today"; "What a poor attempt at expressing my thoughts this is." A similar urgency toward communication paired with a recognition that somehow words are never quite enough runs throughout the letters. In letters 3 and 6

Glasgow writes of her longing for "some long, long talks," "those long, dear talks." The language of letter 2—there is "so much . . . to say"— recurs in letters 4 and 5. In letter 4, Glasgow's desire to communicate leads her to write only to say that she plans to write more: "This is a little note to say that in a few days I shall write you a letter. . . . I feel that I can't wait—that I must let you hear of my love."

The reciprocal language that concerns Glasgow impinges upon another characteristic issue in the letters: the female community shared by Glasgow, Moulton, and Amélie Rives Troubetzkoy. That all three women are writers lends a professional immediacy to their personal questions about language. Glasgow reveals her gradual acceptance of Moulton into the friendship she already shares with Rives Troubetzkoy in two telling pronoun references. In her initial letter, Glasgow announces that "*My* Amélie has sent me the enclosed little letter to you"; five months later, she assures Moulton that "indeed, I'll give *our* Amélie your messages" (my emphasis). That Glasgow means also to describe a larger female community is evident when she includes her sisters (see letters 2, 8).

Glasgow often represents this implied female community in her letters to Moulton in mystical or spiritual moments. As Raper in particular has discussed exhaustively, this mysticism characterized much of Glasgow's writing in the early years of the twentieth century ("Ambivalence"; *Without Shelter*). And usually, as I have suggested, critics attribute Glasgow's grounding in "otherworldly" philosophies to her "very real problems in this world, the most urgent of which was likely the collapse of her affair with a married lover called 'Gerald B.'" (Raper, "Ambivalence" 12–13). But this spirituality typically appears in Glasgow's work, including her letters, when her theme is female relationships (see, for example, *The Descendant* [1897], *Phases of an Inferior Planet* [1898], *The Wheel of Life* [1906]; *Letters*, Glasgow to Johnston, Moulton, Patterson, and Rawlings). Glasgow evokes a spiritual quality, similar to that which pervades many of her letters to women, when she expresses her sense of connection with Moulton (and also with Rives Troubetzkoy): "You brought the spirit very close to me and because of this I know—I feel, oh, my dear friend, with a sense that is above and beyond knowledge that we have come together—as Amélie and I have come—for some wonderful and lovely end" (letter 2; see also letters 3 and 7). Similar expressions characterize Glasgow's letters to Marjorie Kinnan Rawlings (*Letters* 286–87) and to Signe Toksvig (*Letters* 321, 332–34) more than thirty-five years later. Thus, a sense of women's spirituality, especially in their relations to one another, marks Glasgow's spiritualism more emphatically than despair over a failed love affair. In expressing to

Moulton her feeling that their friendship existed before they met—the "sweet familiar recognition" of letter 2—Glasgow legitimates a belief that women's friendships exist in some superior, even *a priori*, spiritual world. The implication is that female friendships inhabit a realm out of ordinary bounds and therefore are not subject to patriarchal rules and standards. Moreover, the "recognition" carries with it the sense of a female self as a second self that is "familiar," spiritual, and natural.

This spirituality attached to women and to the connections among them also can be contextualized historically. Feminist scholars note that this spirituality functions with particular significance in nineteenth-century female relationships (Cott; Sahli; Vicinus, "Distance and Desire"). Whether attributable to a displaced religiosity, to apologies for homoerotic attraction, or to some other source, the language of spiritualism characterizes nineteenth-century correspondence between women and is evident later as well. Glasgow's impulse toward spiritualism springs from all of these, I think. Certainly she would have imbibed the pervasive contemporary literary conventions of female letter-writing. Her well-known rebellion against her father's "rock-ribbed" Calvinism, as she calls it (*The Woman Within* 16), may have necessitated replacing the religion she repudiated along with her father. An increasing suspicion that the marriage plot was not the story she wanted for her life (and, perhaps, a suspicion that women, in Virginia Woolf's words, stirred her imagination) may have required justification. Glasgow served all these purposes in associating spirituality with women and with women's relationships.

These possible explanations for Glasgow's female spirituality also gesture toward resistance to male standards. Accepting the conventional language of women writing letters to other women meant inclusion in a female community and tradition that challenged male hegemony. Similarly, in acknowledging the importance of women's relationships in her life, Glasgow simultaneously acknowledged the relative insignificance of men and their cultural expectations for women. Standing up to her father's religion at all was a bold move for Glasgow; replacing it with a spirituality obtaining in women's friendships was downright rebellious. Glasgow's letters to Moulton and the impulses toward connection to women that they reveal mark a significant moment in Glasgow's personal and professional development. They indicate Glasgow's willingness to separate herself not only from the cultural expectations that pressured her to marry and inhabit traditional domestic space but also from the narrative implications of those expectations. "Writing beyond the ending" as a strategy inextricably unites both a narratological and a personal commitment. Challenges to male-dominated discourse extend from personal to fictional worlds, and Glasgow's letters to Moulton show her readiness to ally herself with these challenges.

Female Friendship in *The Wheel of Life*

Glasgow completed *The Wheel of Life* about two months after she met Louise Chandler Moulton, as her fourth letter indicates, and she visited Moulton in Boston just after her trip to New York in January 1906, the month her novel was published (see letters 5, 6). This novel tells the story of Laura Wilde, a poet, like Moulton, to whom others pay homage. Despite Laura's belief that no one who has "dreamed dreams" could possibly "fall in love and marry," she does just that (Glasgow, *Wheel* 37). Rejecting the undeserving Arnold Kemper on the eve of their marriage, Laura finds comfort first in her friendship with Gerty Bridewell and, if we accept the novel's conclusion, in a future relationship with Roger Adams, editor of an international journal. Despite the seemingly traditional romantic ending of *Wheel*, however, the novel gathers force primarily from the relationship "between Laura and Gerty," as the penultimate chapter's title suggests.

Though *The Wheel of Life* largely resists capitulation to the traditional heterosexual marriage plot, most critics, encouraged in part by Glasgow, have conspired in the forced marginalization of the novel's woman-centered plot. Godbold finds *Wheel* not only the "greatest mistake of Ellen's writing career" but also "tedious" in its "descriptions of ladies' fashions and soliloquies by women who are dying of boredom" (75). Usually—indeed, almost invariably—readers participate in overemphasizing the novel's interest in heterosexual relationships by embedding discussion of the novel in the context of Glasgow's own ostensible love affairs, especially *the* affair with "Gerald B—," at the time the novel was written. In the earliest scholarly book in English on Glasgow (1960), McDowell begins his analysis of *The Wheel of Life* and its immediate successor in such a way that it would be difficult for readers to view these novels as anything other than dramas of heterosexuality: "With the death of her lover Gerald B— in 1905 Ellen Glasgow entered her 'mystical' phase; and in two books, *The Wheel of Life* and *The Ancient Law*, she reflected her endeavor to find solace deep within herself for her grief" (82). In 1971, Richards, after a glancing reference to women's friendship in *Wheel* and elsewhere in Glasgow's work (97), nevertheless similarly emphasizes Gerald B—: "For seven years, Ellen Glasgow came closer to happiness than at any other period of her life. . . . Her relationship with Gerald made her feel for the first time like an attractive woman" (91).

Godbold asserts confidently that "the key to the truth of her relationship with Gerald is to be found in this novel" (75). These early studies, in emphasizing Gerald B— in their discussions of *The Wheel of Life,* set the tone for most of the work that has followed.

Focusing so exclusively on the novel as a response to Glasgow's relationships with "Gerald" and the other men in her life centralizes those relationships and marginalizes her close friendships with women. As Wagner has noted, *The Wheel of Life* demonstrates Glasgow's ability "not only to attack romantic myths but also to provide alternatives for them" (36) partly through women's friendship. Glasgow's letters to Moulton (along with others written about this time to Mary Johnston and Lizzie Patterson) suggest that, regardless of "Gerald," Glasgow's emotional life was far from impoverished and indicate that much of her fulfillment came from her relationships with women friends. Focusing on the Moulton correspondence, which spans the year that ended Glasgow's relationship with "Gerald," serves as a reminder that Glasgow's supposed overwhelming despair over the end of the "Gerald" affair did not prevent her seeking out and nurturing close friendships with women.

Glasgow's claim years after publishing *The Wheel of Life* that she regarded the novel as a "failure" (*The Woman Within* 171) does not confirm views of her book that Glasgow expressed earlier. In 1904 she called it "another big, . . . human document" that was "wrung from life itself" rather than from "sugared romance."[13] She sought not approval but self-satisfaction, she says, in writing *Wheel:* "I could no more help writing it than I could live and not breathe the air about me. It was this or death for me" (*Letters* 41). Twenty-four years later (and perhaps even close to the time she pronounces *Wheel*'s "failure" in her autobiography),[14] she expresses delight in a critic's discovering "the autobiographical basis" of *The Wheel of Life* (*Letters* 238). That novel, Glasgow goes on to say, was "the only one of my books that was taken directly from experience"; the book's "mystic phase, and even the incident of the little blue flower, really occurred" (238). Though critics have always assumed that the relationship with "Gerald" forms the only "autobiographical basis" to which Glasgow refers, Laura's mystical awakening during her trip with Gerty to the Adirondacks has its parallel in an experience that Glasgow relives as she describes it to Mary Johnston in 1906 (Johnston Papers, September 15th 1906; *Letters* 55–56).[15] In these letters, as in her letters to Moulton, Glasgow clearly associates her mystical experiences with her women friends, a pattern of association also evident in Glasgow's letters to Lizzie Patterson and Mary Johnston about the same time (Glasgow Papers, Accession #5060, Box 28; Johnston

Papers, Accession #3588, Box 2; also *Letters*). The friendship between women in *The Wheel of Life* is as much or more "wrung from life" as any heterosexual love.

The Wheel of Life's first chapter, "In Which the Romantic Hero Is Conspicuous by His Absence," calls the reader's attention away from the traditional novelistic marriage plot, as Wagner also notes (35). Much as the letters to Moulton refuse male intervention by excluding any reference to men, *Wheel's* opening chapter pointedly omits the male romantic hero who would make possible that plot which the novel's conclusion, with its hopeful suggestion of future love between Laura and Roger, appears to support. Glasgow's beginning thus calls into question the conventional romantic ending, both as a narrative and, by extension, as a real-life choice. Here, Glasgow goes even further than "writing beyond the ending." She writes beyond the beginning, as well, as she forces us to look back to her book's opening for clues to the *other* ending—the one that does not satisfy the beginning's nontraditional, heroless terms. That other ending, it turns out, is contained not in the romantic plot suggested by the last few pages of the final chapter, "Renewal," but in the healing women's friendship that dominates the penultimate chapter, "Between Laura and Gerty," and lingers in the first pages of the concluding chapter. Just as Glasgow feels a "thrill of joy" in the transcendent love that "returned" to her after meeting Moulton (letter 2), it is the "renewal" between Laura and Gerty that makes Laura's rebirth possible. The renewal in the final chapter depends not upon the reentry of the "romantic hero" but upon the women's friendship at the center of "Between Laura and Gerty" and at the center of Laura's renewed faith in life. By refocusing attention on what has been traditionally viewed as marginal—not the traditional "ending" but the penultimate chapter, and not the romantic heterosexual plot but the women's relationship—Glasgow at once asserts the misunderstood centrality of female friendship, the misplaced devotion to traditional heterosexual love plots, and the misrepresentation of female life inherent in conventional narrative.

Early in the novel, an acquaintance of Perry Bridewell, Gerty's husband, describes Laura Wilde as not "worth much at love-making—the purpose for which woman was created by God and cultivated by man"— because she "writes books" (*Wheel* 10), an attitude that Glasgow, Moulton, and Rives Troubetzkoy no doubt encountered in their professional lives. Laura, writing poetry that is "chastened and restrained" and characterized by a "cloistral vision" and a "conventual purity" (52–53), has clearly separated herself and her "books" from their traditional sexual and narrative requirements: they are "conventual" rather than "conventional." Perry's friend's fusion of narrative and heterosexual love with its prescription that women exist for male-defined roles in life and art becomes precisely Glasgow's target for criticism and provides the impetus for her revisionary emphasis on women's friendship. Molly Merryweather's exasperated rhetorical question in *The Miller of Old Church* (1911) might well be Glasgow's here: "Why do you seem to think that the beginning and middle and end of my existence is a man?" (173). Molly's question inveighs against the literal expectation that a man should be the center of her life, and her language as she does so recapitulates the narrative analog to that expectation: just as her life is supposed to begin, develop, and end with a man, her narrative's convention-bound trajectory with its "beginning and middle and end" is supposed to revolve around the marriage plot and its romantic hero.

If fictional patterns convey Glasgow's rebellion only subtly—*The Wheel of Life*, after all, does end with at least the strong suggestion of a traditional "happy ending," however seriously qualified by the novel— her life's patterns more obviously work against such conventionality. In contradistinction to the usual view of Glasgow as unquestionably (even if complexly) heterosexual in the plots of both her personal and fictional lives, in fact she channeled more of her emotional energy into her relationships with other women than into her much-discussed search for an ideal male mate, a pattern critics have identified in other women writers' lives (Goodman; O'Brien; Sherman, *Sarah Orne Jewett*) and as a few readers have briefly noted in Glasgow's life (Jones; Richards; Wagner). Glasgow's letters to Louise Chandler Moulton reveal a warmth toward other women characteristic throughout Glasgow's life. Glasgow's close friendships with several women have been ignored largely because they do not fit the traditional pattern. The presumed married lover, "Gerald B—"; the adoring minister with the improbable name, Frank Paradise; the aspiring lawyer and politico Henry Anderson—these and others have compelled our attention because they are *supposed* to do so. Recognizing the centrality of the women in Glasgow's life—Lizzie Patterson, Carrie Duke, Mary Johnston, Louise Chandler Moulton, Amélie Rives Troubetzkoy, Radclyffe Hall, Clare Leighton, Signe Toksvig, Marjorie Kinnan Rawlings, members of Glasgow's family, and especially Anne Virginia Bennett—requires a willingness to explode our expectations and to ask complicating questions.

One recurring theme in Marjorie Kinnan Rawlings's notes on interviews with Glasgow's family and friends is discomfort with Glasgow's closeness to Amélie Rives Troubetzkoy. Describing Glasgow's inscriptions to Rives Troubetzkoy in presentation copies of books as "too affectionate" and Glasgow's letters as written "rashly and indiscreetly"

(Rawlings Papers B.29, B.36), Glasgow's lifelong friend, Roberta Wellford, responded much the way readers have responded since then: it's simply too uncomfortable and unfamiliar openly to confront the implications of a woman's life centered emotionally on other women. But by such refusal, we have conspired in disallowing Glasgow's right to tell her own story or to let her life's story speak for itself. I think we can no longer participate in such willful blindness. Instead, we can refocus and, in a sense, save Glasgow's life.

Notes

1. The eight autograph letters are housed in the Louise Chandler Moulton Papers, Library of Congress. I wish to express my gratitude to Alice L. Birney, American Literature Specialist at the Library of Congress, for locating the letters in response to my inquiry. In reproducing the letters, I have chosen as little editorial intrusion as possible. In the case of obvious omissions, I bracket the missing word or words; likewise, I bracket any guessed words and punctuate them with a question mark. Words that are completely illegible are designated as such, again in brackets. I have let Glasgow's spelling, punctuation, and occasional confusing syntax stand as written by her.

2. Though the word *wiser* seems odd here, Glasgow could refer to her earlier characterization in this letter to Moulton as "wiser than I." In this sense, the later use would mean that in the presence of a spiritually inspiring person, "what else can one be but a believer in and a lover of" those "wiser" than oneself.

3. *The Wheel of Life*, which would be published in January 1906 by Doubleday. See also letter 4.

4. Glasgow's "friend" may be her sister Cary Glasgow McCormack or her friend and fellow Virginia novelist Mary Johnston. According to a letter dated "Christmas 1905" Glasgow was in The Glen Springs, Watkins, New York. In it she mentions Cary's illness, though it sounds as if Cary is not with her. Since letter 5 indicates that Glasgow was in New York City by the end of January 1906, it would make sense for her to have been in The Glen Springs [Watkins Glen], not far from Ithaca, New York (see *Letters* 49). Glasgow's letter to Mary Johnston in summer 1906(?) expresses relief at hearing of Johnston's recovery from her "illness" (*Letters* 51). Since Glasgow was very close to Johnston in the early years of the twentieth century, it is possible that she is the "friend" Glasgow refers to in her letter to Moulton.

5. Glasgow refers to Moulton's literary "Friday evenings," held in her Boston home (see above).

6. Castle Hill was the home of Amélie Rives Troubetzkoy and her husband,

Prince Pierre Troubetzkoy. It is located just northeast of Charlottesville, Virginia (*Letters* 47).

7. Rebe Glasgow (later Tutwiler) was Glasgow's younger sister by four years. Rebe frequently traveled with Glasgow, and she may have accompanied her to Boston. Rebe and Cary sailed with their sister to Europe in 1905 when Glasgow first met Moulton.

8. I have been unable to identify this verse, which is not in Proverbs, the Song of Solomon, or Ecclesiastes. Glasgow may be misquoting something she remembered vaguely from her religious upbringing, or even conflating biblical text with something from the philosophical texts she was reading at the time (see Raper "Ambivalence" and *Without Shelter*).

9. Rebe married Cabell Carrington Tutwiler in December 1906. Though Glasgow here refers to the "excitement" of Rebe's wedding, it was a difficult event for Glasgow (see her later statement in this letter that "missing" Rebe "cuts too deep" even to allow articulation). She had been close to Rebe, and she apparently did not like her sister's new husband. These feelings are evident in Marjorie Kinnan Rawlings's notes on interviews with Rebe (Rawlings Papers, folder B.33) and Glasgow's letters to Rebe in 1906 and 1907 (Rawlings Papers, folder D).

10. I have been unable to determine what book Glasgow refers to here. Moulton's best-known volumes were published before 1900; her collected poems did not appear until 1909.

11. She is referring to her sister Cary, who died in August 1911 from cancer.

12. The fact that Glasgow so carefully guarded much of her correspondence from possible publication suggests that she distinguished between letters for public and private consumption and was self-conscious about which letters belonged to each category. In an unpublished letter of 9 September 1937, Amélie Rives Troubetzkoy, for example, admits that she has just destroyed, reluctantly, Glasgow's letter to her, as Glasgow had instructed (Glasgow Papers, Box 18, 9 September 1937).

13. This letter is misdated "1902" in *Letters* (40–41), as Godbold points out (71n).

14. The dates of composition of particular sections of *The Woman Within* are difficult or impossible to determine. She began writing her autobiography in the 1930s and the explanatory letter to her literary executors about its disposition and possible publication is dated 1944. *The Woman Within* was not published until 1954, nine years after Glasgow's death.

15. Two letters from Glasgow to Johnston during Glasgow's 1906 trip to the Adirondacks demonstrate that Glasgow associates Johnston with the transcendent inspiration of nature (August 19 [14?] 1906 and an undated 1906 letter from Hurricane Lodge; Mary Johnston Papers, Accession #3588, Box 2; *Letters* 51–54). Rouse dates the first "August 15," as does Rawlings (Rawlings Papers, folder D).

Works Cited

Published Works

Bauer, Dale M. *Feminist Dialogics: A Theory of Failed Community.* Albany: State U of New York P, 1988.

Cixous, Hélène. "The Laugh of the Medusa." *The Signs Reader: Women, Gender and Scholarship.* Ed. Elizabeth Abel and Emily K. Abel. Chicago: U of Chicago P, 1983. 279–97.

Cott, Nancy F. *The Bonds of Womanhood: "Woman's Sphere" in New England, 1780–1835.* New Haven: Yale UP, 1977.

de Lauretis, Teresa. *Alice Doesn't: Feminism, Semiotics, Cinema.* Bloomington: Indiana UP, 1984.

DuPlessis, Rachel Blau. *Writing Beyond the Ending: Narrative Strategies of Twentieth-Century Women Writers.* Bloomington: Indiana UP, 1985.

Edgerly, Lois Stiles, ed. and comp. *Give Her This Day: A Daybook of Women's Words.* Gardiner, ME: Tilbury House, 1990.

Glasgow, Ellen. *Letters of Ellen Glasgow.* Ed. Blair Rouse. New York: Harcourt, 1958.

———. *The Miller of Old Church.* 1911. Vol II of the Virginia Edition of the Works of Ellen Glasgow. New York: Scribner's, 1938.

———. *The Wheel of Life.* New York: Doubleday, 1906.

———. *The Woman Within.* New York: Harcourt, 1954.

Godbold, E. Stanly, Jr. *Ellen Glasgow and the Woman Within.* Baton Rouge: Louisiana State UP, 1972.

Goodman, Susan. *Edith Wharton's Women: Friends and Rivals.* Hanover, NH: UP of New England, 1990.

Jones, Anne Goodwyn. *Tomorrow Is Another Day: The Woman Writer in the South, 1859–1936.* Baton Rouge: Louisiana State UP, 1981.

Kelly, William W., ed. *Ellen Glasgow: A Bibliography.* Charlottesville: UP of Virginia, 1964.

Lanser, Susan S. "Toward a Feminist Narratology." *Feminisms: An Anthology of Literary Theory and Criticism.* Ed. Robyn R. Warhol and Diane Price Herndl. New Brunswick: Rutgers UP, 1991. 610–29.

McDowell, Frederick P. W. *Ellen Glasgow and the Ironic Art of Fiction.* Madison: U of Wisconsin P, 1960.

Meese, Elizabeth A. *Crossing the Double-Cross: The Practice of Feminist Criticism.* Chapel Hill: U of North Carolina P, 1986.

Miller, Nancy K. *The Heroine's Text: Readings in the French and English Novel, 1722–1782.* New York: Columbia UP, 1980.

O'Brien, Sharon. *Willa Cather: The Emerging Voice.* New York: Oxford UP, 1987.

Ostriker, Alicia Suskin. *Stealing the Language: The Emergence of Women's Poetry in America.* Boston: Beacon, 1986.

Raper, Julius Rowan. "Ambivalence toward Authority: A Look at Glasgow's Library, 1890–1906." *Mississippi Quarterly* 31.1 (Winter 1977–78): 5–16.

———. *Without Shelter: The Early Career of Ellen Glasgow.* Baton Rouge: Louisiana State UP, 1971.

Richards, Marion K. *Ellen Glasgow's Development as a Novelist.* The Hague: Mouton, 1971.

Roman, Judith A. *Annie Adams Fields: The Spirit of Charles Street.* Bloomington: Indiana UP, 1990.

Sahli, Nancy. "Smashing: Women's Relationships before the Fall." *Chrysalis* 8 (Summer 1979): 17–27.

Sherman, Sarah Way. "Louise Chandler Moulton." *American Women Writers: A Critical Reference Guide* (abridged ed.). Ed. Langdon Lynne Faust. New York: Ungar, 1988. 520–23.

———. *Sarah Orne Jewett, An American Persephone.* Hanover, NH: UP of New England, 1989.

Smith-Rosenberg, Carroll. *Disorderly Conduct: Visions of Gender in Victorian America.* New York: Knopf, 1985.

———. "The Female World of Love and Ritual: Relations between Women in Nineteenth-Century America." *Signs* 1.1 (Autumn 1975): 1–29.

Spiller, Robert E., et al., eds. *Literary History of the United States.* 3rd ed. Vol. 1. New York: Macmillan, 1963.

Todd, Janet M. *Women's Friendship in Literature.* New York: Columbia UP, 1980.

Vicinus, Martha. "Distance and Desire: English Boarding-School Friendships." *Signs* 9.4 (Summer 1984): 600–622.

———. *Independent Women: Work and Community for Single Women, 1850–1920.* Chicago: U of Chicago P, 1985.

Wagner, Linda W. *Ellen Glasgow: Beyond Convention.* Austin: U of Texas P, 1982.

Yaeger, Patricia. *Honey-Mad Women: Emancipatory Strategies in Women's Writing.* New York: Columbia UP, 1988.

Manuscript Collections

Ellen Glasgow Papers, ms. U of Virginia, Charlottesville.

Mary Johnston Papers, ms. U of Virginia, Charlottesville.

Louise Chandler Moulton Papers, ms. Library of Congress, Washington, D.C.

Marjorie Kinnan Rawlings Papers, ms. U of Florida, Gainesville.

The Framing of Glasgow's *Virginia*

Phillip D. Atteberry

Ellen Glasgow's early novels are often interesting but seldom aesthetically satisfying because their realistic openings inevitably give way to sentimentalized endings.[1] Not until her tenth novel, *Virginia* (1913), does Glasgow resolve this inconsistency, keep to her original purpose, and explore a complex subject in a consistently complex manner.

Most discussions of *Virginia* have been thematically centered, and for good reason. Glasgow daringly focuses on a character whose mind has been incapacitated by cultural conditioning, a character who, in most fictional contexts, would become yawningly tedious. But in the same way that Tolstoy's *Death of Ivan Ilych* explores, with excruciating precision, an unthinking man's growing awareness of his own mortality, Glasgow's *Virginia* explores, with equally excruciating precision, an unthinking woman's growing awareness of her own unhappiness, an unhappiness made all the more poignant because, as is the case with Ivan Ilych, Virginia's intellectual limitations (together with the intellectual destitution of her environment) place her fate beyond her control.

And yet *Virginia*'s narrative structure, not its subject, distinguishes it most notably from Glasgow's earlier books. *Virginia* is so aesthetically successful because its thematic elements are so effectively framed. Scenes of youth are muted by images of age; episodes of health are qualified by reminders of death; assertions of fidelity are offset by demonstrations of betrayal. Such contrasts are established in the earliest pages and expand as the book develops, making for a texture that gathers richness throughout.

Book One, for example, concerns, most centrally, Virginia Pendleton's eye-fluttering courtship with Oliver Treadwell. But in this, the lightest section of the book, Glasgow initiates the contrasts that will later

darken the novel's tone and deepen its thematic texture. Introducing
Virginia Pendleton as the archetypical embodiment of feminine youth
and beauty (with a laugh like "the song of a bird" [7], eyes as blue as
"wild hyacinths after rain" [5], and blushes as red as "a rose" [9]) implies timelessness and indestructibility. But built into this section are
three disturbing images of middle age that not only refute the implication
but prefigure the intellectual paralysis, the social rigidity, and the marital
frustrations that will ultimately afflict the middle-aged Virginia.

The novel opens, for example, not with young Virginia but with
Miss Priscilla Batte, a "shapeless" woman "of some fifty years" (3) who
represents all that is "static" and "obsolete" in the Virginia of the eighties (12–13). Miss Priscilla's physical decline is an obvious symbol of the
decaying old order, but she also represents the intellectual immobility
that later characterizes the adult Virginia. Miss Priscilla's central intellectual inadequacy is not that she has "a poor head" for spelling (11) or
that she believes "poetry was the ruination of Poe" (20), but that she
sees no connection between learning and life. This is why she regards
history "strictly as a branch of study" and visualizes it "as a list of dates
or as a king wearing his crown" and never pauses to brood "over the
tremendous tragedies through which she [has] passed" (10). As the local school mistress, she not only thwarts Virginia's intellectual development but foreshadows her intellectual destiny.

Lucy Pendleton, Virginia's mother, represents the social rigidity
from which the adult Virginia will suffer. Lucy's purpose in life is to
remain a great lady even though "the props and the background of
[greatness have] crumbled around her" (39). This means "keeping an
open house on starvation fare" (39), maintaining servants who won't
work, and scrubbing floors before dawn to avoid being seen (40). She
is the victim of an antique propriety whose existence is a "divine ecstasy of martyrdom" (146). Lucy's real fault, however, is not her Old
World demeanor, but her inability to acknowledge that life necessarily
involves change. She clings to the "impassioned memory" of things that
are dead to sweeten the less romantic elements of things that are living
(39). Like Miss Priscilla, and later Virginia, Lucy believes that "a natural curiosity about the universe is the beginning of infidelity" (22) because such curiosity destroys the sentimental "tissue of illusion" she
weaves around life (35). Because she lives "in a small place" among
"simple and guileless" people who cherish the same opinions as she (35),
Lucy's social rigidity is admired. But the adult Virginia must make her
way in a more diverse, free-thinking world that has no patience for
such calcified domestic values.

Unhappy Belinda Treadwell, Oliver's aunt and the wife of tobacco baron Cyrus Treadwell, prefigures Virginia's marital frustrations. The young Belinda's "terror of . . . spinsterhood" (89) caused her to ignore "the personal peculiarities or possibilities of a husband" (94) and "[entwine] herself . . . around the nearest male prop that offered" (89). Not surprisingly, that prop turned out to be unsuitable, rendering Belinda miserable. Her paralyzing stroke symbolizes her incapacity to understand marriage or to deal with life.

Virginia, of course, does not suffer physical paralysis, but her marital difficulties are much like Belinda's and, metaphorically, she is just as paralyzed in her capacity to understand or deal with them. Cyrus and Oliver, for all of their surface differences, admire women of judgment and independence, and yet because they yield to springtime "attack[s] of indiscretion" (88), they end up with precisely what they don't want.

These three images of aging, juxtaposed as they are against Virginia's youth and exuberance, do not dominate the tone of part 1, but they establish a sober counterpoint to the more pervasive atmosphere of excitement and gaiety.[2] As Oliver and Virginia's relationship advances, however, Glasgow initiates an illness motif that climaxes near the end of part 2. Like the early images of aging, the illness motif is barely perceptible at first, consisting only of scattered images,[3] but when Oliver and Virginia marry, illness becomes an integral part of the plot and helps chart the deterioration of their diseased relationship.

Illness first becomes a plot preoccupation when Oliver's play, *The Beaten Road,* fails on the New York stage. Virginia, who has stayed home with the children, learns from a newspaper reference that Oliver is ill and confined to his hotel. That Oliver's illness is anything but physical never occurs to the naive Virginia:

> Her mind, unable to grasp the significance of a theatrical failure, had seized upon the one salient fact which concerned her. Plays might succeed or fail, and it made little difference, but illness was another matter—illness was something definite and material. Illness could neither be talked away by religion nor denied by philosophy. It had its place in her mind not with the shadow, but with the substance of things. It was the one sinister force which had always dominated her, even when it was absent, by the sheer terror it aroused in her thoughts. (273)

Virginia hastily goes to Oliver and finds New York nothing but "the dreary background of . . . illness" (283). Even the walls are "frowning" so that the sunbeams can bring no color to the grey streets, a scene so repulsive to Virginia that she holds her breath for "fear of 'catching' some malign malady from the smells and filth" (282). Upon reaching

Oliver, she is confronted "as grimly as a physical sore" with the fact that he has changed (295). He is not ill as she thought, but "wounded" more deeply, so deeply and mysteriously that the "balm" of her affection is like "bungling touches on raw flesh" (286, 290). Virginia rejoices in their prompt return home, thinking that Oliver's malady "had been in some mysterious way produced by New York, and that it existed merely within the circumscribed limits of this dreadful city" (290). But upon returning, Oliver's "strange, almost physical soreness" continues. He craves solitude, which Virginia fears "as if it were the smallpox," and becomes more irritable the more Virginia "ministers" to him (297).

The episode reveals the root of Virginia and Oliver's difficulties. Oliver's is an illness of the spirit, for which the only antidote is "an intelligent justification of his work" (286), but Virginia, who has no knowledge of intellectual concerns, can only provide "pitiful attempts at flattery" (290). To Oliver, life's ultimate significance lies in activities beyond the home. To Virginia, the universe beyond the home scarcely exists.

Illness next becomes a preoccupation when Harry, Virginia and Oliver's son, contracts diphtheria. Though quite literal and deadly, this illness also assumes metaphorical significance. The day before Harry falls ill, Virginia and Oliver are scheduled to travel with friends to Atlantic City. But at the last minute Virginia refuses to go, asserting that Harry is sick, even though he has "never looked healthier" (338). To Virginia, the Atlantic City trip represents irresponsibility and self-indulgence, those qualities most abhorrent to her notion of motherhood and a healthy home. To Oliver, it represents freedom. In short, the trip takes on symbolic significance; both refuse to yield, and Oliver leaves, furious at what he calls Virginia's "'sensational motherhood'" (338).

Virginia, however, is right about Harry's being ill and ends up hovering over a desperately ill child while Oliver takes a holiday. As the imagery suggests, the illness affects Virginia's emotional fiber as severely as Harry's physical. A feeling of isolation permeates her "like a physical chill" (358). Even her physical frame is emaciated by the vigil. Her sleeplessness not only causes her complexion to turn "ashen" (355) but reduces "the flower-like blue" of her eyes to "a dull grey" (350), while beneath her dressing gown the shoulder blades of her once shapely figure show "sharply under their fragile covering of flesh" (350).

Not surprisingly, Virginia's physical changes parallel a change of character. She prays repeatedly for her son's recovery: "If he only lives, I will let everything else go. I will think of nothing except my children. . . . Nothing [else] on earth will make any difference" (353). And she remains true to her vow. Harry recovers, but Virginia does not. Oliver arrives only hours after Harry's crisis has passed, but Virginia thinks of him now as "a person whom she had known in another life" (360). Of course, they settle into a domestic routine once again, but Virginia is more rigidly committed to limiting her thoughts and activities to the home while Oliver is more committed than ever to escaping its claustrophobia.

After its focus on Harry's illness, the narrative shifts abruptly to Cyrus Treadwell. We learn that his Negro servant, Mandy, bore a child by Cyrus twenty years earlier, a young man who is now in trouble and whom Cyrus refuses to acknowledge or assist (367). The episode is important for two reasons. First, it extends the image of a sick marriage that Cyrus and Belinda's union has represented all along. But most importantly, it parallels Oliver's treatment of Virginia. The young Oliver develops a passion for and avails himself of Virginia's sexual attractions just as Cyrus does Mandy's. Both, moreover, abandon the women when they lose their appeal. In Oliver's case, of course, mitigating circumstances do exist. He does make efforts to reconcile with Virginia, and he does genuinely regret their separation, but such circumstances do not change the central issue. When Virginia was at her most attractive, Oliver was willing to give up everything for a life with her, just as Cyrus was willing to risk everything to enjoy Mandy. But with the passing of time has come a change in priority, a change that, in each case, results in an abandoned woman.

The subplot of Cyrus and Mandy, small though it is, functions as an image of infidelity and abandonment. Throughout the book, Cyrus and Belinda's marital difficulties have prefigured Oliver and Virginia's, so it is appropriate that in this, Cyrus's last significant appearance, his actions foreshadow Oliver's final abandonment of Virginia.

Thus far, we have examined the novel's darker elements, and indeed the tone does darken as the plot develops, but the book never gives way to pervasive bleakness. Just as images of aging, disease, and infidelity serve as sober counterpoints to the lightness of the novel's first half, images of youth, health, and fidelity arise near the end, contrasting with the gathering anxieties of the middle-aged Virginia.

Susan Treadwell, for example, functions as a physical and temperamental contrast to Virginia throughout the book, being introduced early on as one whose "natural intelligence [has] overcome the defects of her education" so that unlike Virginia she thinks "not vaguely, but with clearness and precision" (29). At the beginning, Susan is a plot vehicle rather than a thematic element, helping (though inadvertently) to bring Virginia and Oliver together and helping us get to know both characters.[4] In the book's last section, however, Susan represents an image of physical and intellectual vitality that contrasts with Virginia. She is a "superbly vigorous woman of forty-five, with an abundant energy which overflowed outside of her household in a dozen different directions. . . . She had kept her mind as alert as her body, and the number of books she read had always shocked Virginia a little" (446).

In addition to being an image of intellectual vigor, Susan and her husband, John Henry, represent a healthy marriage. John Henry, though busy and successful at his trade, is sincerely devoted to Susan and, unlike Oliver and Cyrus, he doesn't allow his business to assume more importance than his marriage. Susan, for her part, loves John Henry but, unlike Virginia, she doesn't place boundaries on her affections: "[S]he did not love him [John Henry] to the exclusion of other people; [just as] she loved her children, but they did not absorb her" (446).

In virtually all of Glasgow's early novels, healthy, well-directed characters are notable for their capacity to love sincerely but to keep that love in perspective, to maintain an emotional balance.[5] Neither Virginia nor Oliver do that. Virginia preoccupies herself with domestic concerns, and Oliver, with professional, so that, unlike Susan and John Henry, they have no common interests to strengthen their relationship.

The other prominent image of youth, health, and fidelity near the book's end is Virginia's son, Harry, a "tall, lean, habitually towselled-headed" boy who combines a Treadwell regard for "material success" with the "genial temper" of the Pendletons (401–2). Harry, though unsentimental in every detail, is devoted to his mother in spite of her intellectual limitations. While at college, he writes to her every week, and when at home he dotes on her with playful gallantry, recognizing that his is all the attention she gets. When his sisters try to convince Virginia to change her old-fashioned hairstyle, Harry defends her vociferously, if none too logically: "You let them fuss all they want to, mother . . . , but your hair is a long sight better than theirs, and don't you let them nag you into making a mess of it" (418). It is no doubt because of his devotion to Virginia that Harry consistently "rubs" Oliver "the wrong way" (403). Harry is a constant reminder to Oliver that he is not treating his wife well. Glasgow's portrayal of Harry's devotion avoids sentimentality by keeping Harry largely in the background. He is just prominent enough in the last chapters to provide, along with Susan and John Henry, a thematic contrast to the dominant themes of betrayal and decay.

The book ends as it begins, not with a thematically dominant image or character, but with one of the many counterpoints, a note from Harry (who has just learned of Oliver's abandonment) to Virginia: "'Dearest mother, I am coming home to you'" (526). But this ending, like the entire book, is more complex than it first appears. What will Harry do when he arrives home? Quit school and stay with his mother?

Console her for a time and leave again? There is, in fact, nothing he can do to alleviate, in any substantial way, Virginia's dilemma, making his gesture of fidelity of limited plot significance. This gesture, however, has considerable thematic and tonal significance because it qualifies the atmosphere of abandonment and despair that has climaxed in the final chapters.

Virginia, in short, explores both the multifaceted effects of aging and the social tensions of the changing South, but unlike Glasgow's earlier books, it doesn't simplify life's great complexities. It is a book full of tonal contrasts and structural counterpoints that qualify every presentation and question every assertion.

Notes

1. Glasgow's book of self-criticism, *A Certain Measure,* discusses with considerable insight the thematic and stylistic imperfections of the early novels. Chapter 2, "*The Deliverance,*" focuses most directly on their thematic inconsistencies. For a more complete discussion of the aesthetic difficulties in Glasgow's first nine novels, see my essay, "Ellen Glasgow and the Sentimental Novel of Virginia."

2. The significance of these initial juxtapositions is underscored nicely in chapter 3 when Virginia accompanies her mother to market. Because Virginia is less interested in gathering provisions than in gaining a glimpse of Oliver, she is frustrated by the delays that occur along the way: "At every corner, it seemed to Virginia, middle-aged ladies, stout or thin, wearing crape veils and holding small black silk bags in their hands, sprang out of the shadows of mulberry trees" impeding their progress with insignificant chatter (60). Though the reader is sobered by these reminders of youth's brevity, Virginia never perceives, in these early chapters, a connection between herself and the aging women surrounding her. In fact, she believes with glorious certainty that her life will be altogether different from theirs, triumphing in the "thought that her own dreams were larger than the actuality that surrounded her" (61).

3. For a sampling of such images, many of which are applied to the marriage of Cyrus and Belinda Treadwell, see pages 22, 90, 94, 97, 167, and 260.

4. The best discussion of Susan Treadwell's evolving role in the novel occurs in Linda Wagner's *Ellen Glasgow: Beyond Convention.* See particularly the chapter on *Virginia.*

5. Achieving this balance is often contingent upon a character's ability to learn from experience. Betty Ambler and Dan Montjoy in *The Battle-Ground,* for example, acquire a "deeper knowledge" of life through their wartime depriva-

tions, thus transforming their prewar flirtatiousness into a love forged "out of many struggles and the fulness . . . of experiences" (419).

Maria Fletcher of *The Deliverance,* though less successfully drawn than Betty Ambler, acquires this balance from suffering through a failed marriage—with a mentally unstable man whose mustache goes "to bed every night in curl papers." Such suffering prompts her reassessment of Christopher Blake and results in a love that "delivers" them both from hatred and insensitivity.

The marriage of Molly Merryweather and Abel Revercomb near the end of *The Miller of Old Church* is yet another example of a couple whose love achieves balance by the vicissitudes of experience—by misunderstanding, separation, and the death of loved ones. The strength of their relationship contrasts with Jonathan Gay's attraction for Blossom Revercomb (like Oliver's for Virginia), which is a thoughtless impulse: "His passion had run its inevitable course of desire, fulfillment, and exhaustion. So closely had it followed the changing seasons, that it seemed, in a larger and more impersonal aspect, as much a product of the soil as the flame-coloured lilies that bloomed in the Haunt's Walk" (369).

The point is that in Glasgow's early novels the characters who grow emotionally from life's experiences are able to develop healthy, well-balanced relationships. Others, like Virginia and Oliver, do not. This generalization does not apply as well to Glasgow's later novels. In *Barren Ground,* to cite the best-known example, Dorinda Oakley learns much from her experience but is never able to sustain a stable relationship.

Works Cited

Atteberry, Phillip D. "Ellen Glasgow and the Sentimental Novel of Virginia." *Southern Quarterly* 23.4 (Summer 1985): 5–14.

Glasgow, Ellen. *The Battle-Ground.* New York: Doubleday, 1902.

———. *A Certain Measure: An Interpretation of Prose Fiction.* New York: Harcourt, 1943.

———. *The Deliverance.* New York: Doubleday, 1904.

———. *The Miller of Old Church.* Garden City: Doubleday, 1911.

———. *Virginia.* Garden City: Doubleday, 1913.

Wagner, Linda W. *Ellen Glasgow: Beyond Convention.* Austin: U of Texas P, 1982.

"The Problem of the South"
Economic Determination, Gender Determination, and Genre in Glasgow's *Virginia*

Francesca Sawaya

In *A Certain Measure,* Ellen Glasgow describes how her first novel, *The Descendant,* came to be published. After signed versions of her manuscript had been rejected by three publishers, a friend suggested she submit it anonymously to Harper's. Writes Glasgow:

> Fortunately for me, one of the critics for that eminent firm proved to be so lacking in discernment that he pronounced *The Descendant* an unsigned book by Harold Frederic, the author of a then popular novel, with a depressing theological flavour. . . . With this unmerited endorsement, my book was immediately accepted. (*ACM* 106)

This anecdote, which she tells again and at greater length in *The Woman Within* (106–13, 121), and particularly her ironic term "unmerited endorsement" for the acceptance and publication of her first book, is telling on two counts. According to Glasgow, her writing was seen as having merit because it was felt to be the writing of the naturalist author, Harold Frederic, a writer with whom she seems to feel no affinity and for whom she expresses no admiration. More generally, her book was endorsed on the "unmerited" assumption of male authorship, pointing to the difficulty facing women writers, like herself, who wrote on "unpleasant subjects" (*ACM* 106) at the turn of the century.

But despite Glasgow's critique of what she sees as a misreading of her work, that misreading does point to two problems critics have had in reading Glasgow: how to categorize her work in terms of genre, and how to understand her work in relation to gender issues. She has been variously read as a realistic, sentimental, ironic, comedic, or, as in the case above, naturalist novelist, and frequently her work has been criticized for not remaining consistently within the confines of whatever genre is ascribed to her.[1] At the same time, while her texts foreground feminist issues, feminist critics have frequently found her accounts of these issues disappointing, even antifeminist.[2]

These problems of reading Glasgow, I will argue, are related to the two sides of her struggle to create a genre that could express the complicated social problems her texts engage. Her struggle with generic issues can be seen in the seemingly contradictory analyses of her work that she provides in *A Certain Measure*. On the one hand, she recounts obsessively her "solitary revolt" (*ACM* 8) against what she calls the "sentimental fallacy" (11, 14), or "evasive idealism" (50), which she argues characterized turn-of-the-century southern writing. On the other hand, though her critique of sentimentalism was clarified by reading *The Origin of Species* (58), she rejects naturalism, finding herself at odds with what she calls the "barbaric fallacy" (54) or the "whole-hearted retreat to the Neanderthal" (53). Her objections against these two opposed genres are clarified later when she traces the historical roots of each. Sentimental literature, she says, rose out of the "congenial hedonism" and complacency of the old South, where "as elsewhere, expression belonged to the articulate, and the articulate was supremely satisfied with his own fortunate lot, as well as with the less enviable lot of others" (135). She goes on to argue, "Only the slave, the 'poor white,' or the woman who had forgotten her modesty, may have felt inclined to protest," but "even if they had protested, who would have listened?" (135–36). The sentimental novel is not only silent about social conflict but also works to silence this conflict. However, the naturalist novel is equally problematic. It is a literature of standardization, rising out of the "uniform concrete surface of an industrialized South" (147). "Noise, numbers, size, quantity, all are exerting their lively or sinister influence. . . . Uniformity . . . has become the established ideal" (145). Thus, naturalism does not so much silence social conflict as flatten it.

Her rejection of both genres, then, is part of an economic and political critique of them. Not only does she believe that both sentimentalism and naturalism fail to depict all aspects and levels of society, but also, and more crucially, she believes those two genres are determined by specific economic systems. In Glasgow's equation, slavery leads to sentimentalism, just as industrial capitalism leads to naturalism. Dorothy Scura has shown that Glasgow saw herself as a socialist (39), and the Marxist idea of the base's determination of the superstructure, of how economic structures define ideological structures, is clearly at work in Glasgow's equation. Such a vision of the determined nature of writing leads Glasgow to criticize sentimental literature as representing an outmoded and oppressive economic system and embrace naturalism, but then to criticize naturalism to the extent that it is an outgrowth of a new but also oppressive economic system. That is, in order to escape this circular dilemma, where genres determined by economic systems necessarily reduce the author's ability to represent the complexity of social problems, Glasgow suggests that one can only rebel against the discredited genres through the available modern means, but then criticize these very modern means through the discredited ones.

However, this use of two oppositional genres, in order to create a genre adequate for expressing social problems, represents not only a kind of socialist response to the determination of economics; it represents also a feminist response to the "determination" of gender. That is, Glasgow associates sentimentalism and naturalism with different genders, as well as with different economic systems. While Glasgow does not make this association explicit, it is implicit, as we have seen in her description of *The Descendant*'s reception. Her "unmerited endorsement" rests in part upon the assumption that a woman would not and could not write such a book. Naturalism is associated with masculinity and male authorship. Similarly, sentimentalism is associated with femininity and female interests (*ACM* 11, 14).[3] Such associations are understandable in that naturalism, as Mark Seltzer has argued, is an "emphatically 'male' genre" (121) that typically "displaces the . . . mother" (124), or narratives of female reproductive power, and "places power . . . into the hands of the immortal and autonomous male technology of generation" (124). That is, the naturalist novel wants to "project an alternative to biological reproduction, to displace the threat posed by the 'women people' . . . and to devise a countermode of reproduction (the naturalist machine)" (125). By contrast, while contemporary critics disagree about the purpose and effect of sentimental literature, they agree that it dealt particularly with the domestic sphere and glorified the role of the mother/wife in that sphere and her supposed moral influence upon her children and husband.[4]

The significance of the associations Glasgow makes between genres and gender becomes clear in one of her pronouncements on domestic regional women writers, her "sentimentalist foremothers" (Donovan 131). She writes:

> I had always wished to escape from the particular into the general, from the provincial into the universal. Never from my earliest blind gropings after truth in art and truth in life had I felt an impulse to write of a single locality or of regional characteristics. . . . I knew my part of the South,

and I had looked deep enough *within* and far enough *without* to learn something of human beings and their substance. (*WW* 128–29; the italics are mine.)[5]

While she criticizes regional writing for focusing only on the particular and the subjective (what lies "within") and not the general and the objective (what lies "without"), a charge typically leveled at women writers, and she figures herself as able to escape the particular "within" by looking to the general "without," finally she combines the particular with the general. Rather than rejecting the particular for the general, she wants to create a dialectical engagement between them. Feminine vision is limited to individual, subjective interiors (by convention, Glasgow seems to suggest, for she "escaped" to the "without"), but in combination with masculine vision it will reveal "truth."

It is in *Virginia,* the novel Glasgow identified as "the first book of my maturity" (*WW* 188), that the struggle for a genre that encompasses both socialist and feminist ideas is most clearly delineated. The novel begins as a social Darwinistic account of economic and social change in the post-Civil War South. These changes are embodied in the life of Virginia Pendleton, the quintessential southern lady, who remains always the lady in face of the historical changes that render her obsolete. Divided into three sections, "The Dream," "The Reality," and "The Adjustment," the novel follows Virginia from her romance with and marriage to the aspiring playwright Oliver Treadwell, through her self-immolation in marriage and motherhood, to her abandonment by her children, her husband, and "Life" in general, and finally to a temporary "rescue" by her son. Not merely the story of Virginia the individual, but also the story of Virginia the state, the story of the backwards agrarian South confronting the modern industrial South, the novel depicts change as the struggle between successful and failing types, rather than individuals, and power is transferred figuratively from, as Seltzer would argue, the mother to the male machine. But while this account of change as necessary is the dominant one throughout the text, particularly in the last section of the novel, there is an oppositional account that ironizes this central thesis of the necessity of change. In this account, rather than the objective failure of the type, the subjective experience of Virginia Pendleton's individual failure is described. While the machine is dominant, in this last section of the novel, a kind of ideal or moral power is returned to the mother.[6]

Characteristic of the first two sections of the novel is a distanced and knowing narrator who sets forth the characters in the novel not only as unwitting pawns of an unknowable power and purpose, but also as biologically determined to succeed or fail. Individuals are "medium[s]" (37), or "vehicle[s] of . . . expression" (140; also 118) to "the purpose of Life" (37), to an "outside Power" (140) that guides even their most minute actions; depending on biological circumstances, on their heredity, they are predetermined to act and think in certain ways. Biologically determined types who become outdated are crushed by those who are biologically determined to move with the times and succeed. The "very structure of life" is such that success is not that of "the individual" but that of "the type" (364).

More specifically, however, the narrator reveals that what determines individuals is their predestined and hereditary adaptability to the changing mode of production, namely, to the change from slavery to industrial capitalism. From the beginning of the novel, the narrator makes clear that "the Problem of the South" (34) is an economic one based on the black/white conflict or the "primitive antagonism of race" (130). However, this "race" conflict, while providing the structure for the South's "Problem," is only one manifestation of it, for *race* is a term the narrator uses to describe any group of individuals with similarly inherited characteristics. For example, the white southern lady's "narrowness of vision, and uncompromising devotion to an ideal . . . were the qualities which had passed from the race in to the individual and through the individual again back into the very blood and the fibre of the race" (100). The "Problem of the South" in the novel, then, is the struggle between the biologically determined types I discussed above, a struggle between "two forces" "embodied in classes, in individuals, in articles of faith, in ideals of manners" (10). One is the "obsolete and outgrown" "vanquished idealism"; the other is the "new" "spirit of commercial materialism" (10). Those individuals associated with slavery are biologically predetermined to fail just as those associated with capitalism are biologically predetermined to succeed.

The text narrates this struggle between races embodying slavery and capitalism as that between two families in the town of Dinwiddie, the Pendletons and the Treadwells. By tracing out the relationship of Pendletons to Treadwells over two generations, the narrator reveals the differences between the old defeated South and the new rising one. The naturalist account of change poses these differences as concomitant with femininity and masculinity, so that the relations between the two families are figuratively and then literally heterosexual, the feminine/maternal type losing power to the masculine/machine type. But such a figuration of relations between the two families finally reveals the problems inherent in the naturalist account of change and becomes the grounds on which Glasgow can deploy her sentimental account of change as a critique of it.

The first relationship the narrator traces out is the friendship between Gabriel Pendleton and Cyrus Treadwell, who are bound together by their experience as Confederate soldiers in the Civil War. Gabriel is idealism and sentiment embodied, impoverished but living genteelly off his "whitewashing of . . . actuality" (26) and the kindness of neighbors. "To reach his mind," the narrator writes, "impressions of persons or objects had first to pass through a refining atmosphere in which all baser substances were eliminated, and no fact had ever penetrated this medium except in the flattering disguise of a sentiment" (26). His domestic relations are blissful not only because "he had married by accident the one woman who was made for him" (27), that is, a woman who is "an idealist only less ignorant of the world than himself" (26), but also because his "militant idealism" (26) enables him to believe that "the only form of activity" his wife really enjoys is "working herself to death for his sake" (32), his wife sharing this conviction. The two, in fact, are "so sensitive to pain" that they exist "only by inventing a world of exquisite fiction" (51), fiction that enables and enforces the slave system and the different forms of oppression that stem from it. Most important, in the logic of the text, Gabriel is a minister, a figure at this time seen as marginal and feminized, uninvolved in the "real" world of men, politics, and business (see Douglas). He is a member of an obsolete caste to whom "[n]ot progress, but a return to the 'ideals of our ancestors,' was his sole hope for the future" (27).

By contrast, Cyrus is the pure materialist. The narrator describes him at first as "aloof and indispensable, like one of the gaunt iron bridges of his great railroad" (55), suggesting that he is the link in Dinwiddie between the old and new economic systems. But this description also reveals him to be simply a carrier of the force of change, an iron bridge, inhuman and inanimate, machinelike. As the narrator tells us explicitly, "Success . . . had controlled his thoughts and even his impulses so completely for years, that he had come at last to resemble an animal less than he resembled a machine" (122), adding that Cyrus is "as soulless as a steam-engine" (123), simply "force" (272). So his unhappy marriage arises less from his brief "April . . . mating impulse" (135) than from his "dogged male determination to override all obstacles, whether feminine or financial" (67). The feminine and the financial are one and the same to Cyrus and, the narrator suggests, to the male or masculine type more generally.

The friendship between Gabriel and Cyrus, then, is one between opposites, figuratively heterosexual. Against the sentimental and feminine figure of the minister, the narrator poses the machinelike and masculine figure of the "great man" (18), the successful businessman. Cyrus is attracted to Gabriel because "the caged brutality in his heart was soothed by the unconscious flattery of the other's belief in him" (279), an attraction that the narrator describes as being much like romantic love between man and woman: "The charm that Gabriel exercised over him [Cyrus] was almost feminine in its subtlety and in its utter defiance of any rational sanction" (279). At the same time, Gabriel is an object of contempt to Cyrus, for Gabriel knows nothing about business and must request personal and financial favors from Cyrus. The dynamics, as well as the "genders," of this first relationship of Gabriel and Cyrus are carried on in the next generation, in the literally heterosexual relationship between Virginia Pendleton and Oliver Treadwell.

At first, their marriage is figured as that between two idealists. Virginia's "inheritance" (20) is the old "vanquished idealism" (10) so that, for example, when shopping with her mother and a cousin, she is unable to see the history of the "market"—slavery—or even its present-day reality:

> [T]he three stood in silence, gazing dreamily, with three pairs of Pendleton eyes, down toward the site of the old slave market. Directly in their line of vision, an overladen mule with a sore shoulder was straining painfully under the lash, but none of them saw it, because each of them was morally incapable of looking an unpleasant fact in the face if there was any honourable manner of avoiding it. (49)

If Virginia's inability to see material realities, both past and present, reveals her obsolescence as a type in the new age of "materialism" (10), even more so does her maternity. The text equates maternity with slavery. As a girl, Virginia "let her mother slave over her because she had been born into a world where the slaving of mothers was a part of the natural order," "a racial custom" (41), while later, she makes "a slave of . . . [herself] over the children" (251; see also 284, 336). Virginia's "Madonna-like" (183, 200) qualities only illustrate the fact that she remains always in the past, "utterly stationary" (349).

By contrast, while the young Oliver Treadwell falls in love with Virginia because he is "intellect in revolt against the tyranny of industrialism" (95) and because she appeals "to the strongest part of him, which was not his heart, but his imagination" (117; see also 104, 304), he finally is "only a romantic variation from the Treadwell stock"; "in the depths of his being, the essential Treadwell persisted"—"he revolted from materialism as only a materialist in youth revolts" (75). This becomes more

and more evident as the novel progresses. Susan Treadwell, echoing
the narrator's description of Cyrus, warns Virginia that the Treadwell
type always "is going to get the thing he wants most . . . whether it is
money or love" (156), and in fact, Oliver uses his idealism like a materialist; he uses "love, as he had used life, merely to feed the flame of the
unconquerable egoism which burned like genius within him" (341). His
materialistic nature eventually manifests itself: "Comfort was almost
imperceptibly taking the place of conviction" (292), and he comes to
"doubt if there's anything much better than money" (294).

This transformation of Oliver back into the "essential Treadwell" is
traced in his writing. At first, Oliver has "a feeling for reality" (97) and
so writes a realistic play about "the new woman" (96). But after the
failure of this play, which is perceived as *"immoral,"* "an attack on
American ideals" (206), he begins to produce mechanically, as he himself says, the "trash" that "the public wants" (294), "perfectly innocu-
ous" "rot" (317, 342). His desire for material comfort helps him produce
comfortable plays, plays that match the desire for comfort of his audience. Like all Treadwells, he is at one with, and *reflects,* his age:

> His eyes . . . reflected the restless animation, the pathetic hunger, which
> made each of those passing faces appear to be the plastic medium of
> an insatiable craving for life. Handsome, well preserved, a little over
> coloured, a little square of figure, with his look of worldly importance, of
> assured material success, he stood to-day, as Cyrus had stood a quarter of
> a century ago, as an imposing example of that Treadwell spirit from
> which his youth had revolted. (351)

Consequently, the woman he now falls in love with, Margaret Oldcastle,
though "honest" (331), is also a materialist. A "woman of power" (330),
she reaps "a small fortune" (317) by acting the role of the traditional
woman onstage (and only onstage), producing mechanically—we could
say—the unauthentic emotions of Oliver's plays and making the plays
financially successful (315). She is like a Treadwell in that she is biologically determined to succeed, is at "one with evolution and with the
resistless principle of change" (364). And like a Treadwell, she is figured
as masculine: "her freedom, like that of man, had been built upon the
strewn bodies of the weaker" (364).

To recapitulate for a moment, change in these first two sections of
the novel is the transformation of the mode of production from a slave
to an industrial economy. Those races or types associated with the slave
order are deemed historically backwards. Thus, according to the logic
of the book, there appears on the same register the racist analysis of

blacks as being of "the more primitive forms of life" (34), even apelike or animalesque (129, 276–77), and the critique of the Pendleton "ideal-ism."[7] But while the text suggests that the "primitive" blacks must give way to the "superior" (129) whites, as our exploration of the relation-ship between Pendleton and Treadwell "types" has shown, even more clearly must a nonrationalized mode of production give way to a ratio-nalized and scientific one, idealism to materialism, the mother to the ma-chine, and finally femininity to masculinity, literally women to men—in Virginia and Oliver's case. Survival of the fittest means survival of the white male capitalist or his counterpart, the white woman capitalist. Be-cause Glasgow is less interested in the racism of this "logical" conclusion to the naturalist account of failing and succeeding types than in the misogyny of it, after reaching this "logical" conclusion, she proposes an oppositional account to it. Upon showing the success of the white male capitalist type, she returns to a sentimental vision of change that the naturalist account has discredited. The last third of the novel—while largely naturalistic—is also a sentimental protest against the logic of the naturalist account.

In this last section, the ironic and distanced narration of failing types gives way to a nonironic and sympathetic one of the personal tragedy of one failing type. That is, throughout the novel, the struggle of old and new has been personified as the transfer of power from the Pendleton type to the Treadwell type, and this transfer of power has occurred rather discursively and objectively. Now, the transfer of power is seen subjec-tively; Virginia's conflicting emotions and her understanding of her predicament are traced out in detail. The narrator can no longer com-ment with detachment on Virginia's thoughts and actions, for Virginia herself is suddenly given "some outside vision" (332), the vision, in fact, of the narrator: "she realized that she was fighting, not a woman, but the very structure of life" (364; also 332, 357). One result is that change becomes less an objective fact than a redundant cruelty: "So little was needed to make her [Virginia] happy—that was the pathos! She was satisfied with the crumbs of life, and yet they were denied her" (346), thinks Oliver (who is himself one crumb that life denies Virginia). Even Virginia's daughters for whom she sacrifices so much are redun-dantly vicious toward her (300, 322, 374).

Most important, however, the more life passes Virginia by, the more spiritual and ethereal she becomes. In contrast to the first sections of the book, where spirituality is depicted as purely physical in nature—the effect of an instinct, or an emotional state created by coffee, food, or whiskey (98, 139, 137)—Virginia's physical characteristics are increas-ingly described as timeless and undetermined spiritual characteristics, as belonging "not to her flesh, but to an unalterable quality of her soul" (355). It is the very timeless nature of her spirituality, undetermined by the mode of production, that gives her a moral victory over that successful male type, Margaret Oldcastle. The narrator writes of their confrontation that Oldcastle becomes almost coarse in her inability to understand Virginia, an inability clearly determined by the fact that she is "one with evolution" (364) so that "the dignity which had been on the side of . . . [Oldcastle] appeared to have passed from her to Virginia" (365), a "dignity, which was not that of triumph, but of a defeat which surrenders everything except the inviolable sanctities of the spirit" (365). While the naturalist account shows us how Virginia's emotions and actions are determined by history, we also see that she is "unalterable," "inviolable," outside the *current* determination of history. If her Pendleton idealism does not allow her to see the market for what it is, it has also left her able to stand outside it: "She could no more have bared her soul to . . . [Oldcastle] than she could have stripped her body naked in the market-place" (365). The implication is that both Oliver and Oldcastle could and do strip their bodies naked in the market-place and sell themselves in order to succeed.

Just as the naturalist critique of sentimentalism has transferred power from the mother to the male machine, so the sentimental critique of naturalism works to reestablish the power of the mother over the machine. This power is not figured as a material reality but as a moral and emotional one, the typical sentimental appeal, Ann Douglas has argued, of the powerless. In this novel, however, while the shams and artifices of sentimentalism that support an oppressive system are continually spelled out, at the same time, sentimentalism is represented as a feminine capacity for understanding certain truths outside current materialist hegemonic ideology. In a text where violence against blacks occurs frequently and goes almost unnoticed, only Virginia at her most maternal—when nursing her gravely ill child—is shown as transcending "the Problem of the South," or race barriers. She suddenly has a "feeling of oneness" with her children's black nurse, feels "the barriers of knowledge, of race, of all the pitiful superiorities with which human beings have obscured and decorated the underlying spirit of life, had melted back into the nothingness from which they had emerged in the beginning" (267).

Virginia's ability to transcend, even momentarily, "the Problem of the South" is crucial for understanding the sentimental protest in the novel. For while the naturalist narrative has revealed to us the sentimental claptrap that hides the reality of predetermined failing and succeeding types, the sentimental narrative highlights the fact that the "change" the naturalist account depicts is merely repetition of the same, that social "evolution" is not occurring. The "Problem of the South" is certainly not solved over the course of the novel. At the beginning of the story, blacks are identified as former slaves of the white characters; by the end of the book, they have become their servants: "Out of the problem of the South 'the servant question' had arisen" (307). Continuity rather than evolution is in evidence.

Such continuity is highlighted by the text's sentimentalization of the relations between the Pendletons and their former slaves and black servants, as opposed to its harsh depiction of the relations between the Treadwells and their former slaves and black servants. Mrs. Pendleton visits her old slaves, bringing them food while nursing those that remain with her. Gabriel, in fact, dies defending the grandson of one of his former slaves from a lynching. By contrast, toward Gabriel's feeling of "grave . . . responsibility" and "compassion" (278–79) for the former slaves, Cyrus feels "an immediate suspicion," "as if it were insidiously leading the way to an appeal for money" (278). He has no sense of relations between individuals outside of business and the market:

> It was well enough to go on like that [about responsibility and compassion] in the pulpit; but on weekdays, when there was business to think of and every minute might mean the loss of a dollar, there was no use dragging in either religion or sentiment. Had he put his thoughts plainly, he would probably have said: "That's not business, Gabriel. The trouble with you—and with most of you old-fashioned Virginians—is that you don't understand the first principles of business."
> (279)

While the depiction of the Pendletons' relationship to their former slaves, and the condescension implicit in it, strikes the modern reader as racist, in the text, it stands in opposition to Cyrus's completely rationalized view of his relation to the former slaves. He sees them, as he sees everyone, only in terms of "the first principles of business."

In fact, it is Cyrus, the representative of the new order, who most brutally reveals that "the Problem of the South" is not solved by the new materialism or capitalism. Rationalization, as we have seen, blinds the individual to any relationship with people outside the market. Cyrus's inability to see anything except profit, at first, is comparable to the Pendleton inability to see anything but romance:

> [W]hile Cyrus watched from his height, there was as little thought in his mind for the men who drove those waggons through the parching dust as for the beasts that drew them. It is possible even that he did

not see them, for just as Mrs. Pendleton's vision eliminated the sight of suffering because her heart was too tender to bear it, so he overlooked all facts except those which were a part of the dominant motive of his life. (61)

Particularly, Cyrus is unable to see the "negro hovels" (61) and "the swarms of mulatto children" because "to his mind that problem, like the problem of labour, loomed vague, detached, and unreal—a thing that existed merely in the air, not in the concrete images that he could understand" (62).

In addition, even "concrete images" elude him. Despite his "strong physical liking for children" (63), despite his "strongest instinct, . . . that of race" (56) or family, he looks "with unseeing eyes at the mulatto boy" (66) who is his own illegitimate child. His relations with blacks are completely reified. In fact, when his son is about to be lynched for shooting a white policeman, Cyrus—the most powerful man in Dinwiddie—not only refuses to interfere but is disgusted by the "emotion" (275) displayed by Mandy, his son's mother. His two reactions are to wish that she were merely an object that he could have disposed of once she had served his purpose ("If only one could get rid of such creatures after their first youth was over!" [276]) and to "buy off" his responsibility by giving Mandy fifty dollars. Even Susan Treadwell, his daughter, who represents the most positive version of the new South, comes off badly during this race crisis. As an afterthought, she remembers to tell her father about the lynching of her half-brother, and then merely comments before running off on a trivial errand that Mandy "'was very pitiable; but, after all, what can one do for a negro that shoots a policeman?'" (275). As Gabriel has revealed, something can be done to prevent lynching, but an egoistic and purely materialistic Treadwell—no matter how "refined" (273)—is unable to imagine this. The blindness of the Treadwells to social injustice, their inability to see truth outside of what serves their material interests, which was, at first, compared to the Pendleton blind idealism, becomes finally more sinister than that idealism.

In the last pages of the novel, like one of Oliver's sentimental heroines, Virginia "comes back to her old home" (359), apparently to a defeated and solitary life, only to find a telegram from her sympathetic son, who is rushing home to be with her. This ending is doubly ironic. Just as Virginia's transcendence of racial barriers is momentary and individual, so also the home and the mother's sentimental power are represented here as momentary, individual, and finally illusory. At the same time, just as Virginia's transcendence of racial barriers is one of the text's few moments of escape from economic determination, so also is this ending represented as the only possible moral and redemptive response to economic determination. In this ending, the problems with naturalism and sentimentalism are apparent and irresolvable. The naturalist account of change is enabling in that it uncovers how sentimentalism has disguised and supported the institutions of oppression by race (meaning color or gender in Glasgow's South); however, "the naturalist machine," as Seltzer calls it, which opposes sentimentalism, in fact reproduces the same kind of oppression on a more scientific level—power is again male and white. The sentimental account of change is utterly disenabling until the moment when, confronted with the dominant naturalist account of change, it reveals that the new justifications for race and sex oppression are standardized and consequently as pernicious as the sentimental ones. *Virginia*, then, is a naturalist text. But it is a naturalist text that puts into question the naturalist project in relation to race and sex, puts into question the naturalist project through sentimentalism—its opposite and its double.

Notes

1. I use the word *genre* to describe naturalism and sentimentalism. For an analysis of the different literary genres and styles Glasgow employs, and the criticism leveled at her, see J. E. Bunselmeyer.

2. Anne Goodwyn Jones finds Glasgow's work problematically feminist; Linda Wagner argues that Glasgow's novels before *Virginia* are male-identified; Josephine Donovan sees evidence of "phallic-worship" (131) in many of Glasgow's texts.

3. For example, Glasgow describes how every year she received "romances of the Confederacy," typically recounting the story of a "gallant Northern invader" rescuing "a spirited yet clinging Southern belle," romances given to her by and inscribed "in the fine Italian penmanship of a maiden aunt" (*ACM* 11). She explicitly rejects this kind of story that women read and exchange with each other.

4. The relation of sentimentalism to domesticity has been charted extensively in recent years. For three differing accounts of the significance of this relation, see Ann Douglas, Mary Ryan, and Jane Tompkins.

5. In *A Certain Measure* (152–53), there is a longer—if less revealing—discussion of this issue.

6. In her lively and helpful discussion of *Virginia,* Jones describes the tension in the novel as that between traditional or romantic and feminist or realistic ideas about the Southern lady. My essay differs from hers in that I see this tension as having to do with racial and economic issues, as well as with gender ones.

7. While I touch upon the racist representations of blacks in *Virginia,* another essay would be required to explain it fully.

Works Cited

Bunselmeyer, J. E. "Ellen Glasgow's 'Flexible' Style." *Centennial Review* 28.2 (1984): 112–28.

Douglas, Ann. *The Feminization of American Culture.* 1977. New York: Doubleday, 1988.

Donovan, Josephine. *After the Fall: The Demeter-Persephone Myth in Wharton, Cather, and Glasgow.* University Park: Pennsylvania State UP, 1989.

Glasgow, Ellen. *A Certain Measure: An Interpretation of Prose Fiction.* 1938. New York: Harcourt, 1943.

———. *Virginia.* 1913. London: Virago, 1981.

———. *The Woman Within.* New York: Harcourt, 1954.

Jones, Anne Goodwyn. *Tomorrow Is Another Day: The Woman Writer in the South, 1859–1936.* Baton Rouge: Louisiana State UP, 1981.

Ryan, Mary P. *The Empire of the Mother: American Writing about Domesticity, 1830–1860.* 1982. New York: Harrington Park, 1985.

Scura, Dorothy M. "A Knowledge in the Heart: Ellen Glasgow, the Women's Movement, and *Virginia.*" *American Literary Realism* 22.2 (Winter 1990): 30–43.

Seltzer, Mark. "The Naturalist Machine." *Sex, Politics, and Science in the Nineteenth-Century Novel.* Ed. Ruth Bernard Yeazell. Baltimore: Johns Hopkins UP, 1986. 116–47.

Tompkins, Jane. *Sensational Designs.* New York: Oxford UP, 1985.

Wagner, Linda W. *Ellen Glasgow: Beyond Convention.* Austin: U of Texas P, 1982.

Barren Ground and the Transition to Southern Modernism

Julius Rowan Raper

A number of Ellen Glasgow's contributions to American culture are well known. The role she played, as early as 1897, in bringing Critical Realist and Naturalist perspectives to the fiction of the New South has earned her a central place in literary histories of the South and, in view of the contribution of southern fiction to the nation's literature, a place in the history of American writing as well. Although she received help from Kate Chopin, she wrote so precociously and frequently after 1895 of the revolt of women against the roles our culture inscribes for them that, to readers who know Glasgow well, much contemporary writing brings a strong feeling of déjà vu. Her experiments from 1913 onwards with a modified Expressionist and Cubist technique that turns major characters inside out by having minor characters mirror them may not be as well known, but they are nonetheless important. The degree, however, to which she, along with James Branch Cabell, Evelyn Scott and Jean Toomer in *Cane* (1923), brought the psychological complexity of Modernist writing to southern fiction in the 1920s is not generally appreciated; this in part may be because reception of Southern Modernism quickly came under the control of the Nashville Agrarians and they could most commonly express only a startled ambivalence in response to Glasgow's unexpected and precocious brilliance. It is on the psychological complexity of *Barren Ground*—especially as that richness relates to Glasgow's life and affects the reader—that I wish to focus here.

Near the end of *Barren Ground*, long after Dorinda Oakley has been seduced and abandoned by Jason Greylock, has fled to New York and miscarried Jason's child, and has returned to Pedlar's Mill to redeem her family's land by turning it into a prosperous modern dairy farm,

Dorinda, now the widow of Nathan Pedlar, thinks back over her years; the narrator tells us:

> In her own life she could trace no logical connection between being and behavior, between the thing that she was in herself and the things she had done. She thought of herself as a good woman (there were few better ones, she would have said honestly) yet in her girlhood she had been betrayed by love and saved by the simplest accident from murder. Surely these were both flagrant transgressions according to every code of morality! They were acts, she knew, which she would have condemned in another; but in her memory they appeared as inevitable as the rest of her conduct, and she could not unravel them from the frayed warp-and-woof of the past. (460)

It is, I suggest, Dorinda's inability to understand the gap between the woman she thinks herself to be and the things she has actually done, the distance between her character and her conduct, between her "being" and her "behavior," that gives *Barren Ground* the added dimensions that have led readers and critics to take such wildly differing positions on the meaning and value of the novel. For this distance, between the conscious and the unconscious Dorindas, allows us to read the novel simultaneously on two totally different levels. The nature of a given reader's interpretation will likely depend on how strongly he or she draws from each of the two levels; the specific combinations of levels possible—and therefore the responses—may be very nearly infinite in their variety. We will consider several of these interpretations to show the variety. But first I would like to search for sources in Glasgow's own life of this extraordinary ability to create a character about whom readers may feel great ambivalence. Later, we will focus on two sections of *Barren Ground* that show how the author has built this added dimension into her story.

When we look at Glasgow's early years, we find that a mixture of sensations, of contentment and terror, marked the author's life from the start. The earliest memories described in her autobiography, *The Woman Within,* are the rhythm and caress of her mother lulling her to sleep and, then, "a vacant face, round, pallid, grotesque, malevolent"—perhaps the setting sun—staring in on her when she opens her eyes (3–4). Because she came to view her parents according to a parallel split between a caring mother and a threatening father, this alternation between gentle affection and fear dominated her childhood as she records it. But even that seemingly clean division between mother and father contained ambiguities, for both parents possessed qualities that complicated their daughter's fundamental view of them.

When she recalled her mother, she had "two images of her, one a creature of light and the other a figure of tragedy. One minute I remember her smiling, happy, joyous, making gaiety where there was no gaiety. The next minute I see her ill, worn, despairing, yet still with her rare flashes of brilliance" (13). On the one hand, her mother was a fragile flower of the Tidewater, related to several of the oldest families in Virginia, including the Randolphs and the Woodsons. On the other hand, her line backwards to Virginians of distinction was weak, running chiefly through orphaned women. In fact, her mother was the orphaned daughter of a woman who had herself been adopted—and by the same relatives who later adopted Glasgow's mother (Raper, *Shelter* 14–15). Even though Glasgow's mother's "whole nature was so interwoven with sympathy" that she became the center of her daughter's world, she was so completely the victim of a long anguishing nervous illness that, too weak to care for her daughter properly, she extended her love through the agency of a black nurse (Glasgow, *Woman* 13–14). In Glasgow's mature years, especially when she came to write her autobiography, she identified herself closely with her mother's compassion for the unfortunate, her feeling for animals, her suffering as the victim of an inhumane age and an unfeeling husband.

About her father, Glasgow felt altogether differently: "we were made of different clay," she wrote, "and I inherited nothing from him, except the color of my eyes and a share in a trust fund" (16). She thought of him as Romanlike in his "complete integrity," his lack of love, his total unselfishness, his inability to ever commit a pleasure (*Woman* 15–16). He was a hard-shell Scotch-Irish Presbyterian with whom Glasgow later fought bitter religious wars. At the back of her mind she appears to have associated him with the malevolent red face staring in on her, the terror that oppresses the victims of life; for it was he who forbade her bringing a small pointer home, who refused to buy her a doll with real hair, and who stuffed the family's pet dog in a bag to get rid of him (*Woman* 27–28, 51–52, 69–71; *Measure* 12). Consciously, Glasgow so identified herself with victims like the pets (and her mother) that she only felt a "passionate, tormented hatred" of such "merciless strength" as that her father demonstrated (*Woman* 9–10).

And yet she owed far more to her father than she admitted. For her mother's Tidewater, Anglo-Episcopal, planter background contributed less to her economic status in postwar Richmond, perhaps even to her social standing, than did her father's Scotch-Irish, Presbyterian, industrialist position. Mr. Glasgow's uncle and employer, Joseph Reid Anderson, since branded "the most conspicuous manufacturer of the slavocracy," owned Tredegar Iron Works of Richmond, the chief supplier of munitions of war for Lee's army of northern Virginia. Tredegar also over-hauled and outfitted the Confederate ram, the Merrimac, with iron plates and guns. After the war, Glasgow's father became managing di-rector of Tredegar, a firm still worth more in December 1865, though par-tially burned, than before the Civil War began (Raper, *Shelter* 17–19). In a more personal way, Glasgow's inheritance from her father must include a certain willfulness and strength of character that saw her through her rebellion against him and her revolt against elements of her region, in-cluding its tradition in literature. Indeed, it would be difficult to sepa-rate him from the vein of iron that fortified her throughout the fifty years during which she published over twenty of the more original books in our national literature. Glasgow's affection for this part of her heritage shows through, of course, in the warmth she lavishes upon various hero-ines blessed with a vein of iron, especially Dorinda Oakley of *Barren Ground*, Ada Fincastle of *Vein of Iron*, and Roy Timberlake of *In This Our Life*. Apparently some of the positive qualities she had, for the sake of consistency, to reject when she rejected her father returned projected not on male characters but onto her own feminine creations.

Other evidence suggests that the attempt to iron out inconsistencies in her feelings about her parents created a significant ambivalence in Glasgow's image of herself. To the public she frequently presented her-self in a rather grand fashion presiding over literary and social gather-ings as the great lady of southern letters. In this grandiose pose we may find a reminder of her father's manner as she saw him: "A man of fine presence, with an upright carriage, I have heard old ladies say that they used to wait, at the window, to see him pass in the street" (*Woman* 15).[1] This is the Glasgow that Gertrude Stein and Alice Toklas encoun-tered in 1935; in Toklas's words: "We met Miss Ellen Glasgow in N.Y. and heard her speak at the dinner for Southern Authors. She was quite extraordinary, very brilliant—and gracious and attaching (it may be at-taching) and fearless and all with an incredible smile and charm. I've never known anything suggesting it and was not prepared for it—even after meeting her that lovely night at her house. She was transcendent" (quoted in MacDonald, "Glasgow-Stein" 17). This is also the Glasgow who, in the prefaces to her novels, put herself forth in an imposing manner as a master of the art of fiction.[2] But when she turned to her autobiography, it was her identification with her mother as a helpless victim of the malevolent force of life that she allowed to govern her self-representation. If we take the two works together (along with the implied author created by all her writing), we come up with a far truer image of Ellen Glasgow than we find in either *A Certain Measure* or *The Woman Within*. For she was neither as helpless as the figure in the autobiography nor as grandiose as the mask created in the prefaces: she was the heir, despite what she says in the autobiography, of her father as well as her mother.

The inconsistencies in her early relationships were not limited to these two primary figures. With her mother ill, Ellen depended on substitutes, especially the black nurse, Lizzie Jones, who began caring for her the month after she was born. Of the seven years with Lizzie, the final four, she says, were the happiest of her childhood, the time when she discovered the streets and faces of Richmond, the wind and fields of the Virginia countryside (*Woman* 23–24). To have this loving woman, clearly a major caregiver of Glasgow's early life, suddenly sent away to work for another family came as a great blow to seven-year-old Ellen. Lizzie's departure "was the beginning of that sense of loss, of exile in solitude, which I was to bear with me to the end" (*Woman* 30). The trauma of this separation combined with regional attitudes toward Lizzie's race no doubt complicated Glasgow's feelings toward all persons willing to offer or accept her love.

Even before Lizzie Jones left her, little Ellen had extended her need for maternal support to the encompassing atmosphere of Jerdone Castle, the 485-acre estate in Louisa County (northwest of Richmond) that her father purchased just before her sixth birthday. There Ellen and Lizzie ranged about the fields of corn and tobacco, through the broomsedge and scrub pine, and on into the virgin woods. Summers there she gave to natural things—earth, sky, hills, fields, trees, grass, flowers—for which she developed a lasting affection. She came to love the farm, she writes, "in the way one loves not only a place but a person" (*Woman* 26). Even this sustaining rural presence would eventually gather a cluster of painful associations. For night after night at Jerdone Castle, Ellen and her younger sister lay listening through an open door to a voice from their parents' adjoining room where their mother "walked the floor in anguish, to and fro, back and forth, driven by a thought or a vision, from which she tried in vain to escape." In about 1884, a "severe shock, in a critical period," had caused Mrs. Glasgow's frayed nerves to give way, leaving her "a chronic invalid, whose nervous equilibrium was permanently damaged" (*Woman* 61). The probable cause of the shock, according to one biographer, was Mrs. Glasgow's discovery that her husband had had "illicit relations" with various black women (Parent 137n). Mrs. Glasgow's chronic horror of Jerdone Castle, the only place where Ellen had found a happy support, caused Mr. Glasgow in 1887 to sell the estate (*Woman* 68; Roades 13). Because Jerdone Castle provided young Ellen's most concrete experiences of her remarkable state, the rich mix of emotions she came to associate with the beauty and ambiguities of the land there likely prefigured the complex feelings toward the natural loveliness and sometimes checkered history of Virginia that she would embody in the various novels she would write about her native state.

By the time her father sold the farm when she was fourteen, a basic pattern of positive expectations followed by painful surprises had established itself in Glasgow's important relationships. Similar cycles of pleasure followed by disappointment mark a number of other significant episodes of her girlhood and early mature years as she reports them in the autobiography: her early experience with religion, a revival, ended in "burning humiliation"; her sisters read her first "precious verses aloud" amid bursts of "kindly ridicule and amusement" (*Woman* 37); her first day at school ended in dismal embarrassment and fear; the professional critic who read the manuscript of her first novel so humiliated her when he expressed a wish to see her nude and demanded a kiss that she tossed her book in an open fire and resolved never to write again (*Woman* 36–37, 41–50, 95–99). When she was twenty-one, her mentor and youthful brother-in-law, the man she respected most, was discovered shot in a New York hotel; a strange woman claimed the body (Raper, *Shelter* 32–36, 40–42, 47–49). In memory, each of these events came to carry a double charge of anticipation and bitterness. But the latter episode, the death of her brother-in-law, was especially calculated to confirm her sense that those who loved her were likely to cause her the greatest pain.

With this background of confusing experiences during her first twenty-one years, we would expect irony, paradox, ambiguity, ambivalence to characterize her fiction. Indeed, in her best novels, a large part of the power arises from her ability to create destructive characters whom it is difficult to hate and positive characters who generate the greatest evils. In these works one particular method of presentation—that of allowing the minor figures in the story to mirror conscious and unconscious dimensions of the major figures—enables her to convey the contradictory sides of her fictional people. Nowhere does Glasgow build richer ambivalence into her work than in the representation in *Barren Ground* of the relationship that binds Dorinda Oakley to Jason Greylock. Ambiguities so pervade this novel that critics often reach very different (yet valuable) conclusions.

A helpful book by Edgar MacDonald and Tonette Bond Inge, *Ellen Glasgow: A Reference Guide* (1986), enables us to recognize just how diverse the reactions to *Barren Ground* have been, both in 1925 and over the past sixty years or so. By the start of 1925, Glasgow's career had reached its lowest point ever. Her best early works, *The Miller of Old*

Church (1911) and *Virginia* (1913), were at least a decade behind her. Her two most recent novels, *The Builders* (1919) and *One Man in His Time* (1922), had received a respectable number of notices (about forty-five for the first and about fifty for the second), but opinions of the two political novels were mixed, including charges of unconvincing and distracting characters (MacDonald, *Guide* 50, 59). Glasgow's latest book, a collection of short stories called *The Shadowy Third* (1923), drew much less attention (fewer than twenty-five notices), but it helped reestablish a favorable critical opinion of her skills as creator of fiction.

Like the previous two novels, *Barren Ground* also received mixed reviews. The *New York Times Book Review,* for example, felt that the novel's "overparticularity," its lack of humor, its overextended characterizations, and its forceless, unconvincing story fail to evoke the tragic emotion the book aspires to convey (MacDonald, *Guide* 67). Elizabeth Lay Green, wife of playwright Paul Green, writing in the *Reviewer,* thought the book's "characters lack reality because their descriptions focus on externals"; Dorinda's fight with the land belonged, Green felt, to "a success story from an agricultural magazine" (MacDonald, *Guide* 69). One anonymous reviewer, in the *New Yorker,* concluded that the novel's "five hundred pages of 'a commonplace subjective impersonation, purporting to manifest insight' succeed only in boring the reader to misery" (MacDonald, *Guide* 64).

Some of the barbs, however, came with balancing perceptions. Waspish H. L. Mencken, for example, who eight years earlier had christened the South a cultural desert in his stimulating essay "The Sahara of the Bozart," found Dorinda Oakley more convincing as the Universal Woman than as a particular woman of Pedlar's Mill, because the author "gives no sign of an intimate knowledge of the poor, flea-bitten yokels she sets before us." Yet Mencken also recognized that *Barren Ground* is "boldly imagined and completely planned" (MacDonald, *Guide* 69–70).

Other reviewers had few or no reservations. Stuart P. Sherman compared her to George Eliot and called for a collected edition of her books. Archibald Henderson praised the epic mass of the novel and ranked her with Thomas Hardy, Émile Zola, and other naturalist writers. More significant for our purpose here, the psychologist Joseph Collins wrote that Glasgow's greatest gift was her power of characterization, and he ranked *Barren Ground* with the best American fiction of the generation. Not to be outdone, one anonymous reviewer in Macon, Georgia, threw all restraint to the wind and claimed that the novel was "the greatest book yet written by an American woman" (MacDonald, *Guide* 66–70).

In recent years, the differences in critical responses revolve less around the quality of *Barren Ground* and more around its meaning. But great differences still persist. In an inspired article, for example, Mary Castiglie Anderson speaks of the epic characteristics of Dorinda's success; to Anderson, Dorinda is a "hero engaged in a struggle with the entire history of women in culture" (385); for hers is the "hero's struggle to move out of unconsciousness into consciousness" and by so doing to recreate "the birth of culture" (386), in as much as consciousness is civilization. Anderson concludes that "the epic image drawn of Dorinda in the final pages . . . evokes both the Promethean tragic hero, whose values are freedom and willed effort, and the serene, enduring Earth Goddess, the spirit of containment and continuity. Dorinda unites the two by bridging the culturally assumed gulf dividing man and nature" (392). There can be no question that, at one level, Dorinda's achievements are significant enough and Jason's flaws sufficient to satisfy the need Anderson's article articulates for a feminine epic hero.

Frederick P. W. McDowell, on the other hand, is able to say of the same book: "This excellent novel has as its central insight the paradox that Dorinda is both victor and victim in her struggle with the soil" (151) and that the "strongest sections . . . are those which express Dorinda's sense of futility, despite her intermittent sense of renewal from contact with the land" (155). In other words, McDowell can respond to Dorinda's "[m]astery of the impersonal powers of nature" and yet discover in her dissatisfaction an adequate defense against the antisexual, even castrating, elements of the book (151). As he writes: "By brooding over her lost ecstasy in spite of her determination to forget love, Dorinda tacitly concedes its pervasive power; and by her very aversion to sexual emotion, she tacitly acknowledges its force" (155).

Both Anderson and McDowell, it seems to me, are right. This apparent contradiction arises from the complex nature of Dorinda's emotions, for as Glasgow has portrayed her, she lives in multiple dimensions. In her outward life she is the epic hero Anderson responds to with such passion: the deserted woman who almost singlehandedly triumphs over the fatality of men, history, and nature. This victory is not an illusion; there is no way to take it away from Dorinda, and it counts for something—for a good deal, I would think. But, in her inward life, as McDowell notes, the sense of futility endures; no more than her Presbyterian ancestors has she been able to eradicate the natural instincts that keep her, in her view, weak. Despite her significant triumphs she remains a victim—of her own human nature.

Indeed, she is more a victim than she allows anyone, especially herself, to realize—far more so than the cheering ending, one of her self-sustaining fantasies, would lead the reader to believe. Her heroic will to master her destiny, in itself, blocks her from knowledge of her real self; in fact, she could hardly be the hero she becomes if she accepted the victim she remains. Dorinda's ignorance about herself is the aspect of her character that generates the two levels of the story and makes possible the starkly opposed interpretations of the novel described above. Two episodes aptly illustrate the sort of self-ignorance and parallel levels of action I have in mind. The first occurs in chapter 11 of part 1 ("Broomsedge"), when she goes to visit Aunt Mehitable Green at Whistling Spring one week before she and Jason Greylock are to be married. The second, from chapter 5 of part 2 ("Pine"), describes the conscious *and* subconscious meanings of her decision to leave New York and return to Virginia to start a dairy farm.

In the first, the conscious reason for visiting Aunt Mehitable is that Mehitable's daughter Jemima, who works at Jason's father's farm, Five Oaks, might have heard something (128) about why Jason's business trip to New York has gone on for two weeks rather than the single week he expected to stay away (126). But at the end of this rich chapter, both Dorinda and the reader—the careful reader—discover something very different: that Dorinda is pregnant (138).

Dorinda's pregnancy and miscarriage are among the miracles of the novel. (I have had undergraduate students read the book through and never know she was pregnant, let alone that she aborted from the street accident in New York [214–15].) In an age of ultrarealism, a reader could come away from a first experience with *Barren Ground* feeling cheated that so little is said about events that largely determine the heroine's later life. But on close reading, we discover that in chapter 11 Glasgow has planted at least fifteen references to Dorinda's pregnancy. They are subtle, however, and subject to misinterpretation because we see them through Dorinda's consciousness, and, given her repressive background, she does not yet recognize what is happening to her body.

On the opening page of the chapter we are told, "For days she had felt disturbed" and anxious, but she attributes her anxiety to Jason's extended absence (126). Her mother says to her, "Ain't you feeling well, daughter? You've been looking right peaked the last day or two, and I noticed you didn't touch any breakfast." But Dorinda blames her condition on Jason's not writing as often as he said he would (127). Dorinda tells her mother, "I've been bending over all day, . . . and the weather has been so sultry. It makes me feel kind of faint" (127). A little later, before Dorinda leaves for Whistling Spring, her mother again says, "You ain't so spry to-day yourself, daughter," but Dorinda blames her lack of energy on getting tired from "sitting in church" (130).

During her walk to Mehitable's, she feels such depression, loneliness, and solitude in the rural landscape that the narrator tells us that all external objects around her "lost their inanimate character and became as personal, reserved, and inscrutable as her own mind. . . . [T]he wall dividing her individual consciousness from the consciousness of nature vanished with the thin drift of woodsmoke over the fields" (130–31). Pregnant, she is apparently being caught up in the force of nature without knowing it. As she walks along, she struggles to assure herself that she is "securely happy," that she is to be "married in a week," that "beyond question, beyond distrust," Jason loves her: "For three months she [has] lived in a state of bliss so supreme that, like love, it [has] created the illusion of its own immortality" (134). But at the same time, she feels anxious and cannot understand why.

When she reaches Whistling Spring, one of the first things Mehitable says to her is: "You ain' lookin' so peart, honey"—to which Dorinda replies that worrying has "taken my appetite, and made me feel as if I dragged myself to the store and back every day. . . . I get dizzy too, when I bend over. You haven't got any camphor about, have you?" To the older woman, Dorinda confesses, "I'm afraid something has happened" (135). But again she attributes her concern solely to Jason's absence.

Slowly we recognize that Mehitable is a conjure woman with a "witchlike gaze" and "psychic powers" drawing on "simple, profound, and elemental forces" (136). On a first reading, however, we still do not know what Mehitable means when she tells her visitor, "I'se done been lookin' fur you all de evelin'. Dar's a lil' bird done tole me you wuz comin'" (136). Nor are we initially aware of the implication in what Mehitable says a minute later: "Ef'n you is in enny trubble, honey, hit's mos' likely I kin teck hit erway" (137). Only when Dorinda rises to her feet and "the broomsedge [plunges] forward, like a raging sea" and engulfs her (137) do we finally suspect that there is more to this anxious trip to the conjure woman than simple worry over Jason's absence. And that deeper significance finally becomes as clear as it ever will be when Mehitable brings Dorinda to with camphor (137) and says, "Befo' de week's up you is gwinter be mah'ed, . . . en dar ain't a livin' soul but Aunt Mehitable gwinter know dat de chile wuz on de way sooner—" (138). Of Dorinda's reaction to Mehitable's words, the narrator says: "In the illumination of that instant a hundred mysteries [that had bewildered her for the last three months] were made plain" (138). And that is all the explanation we as readers are ever given regarding the pregnancy.

Rather than feel cheated that nothing more is said, we should reflect on what it tells us about Dorinda that the signs which in retrospect so obviously point to pregnancy told her so little, before Mehitable read them for her. What sort of young woman would have so little awareness of her body and so little knowledge of what her body was saying to her—and in a language another woman reads in an instant—that she could be three months pregnant without knowing it? What sorts of families and cultures produce people whose minds are so completely deaf to the language of the body that the body remains totally outside consciousness? Rather than answer these questions directly, let us say only that whatever else may be true about such families, they produce characters like Dorinda, young women whose lives go on at levels cut off from one another, and that such characters exist in novels that we may read at either the conscious or unconscious level or using any combination of the two.

This recognition leads us to the second episode that effectively illustrates the two major dimensions of the novel, an episode that shows why it is possible to read *Barren Ground* as a story of both triumph and defeat. The first, or conscious, level emerges, after Dorinda has been in New York for two years, in a remark she makes to her friend Dr. Burch. She tells Burch, "If I had the money, I'd go back and start a dairy farm there [on the family's land]" (238). It is an impulsive remark, but the narrator tells us: "While she spoke a vision glimmered. . . . For the first time since she had left home, she felt that earlier and deeper associations [than Jason] were reaching out to her, . . . drawing her back across time and space and forgetfulness. Passion stirred again in her heart. . . . With a shock of joy, she realized that . . . she had come to life again" (239). At this first conscious level, her motives are clearly the positive ones of renewing the barren fields of Old Farm and at the same time revivifying her own suspended emotional life. The surface levels of her self-knowledge, and the article by Anderson mentioned earlier, demonstrate how well she succeeds in this scheme.

But immediately after Glasgow tells us that Dorinda feels the farm calling her "to come back and help it," Glasgow reports the dream Dorinda has that night, a dream that shows the meaning the powerful unconscious side of her personality ascribes to the return to Old Farm (239). In the dream:

> she was ploughing one of the abandoned fields. . . . Dan and Beersheba were harnessed to the plough, and when they had finished one furrow, they [the horses] turned and looked back at her before they began another. "You'll never get this done if you plough a hundred years," they said, "because there is nothing here but thistles, and you can't plough thistles under." Then she looked round her and saw that they were right. As far as she could see, on every side, the field was filled with prickly

purple thistles, and every thistle was wearing the face of Jason. A million thistles, and every thistle looked up at her with the eyes of Jason! She turned the plough where they grew thickest, trampling them down, uprooting them, ploughing them under with all her strength; but always when they went into the soil, they cropped up again. Millions of purple flaunting heads! Millions of faces! They sprang up everywhere; in the deep furrow that the plough had cut; in the dun-coloured clods of the up-turned earth; under the feet of the horses; under her own feet, springing back, as if they were set on wire stems, as soon as she had crushed them into the ground. "I am going to plough them under, if it kills me," she said aloud; and then she awoke. . . . It was the first time she had dreamed of Jason. Long after she had ceased to think of him, she told herself resentfully. (239–40)

That resentment of her inability to control her inner life is the central drama of Dorinda's subsequent career. She intends to put her energies to positive use, but her inner self keeps reminding her that, against her own will, she has unfinished business with Jason. The nature of that business comes through clearly in the dream.

Whether we read the dream from traditional perspectives of fairy tales and myth, or from the twentieth-century perspectives of Sigmund Freud and Carl Jung, whose importance Glasgow claims to have been among the first in the South to recognize (*Woman* 269), we perceive that the force of the dream runs in a direction counter to the renewing and revivifying intention of her return to the South. It is a dream, first and last, of revenge—of death-dealing revenge. The thistles wear the face of Jason, as did everyone she saw on the day she left the hospital after her miscarriage (223). Consequently, the dream reveals a deep misanthropic streak in Dorinda. The thistles, from a Freudian perspective, are snakelike and phallic, an association that exposes a male-destroying impulse in the dream. And the thistles are born from the earth which, to a Jungian, would likely suggest the parallel episode in which Jason Greylock's namesake, the Greek Jason, eradicates the earthborn giants who sprang from the teeth of the dragon he slew to steal the golden fleece. The latter association, likely the most powerful of all, shows that the vengeful force working in Dorinda is at war with the earth itself and therefore probably at war with the shamed and wounded part of her feminine self. Her wound is from Jason, but Dorinda's unconscious has turned her revenge into something much larger, an assault upon the masculine, the feminine, the earthborn—the fate, or fatality, of humankind itself.[3]

But revenge takes two, and, for good or ill, Jason never knows she is pregnant. Consequently, he never knows how deeply he wounded her, how much she hates him, how much she needs to get back at him—even by living well. In effect, as she vaguely realizes in the final scenes with Jason, her revenge and a great part of her life's energy have been wasted on a figment of her imagination (498–99, 506–7). This waste and the associated powerlessness of Dorinda to take complete control of her emotional life constitute the level of the story to which McDowell responds when he reminds us that, in her struggle with the soil, Dorinda is both victor and victim.

Of all the things outside Dorinda's consciousness, least of all does she recognize the complex nature of her tie to Jason. Although Jason seduced and abandoned her, there is nothing Dorinda can ever do to get even—or even to get rid of him. For Jason is not a man who exists simply as an object in her external world. To Dorinda he never was. At the same time he is not a mere figment of her imagination. For Dorinda, Jason resembles what American psychoanalyst Heinz Kohut calls a *selfobject:* a part of the environment that is "experienced as a part of the self," an experience that bridges "the inner world of the self and the outer world of the environment" (Kohut xiv; Wolf 43–44). A selfobject like Jason is neither all subject (self) nor all object (other); it is a third entity, a "psychic reality," that comes into being without threatening the real-world existence of either the subject or the object. To Dorinda, Jason is *the* man she loved, *the* man who ruined her life by abandoning her when she was pregnant. As such, he is the most important person in her adult life—perhaps in her entire life as the novel presents it. To Jason, on the other hand, the significance of his relationship with Dorinda is entirely different. He knows that Dorinda loved him, but from the beginning he can hardly keep his mind on their conversations, an indication that what she sees as their love is largely *her* love alone (35). Because he cannot have known he made her pregnant (she doesn't discover it herself until the day she finds he has married Geneva), he never realizes that for three decades he has existed in Dorinda's mind as an object of hatred formed out of love. Nor is he aware that during those years he was the target of her lifelong project of revenge. Because he does not know, Dorinda's project has, of course, been futile.

But the by-product of her failed vengeance is her outward success. Not even Dorinda realizes that the hidden motive of her struggle to redeem Old Farm has been the desire to get rid of Jason. The techniques of the novel, however, especially her projections onto the other characters and the dream she has the night before she begins her course in scientific farming, make this clear (239–40). In as much as the Jason she wants to destroy is her selfobject, and therefore a part of herself, her attempts to extirpate him from her life are as *self*-destroying as were the struggles of her Calvinistic ancestors to root out the natural instincts from human nature. The side-by-side existence of Dorinda's mythic success and her psychological failure creates the almost electric arc that gives the book its power and enigmatic interest.

Glasgow was able to generate such rich ambivalences around Dorinda because (at least during the creation of the novel) the heroine was the author's own selfobject.[4] Although she later claimed that *The Wheel of Life* was her only novel taken "directly from experience" (*Letters* 238), the more we learn of Glasgow's life the more probable it becomes that, through Dorinda, she discovered deeper levels of her own emotional being than through any other heroine. Through Dorinda, for example, she reclaimed great veins of the iron willfulness and outward strength of character that her father had possessed. Through Jason she split off and embodied the loving cruelness she had experienced from Mr. Glasgow and from other men significant in her life, including her mentor and brother-in-law, Walter McCormack. Her antipathy for her father's religion found expression in Dorinda's mother's crazed missionary dreams and the ironic comments about the Oakley family's Calvinism (43–44). Through Dorinda's care for the earth, Glasgow relived the matrix of support she had known with her mother, with Lizzie Jones, and at Jerdone Castle. At the same time, her deep emotions surrounding the victimization and pain her mother experienced come through, split up, in numerous scenes: the illness of Rose Emily Pedlar, the fondness of Jason's father for women of mixed blood, Geneva's madness, and, of course, Jason's rejection of Dorinda (20–23, 131, 150, 351, 373). Thus divided up and dealt with in manageable pieces, the ambivalences of Glasgow's early life relived in *Barren Ground* give the novel its remarkable emotional authority as well as the psychological complexity that speaks to critics with viewpoints as diverse as those that Professors Anderson and McDowell find mirrored in the story.

Glasgow grew up amid ambiguities; they supplied much of the energy for her best writing. We should not be surprised, therefore, that, called on near her sixtieth birthday to state her credo, she cited complexity of vision as the key. Rationalized into philosophy, what is so rich in fiction and painful in her life becomes relatively simple: she believes, she writes, "that skepticism remains the only permanent basis of tolerance": "that a reasonable doubt is the safety-valve of civilization." Only such openness of mind can fully preserve the complexity of human relationships and permit "that inmost reason which we . . . call the heart" to apprehend "the deepest certainties," certainties that "if they exist," lie beyond the point "where all beliefs disappear."[5] This complexity of relationships based on energies that live beyond the point where beliefs disappear leads the reader to the unconscious dimensions of Glasgow's later works. The various ways she conveys these hidden dimensions to readers constitute her major contribution to Southern Modernism.

Notes

1. Cf. Glasgow, *Sheltered Life* 14, for an additional example of one of her father's traits returning in a female character, Eva Birdsong.
2. See Glasgow, *Measure* vii—viii, for her comments on the hypocrisy of false humility. What I have in mind is more the tone of the prefaces than any specific statement.
3. For a fuller explanation, see Raper, *Garden* 84–88.
4. For a conventional view of Glasgow's objectivity, see Stuckey 509. A selfobject is not "merely" a projection; it is always both subject and object. To grasp the significance of selfobjects one must transcend the Cartesian disjunction.
5. For fuller statements of her reasonable doubts, see "What I Believe" and "I Believe" in Glasgow, *Reasonable Doubts.*

Works Cited

Anderson, Mary Castiglie. "Cultural Archetype and the Female Hero: Nature and Will in Ellen Glasgow's *Barren Ground.*" *Modern Fiction Studies* 28 (Autumn 1982): 383–93.

Glasgow, Ellen. *Barren Ground.* Garden City: Doubleday, 1925.

———. *A Certain Measure: An Interpretation of Prose Fiction.* New York: Harcourt, 1938.

———. *Ellen Glasgow's Reasonable Doubts: A Collection of Her Writings.* Ed. Julius Rowan Raper. Baton Rouge: Louisiana State UP, 1988.

———. *Letters of Ellen Glasgow.* Ed. Blair Rouse. New York: Harcourt, 1958.

———. *The Sheltered Life.* 1932. New York: Hill, 1979.

———. *The Woman Within.* New York: Harcourt, 1954.

Kohut, Heinz. *The Analysis of the Self: A Systematic Approach to the Psychoanalytic Personality Disorders.* New York: International, 1979.

MacDonald, Edgar. "Glasgow-Stein: Second Meeting." *The Ellen Glasgow Newsletter* 15 (October 1981): 17.

MacDonald, Edgar E., and Tonette Bond Inge, eds. *Ellen Glasgow: A Reference Guide.* Boston: Hall, 1986.

McDowell, Frederick P. W. *Ellen Glasgow and the Ironic Art of Fiction*. Madison:
U of Wisconsin P, 1960.

Parent, Monique. *Ellen Glasgow: Romancière*. Paris: Nizet, 1962.

Raper, Julius Rowan. *From the Sunken Garden: The Fiction of Ellen Glasgow, 1916–
1945*. Baton Rouge: Louisiana State UP, 1980.

———. *Without Shelter: The Early Career of Ellen Glasgow*. Baton Rouge: Louisiana
State UP, 1971.

Roades, Antoinette W. "Fertile Ground." *The Ellen Glasgow Newsletter* 8 (March
1978): 13.

Stuckey, William J. "Recent Books on Women Writers of the American South."
Modern Fiction Studies 28 (Autumn 1982): 507–18.

Wolf, Ernest S. "Psychoanalytic Psychology of the Self and Literature." *New Literary
History* 12 (1980): 41–60.

"Put Your Heart in the Land"
An Intertextual Reading of
Barren Ground and *Gone with the Wind*

Margaret D. Bauer

> Yes, she was not broken. She could never be broken
> while the vein of iron held in her soul.
> —Glasgow, *Barren Ground* 180

When Margaret Mitchell's *Gone with the Wind* was first published in 1936, reviewers compared it most often to *War and Peace* and *Vanity Fair;* so it was inevitable that critics would later write extended articles delineating the similarities, as Harold K. Schefski and Paul Pickrel have. Brief mention has also been made by literary critics of the similarities between Mitchell's Scarlett O'Hara and Ellen Glasgow's Dorinda Oakley of *Barren Ground,* published in 1925.[1] An extended comparison of these two characters, their lives, and their fates would serve to replace with a work of literature the David O. Selznick film of *Gone with the Wind,* which is too often used—however unconsciously—as an intertext of the novel. As noted by Amy Levin, "for many, [the movie's] images supplanted any experience with the printed text." She points out a consequential disservice to the novel: "Opinions of *Gone with the Wind* [are] thus frequently based on an abbreviated notion of the story, a [movie] version which emphasized the melodrama inherent in the work" (32). Also remarking on a problem with the movie version of the novel, Gerald Wood notes how "David Selznick purged *Gone with the Wind* of Mitchell's ambiguity. . . . Rather than dramatize, as Mitchell does, an inconclusive conflict between aristocratic idealism and lumpish realism, the film-maker makes a clear preference for days-gone-by" (131). But reading the novel *Gone with the Wind* closely with *Barren Ground* illuminates the heroine Scarlett O'Hara's triumph in the novel's somewhat ambiguous ending and reveals how *Gone with the Wind* defies the conventions of popular romance novels and plantation fiction.

Because the role of Scarlett O'Hara was played by Vivien Leigh in the renowned film, it is easy to forget that the novel opens with the words, "Scarlett O'Hara was not beautiful" (3). The narrator then notes Scarlett's green eyes, "without a touch of hazel" and her "bristly black lashes" and "thick black brows" (3). The narrator explains that in Scarlett's eyes one could see her "true self": "The green eyes in the carefully sweet face were turbulent, willful, lusty with life, distinctly at variance with her decorous demeanor. Her manners had been imposed upon her by her mother's gentle admonitions and the sterner discipline of her mammy; her eyes were her own" (3). This opening description of Scarlett connects her to Glasgow's Dorinda Oakley, despite the differences in the two characters' backgrounds, for in her description of Scarlett, Mitchell has highlighted the same features as Glasgow does in her description of Dorinda. Chapter 2 of *Barren Ground* opens with the comment that Dorinda was "not beautiful," and Glasgow's narrator also remarks that Dorinda's "eyes were her one memorable feature. Large, deep, radiant, they shone beneath her black lashes with a clear burning colour, as blue as the spring sky after rain" (10). Dorinda's thick eyebrows, like Scarlett's, are also remarked upon. Although their eye color is different, the connection between the heroines' eyes and their personalities is clearly similar, and both girls will wear dresses to match their eyes at significant points in their lives.

From an interview with Mitchell, Edwin Granberry determined that she "has not drawn her characters from life. . . . [S]he filled the pages of her book with people of her own creation" (51). Mitchell's brother has also commented, "'Nobody in the book except the historic characters (like Civil War generals) are taken from life'" (Runyon 81). If not influenced by actual people, perhaps these "creations" were influenced by her reading (though Mitchell was never to acknowledge any particular literary influences on her novel). In both of the letters Mitchell wrote to Glasgow, she mentions having read Glasgow's books (Harwell 57, 319), and Anne Edwards, one of Mitchell's biographers, notes that Mitchell's husband gave his wife a copy of *Barren Ground* for Christmas in 1925 (125). Mitchell began writing *Gone with the Wind* in 1926, perhaps with the character and story of Dorinda Oakley still alive in her imagination.

The tenets of being a lady in the antebellum South are so restrictive that in spite of the social life of a belle, Scarlett, like Dorinda in small, uneventful Pedlar's Mill, is unstimulated and thus easy prey for romantic dreaming. The scenes describing how their romantic dreams are each manifested into a living being are quite similar. Glasgow's narrator explains that "[a]t twenty, [Dorinda's] imagination was tinctured by the romanticism which makes a woman fall in love with a religion or an idea" (12), and indeed, Dorinda falls in love with her idea of Jason Greylock, who has just returned to Pedlar's Mill. She transforms him into a man worthy of her adulation, thinking of him as "an irreproachable son who had relinquished his ambition in order to remain with his undeserving old father" (13), when in truth, as Jason will later tell her, he "'hadn't the heart or the courage to refuse to come'" (64). Similarly, Scarlett falls in love with the dashing image that Ashley Wilkes made riding up to Tara to pay his respects to her family upon his return from Europe. Ashley, too, shows evidence early on of his cowardly nature when he lacks the courage to tell Scarlett of his engagement to Melanie Hamilton. Ashley does not, like Jason, express his love or talk of marriage to Scarlett, but he does escort her around the county for two years without telling her that he and Melanie have an understanding that they will marry.

To please Jason, Dorinda decides to have a blue dress made with the money she had been saving to buy a cow. Though surprised by Dorinda's extravagance, the dressmaker thinks, "After all, you weren't young and good-looking but such a little while!" (71). This sentiment is echoed throughout *Gone with the Wind*, beginning at the barbecue with the division of women into belles and matrons, "for there were no married belles in the South." Once married, young girls had to put away their bright colored dresses and were "relegated to arbors and front parlors with staid matrons in dull silks" (101). But, like Dorinda, for the moment Scarlett can wear a bright dress, the color of her eyes, in hopes of attracting the beau of her choice.

From the dressmaker Dorinda learns that Jason had courted Geneva Ellgood the previous summer. Hearing this,

> a wave of dull sickness swept over her. At that moment she realized that the innocence of her girlhood, the ingenuous belief that love brought happiness, had departed for ever. She was in the thick of life, and the thick of life meant not peace but a sword in the heart. Though she scarcely knew Geneva Ellgood, she felt that they were enemies. (68–69)

So Dorinda begins her campaign to attract Jason's attention away from Geneva by ordering a new hat to go with the blue dress. Similarly, when Scarlett learns of the possibility that Ashley might be engaged to Melanie, she, too, must confront a harsh reality of adulthood: "There were pain and bewilderment in her face, the bewilderment of a pampered child who has always had her own way for the asking and who now, for the first time, was in contact with the unpleasantness of life" (22). And Scarlett also immediately perceives of Melanie as her enemy and begins to plan her strategy for making Ashley jealous at the barbecue so that he will recognize that it is she, not Melanie, he wants.

Also when Dorinda learns about her competition, she feels a "primitive impulse" rise within her, "among the orderly instincts and inherited habits of thought. She was startled; she was frightened; but she was defiant. In a flash the knowledge came to her that habit and duty and respectability are not the whole of life" (69). The reader can understand better what is going on within Dorinda by examining her feelings next to Scarlett's actions when she finally confronts Ashley with her love. Although Scarlett's *plans* to win Ashley had ended with, "Of course, she would do it all in a lady-like way. She wouldn't even dream of saying to him boldly that she loved him—that would never do" (72), when she faces Ashley she immediately blurts out a declaration of her love. Like Dorinda, then, her more primitive instincts overpower her notions of respectability.

After seeing Jason with the Ellgoods at church and realizing from his remarks upon her new dress that he does not remember asking her to wear blue, the confused Dorinda questions her mother about marriage. Eudora replies, "'Grandfather used to say that when a woman got ready to fall in love the man didn't matter, because she could drape her feeling over a scarecrow and pretend he was handsome.'" Eudora adds her own opinion that a woman's decision to marry is "'just the struggle to get away from things as they are'" (103). She tries to soften her remarks, which apply so well to Dorinda's attraction to Jason, by telling Dorinda, "'You'll be all right married, daughter, if you just make up your mind that whatever happens, you ain't going to let any man spoil your life'" (103–4). Hearing these words Dorinda feels for the first time "the vein of iron in [her] nature" and "resolved passionately [that] no man was going to spoil her life! She could live without Jason; she could live without any man" (104). Although in the course of the novel, the latter proves to be true, Dorinda suffers from a disappointment that would influence the rest of her life as a result of using her vein of iron to attract Jason's attention rather than to resist his charms.

Interestingly, Scarlett's realization about her love for Ashley, which does not come until the second to last chapter of her novel, echoes remarkably Eudora's grandfather's words about marriage: "'He never really existed at all, except in my imagination. . . . I loved something I made up. . . . I made a pretty suit of clothes and fell in love with it. And when Ashley came riding along, so handsome, so different, I put that suit on him and made him wear it whether it fitted him or not'" (1016). Like Dorinda's, Scarlett's desire to marry Ashley "spoil[s] her life" after she, too, fails to use her vein of iron to resist him once he first resists her.

The scene of Dorinda's discovery of Jason's marriage is quite comparable to that of Scarlett's discovery of Ashley's engagement. Dorinda's chorus of "*It isn't true*" (154) as she waits for Jason's wagon to pass so that she can see if Geneva is with him is echoed by Scarlett as she waits for her father's return from the Wilkes' plantation: "'Oh, it can't be true!'" (25). The imagery used to describe the two girls' reactions to their disappointments is also similar. After Dorinda sees the wagon, "[s]he felt cold and wet. . . . Everything within her had stopped. The clock no longer ticked; it had run down" (156). Similarly, after hearing the twins' secret, Scarlett merely goes through the motions of participating in the rest of their banter until they leave, at which time "she went back to her chair like a sleepwalker," feeling her heart "beat with odd little jerks; her hands were cold" (22). Again echoing Dorinda, who finally says to herself, "'So it is true'" (156), after her father's confirmation of the rumor, Scarlett thinks, "So it was true" (33). And, as Dorinda's body holds onto the earth while she feels her consciousness leave time and space and join temporarily with nothingness, Gerald O'Hara offers Scarlett the consolation of the land's permanence to ease her pain.

Gerald's words are perhaps the most significant echo in *Gone with the Wind* of Glasgow's novel. He tells his daughter, "'Land is the only thing in the world that amounts to anything . . . for 'tis the only thing in this world that lasts. . . . 'Tis the only thing worth working for, worth fighting for—worth dying for'" (36). After Dorinda's return from New York, old Matthew Fairlamb gives her a quite similar message: "'Put yo' heart in the land. The land is the only thing that will stay by you'" (323). Both women recall these messages later as they ponder the losses of their lives and realize that in spite of these losses they have survived.

At this point in their lives, however, neither girl appreciates yet the resilience of land. Dorinda does recognize the permanence of land, but does not view this constancy positively. Surveying the tired, "overworked" landscape, Dorinda thinks, "The country had been like this . . . long before she was born. It would be like this . . . after she and all those who were living with her were dead. For the one thing that seemed to her immutable and everlasting was the poverty of the soil" (11). Although she recognizes the "terrible force" of the land, "whether [this force was] for good or evil she could not tell" (38). And for now she is more interested in marrying Jason and leaving this land. The narrator of Mitchell's novel explains that Scarlett is not conscious of the beauty of her surroundings: "She loved this land so much, without even knowing she loved it" (28). And, to the consternation of her father, she rejects his proffered comfort of her eventual inheritance of Tara. She is only interested in marrying Ashley.

Once Jason's marriage and Ashley's engagement become facts which the two girls can do nothing about, each confronts her betrayer, during which time she glimpses the truth about her romantic hero. After Jason speaks in defense of himself, "with a piercing flash of insight, [Dorinda] saw him as he was, false, vain, contemptible, a coward. . . . Nothing that he said made any difference to her. Nothing that he could ever say in the future would make any difference" (165). Although Scarlett does not so easily shake the influence Ashley will continue to have on her, she does briefly recognize his cowardice, too: "'Why don't you say it, you coward! You're afraid to marry me!'" (117), she lashes out at him, realizing, like Dorinda, that his excuses for marrying another woman are indicative of his weak nature.

Both girls then respond to their situations in such a way as to protect themselves from ridicule—for in spite of their romantic natures, they are both quite pragmatic. Dorinda leaves town to escape people's pity and their eyes, which will soon perceive that she is pregnant with Jason's child. Scarlett marries Charles Hamilton in order to save face in front of the girls who suspect her feelings for Ashley. And the two authors then equally conveniently get rid of these burdens on their heroines: Glasgow has Dorinda miscarry her baby, while Mitchell kills Charles off with pneumonia. The stories of the two survivors, unburdened as yet except for their own heavy hearts, can thus continue.[2]

In *A Certain Measure*, Ellen Glasgow defines the vein of iron she refers to in her characterization of her strongest female characters, including Dorinda Oakley, as "the vital principle of *survival*, which has enabled races and individuals to withstand the destructive forces of nature and of civilization" (169, emphasis added). Writing specifically of Dorinda, Glasgow explains, "In the end, she would triumph through that deep instinct for survival." Indeed, Dorinda "would be hardened by adversity, but hard things . . . are the last to decay" (*ACM* 160). Darden Asbury Pyron compares Glasgow's comments on Dorinda's survival instinct to Mitchell's theme of survival (584). Writing of *Gone with the Wind*, Margaret Mitchell explains, "If the novel has a theme, the theme is that of survival. What makes some people able to come through catastrophes and others, apparently just as able, strong, and brave, go under? . . . [T]he survivors used to call that quality 'gumption.' So I wrote about the people who had gumption and the people who didn't" ("Margaret Mitchell" 38). Scarlett O'Hara, of course, is the central survivor of Mitchell's novel. She, too, is hardened by her experiences and, consequently, becomes less and less mindful of others' feelings and her own reputation. But just as Glasgow's readers find Dorinda admirable for her achievements and sympathize with her losses, Mitchell's readers admire and sympathize with this young woman who, between her sixteenth and twenty-eighth years, loses everyone she loved and life as she knew it, and yet survives to the novel's end and beyond.

As each young woman commences on her journey away from the home which has become loathsome to her since her heartbreak, she feels the stirring of excitement, in spite of her pain. But once gone, each misses the land of her birth. After two years in New York, Dorinda begins to talk about her family's farm, and as she does so her young suitor notices a change in her and comments to himself, "Strange, the hold the country could get over one!" (237). Once in Atlanta, Scarlett misses Tara and "realize[s] dimly what Gerald had meant when he said that the love of the land was in her blood" (155).

Still, neither girl is ready yet to go home. Dorinda does not want to return until "her hate [is] as dead as her love" (228). In contrast, Scarlett stays in Atlanta in large part because as long as she lives with Melanie, she will see Ashley when he is on leave. Paradoxically, although she still loves Ashley, she believes herself "done with passion and marriage" (215), a sentiment that echoes Dorinda's response to Mrs. Faraday's advice that she should get married: "'Oh, I've finished with all that!'" (243). Mitchell's explanation of the seeming contradiction in Scarlett's rejection of passion while still professing love for Ashley is also reminiscent of Glasgow's description of Dorinda's reaction to love since her experiences with Jason. The narrator explains that Dorinda feels a "revulsion from the physical aspect of love" (244). Although she enjoys the company of the young doctor in New York, she retreats from his touch: "the thought of love, the faintest reminder of its potency, filled her with aversion. . . . She simply could not bear . . . to be touched" (244–45). Like Dorinda, Scarlett rejects sex, seeing it as "inexplicable male madness, . . . a painful and embarrassing process that led inevitably to the still more painful process of childbirth" (215). But unlike Dorinda, she does not reject love: "She was done with marriage but not with love, for her love for Ashley was something different, having nothing to do with passion or marriage, something sacred and breathtakingly beautiful" (215). In comparison, as a consequence of their shared distaste for sex, both Dorinda and Scarlett ruin their chances of getting over their first bad experiences with it. Dorinda's refusal to participate in sexual relations again keeps the painful memory of her relationship with Jason alive, so that, when she sees Jason many years later, after not seeing him for ten years, "she felt, with a shiver of terror, that the past had never died." The narrator explains, "In her whole life there had been only that one man. He had held her in his arms. He would remain always an inseparable part of her being" (359). Similarly, Scarlett will not let herself forget Ashley and thus give Rhett a chance to win her heart. And when Rhett does stir up her passions, it does not lead her to thoughts of love for him, for, as noted above, love is something she has separated from sex.

In spite of their arrested sexual development, both girls do mature in other ways into young women during their years away from home. Glasgow's narrator explains of Dorinda, "Young as she was she had acquired the ripe wisdom and the serene self-confidence of maturity; she had attained the immunity from apprehension which comes to those only who can never endure the worst again" (227). As Scarlett returns to Tara, Mitchell's narrator explains, "She was seeing things with new eyes for . . . she had left her girlhood behind her. She was no longer plastic clay, yielding imprint to each new experience. The clay had hardened. . . . She was a woman now and youth was gone" (420). And similar to the narrator's comments about Dorinda, Grandma Fontaine notes that Scarlett has "'face[d] the worst that can happen to her'" and will thus never "'really fear anything again'" (452).

Neither assessment of the two young women is entirely accurate, however, as is indicated by their nightmares. As Dorinda contemplates returning to work Old Farm, her nightmare reflects her fear of seeing Jason again. In her dream, his face appears on the millions of thistles that cover the field she is ploughing. Just before waking she says, "'I am going to plough them under, if it kills me'" (240). Apparently, she is still not over her rage, and it appears, too, that part of her reason for returning to Old Farm is to get even with Jason for the effect he has had on her life. Upon returning to Pedlar's Mill, when she learns the state of affairs at the Greylocks' Five Oaks, she determines to buy it out from under Jason some day. So that she can afford to do so soon, she turns with vigor to her plans to make Old Farm into a productive dairy.

Scarlett, too, suffers a nightmare which reveals that there is something which she still fears—hunger and the insecurity it causes. Her dream is motivated by her actual return to Tara, rather than contemplation of it. In looking forward to returning, Scarlett anxiously anticipates seeing her mother again. Particularly after the ordeals of delivering Melanie's baby and leading her little group safely to Tara after Rhett's desertion of them, she longs to hand everyone, including herself, over to her mother's charge. Arriving to find her mother dead, then, is quite a blow to Scarlett and continues to haunt her in her recurrent nightmare of being hungry and lost in a fog, from which things grabbed at her, trying to pull her down. Ahead, she feels, is security, but she can never reach it in the dream. In her waking life, then, Scarlett determines to find this security for herself and her family, in hopes of stopping the recurring nightmare.

For their own reasons, then, both young women turn their attention to their land. Dorinda begins to feel "earlier and deeper associations" with Old Farm "reaching out to her . . . groping after her, like the tendrils of vines, through the darkness and violence of her later memories . . . drawing her back across time and space and forgetfulness," and with these feelings she "come[s] to life again" (239). She tells her suitor, "'I can't stay away any longer. I'm part of it. I belong to the abandoned fields'" (245). She is soon called home to see her dying father; once there, she immediately proceeds with her plans to revitalize the farm. Finding that she, too, has returned to a disabled father, Scarlett also takes charge of Tara, and in doing so, she, too, realizes that "she belonged to the red acres. . . . Her roots went deep into the blood-colored soil and sucked up life" (420).

The first obstacle that both young women have to confront as they take over the two farms is the obstinacy against change in the people around them. Dorinda describes people of her community as "'in a rut, but . . . satisfied; they don't want to change'" (63). Such was a reason for the Civil War, according to Mitchell's novel: the South did not want to change, and, as Jason points out in *Barren Ground*, "people will fight to stay in a rut, but not to get out of it. . . . [A]ny prejudice, even the prejudice in favour of the one-crop system [or in favour of slavery], is a sacred institution" (111). Evidence of the validity of Jason's assessment can be seen in Joshua Oakley's failure to try something new even after years of unsuccessful farming. Earlier, Dorinda had realized that "'it's being set in a rut . . . that keeps him going'" (118), but now that she has become interested in farming she sees the problem in the fact that "'the experience of generations . . . has taught us nothing except to do things the way we've always done them'" (238). Hence, she believes that her lack of practical experience with farming is to her advantage. She will not be encumbered with the way things have always been done.

Scarlett refuses, too, to allow past ways to hinder the work that needs to be done on Tara. She and her sisters, as well as the house slaves, will all pick cotton. In contrast to Dorinda, however, she looks to the previous generations of her family for strength:

> Gerald, penniless, had raised Tara; Ellen had risen above some mysterious sorrow; Grandfather Robillard, surviving the wreck of Napoleon's

throne, had founded his fortunes anew on the fertile Georgia coast; Great-Grandfather Prudhomme had carved a small kingdom out of the dark jungles of Haiti, lost it, and lived to see his name honored in Savannah. . . . All had suffered crushing misfortunes and had not been crushed. (420–21)

Dorinda plans to transform Old Farm into a prosperous dairy farm, and Scarlett's goal is to bring Tara to some semblance of its former self. In spite of the differences in the two young women's backgrounds, at the time they take over for their fathers, they are starting off with quite similar handicaps. Both are confronting land that has been devastated by the Civil War. In the opening of *Barren Ground*, Glasgow describes the state of the novel's landscape as "impoverished by the war and the tenant system which followed the war" (4). Scarlett takes over Tara after the Union troops have passed through the county, burning the fields and most of the homes, and confiscating all valuable items they could find and carry away with them. Consequently, the O'Haras, like the Oakleys, are described at this point as being "land poor." This comparison is prepared for in the beginning of Mitchell's novel when the narrator notes that at the edges of the plantations stood forests from which "the soughing pines seem to wait with an age-old patience, to threaten with soft sighs: 'Be careful! Be careful! We had you once. We can take you back again'" (8), just as Dorinda remarks upon the threat of broomsedge, pines, and life-everlasting reclaiming her land (237). After the war, Scarlett recognizes that these pines will soon take over the cotton fields, and then the "country folks will go back a hundred years like the pioneers who had little cabins and just scratched a few acres—and barely existed" (495), a description that calls to mind the state of affairs on the Oakley farm before Dorinda's management. Like Dorinda, whose desire is to keep away the broomsedge that threatens Old Farm, Scarlett is determined that the pines will not reclaim Tara.

One of Dorinda's first acts toward improving Old Farm is to buy cows from the Ellgoods. Upon first meeting with Bob Ellgood, "she could see her reflection in his large, placid eyes. . . . It gave her pleasure to feel that she was more distinguished, if less desirable, than she had been two years ago." The narrator explains, however, that "her pleasure was as impersonal as her errand. She had no wish to attract this heavy, masterful farmer . . . beyond the point where his admiration might help her to drive a bargain in cows" (283). Similarly, to save Tara, Scarlett turns to Rhett Butler, wearing the unforgettable dress made from green velvet curtains. She, too, has had misgivings about her current desirability and is thus gratified by Rhett's notice of her fine appearance in the new dress. She has no romantic interest in Rhett. Like Dorinda's, her goal is purely economic in nature: to elicit a marriage proposal or a proposition to be his mistress, whichever, as long as she will have available to her in the future any money that is required of her to keep Tara.

The failure of Scarlett's plans leads to her marriage to Frank Kennedy, of whom she had always thought contemptuously and whose appeal to her sister Suellen she had always questioned. Such irony is reminiscent of Dorinda's marriage to Nathan Pedlar, of whom she had once thought, "There could be no drearier lot . . . than marriage with Nathan for a husband" (86).[3] This marriage brings up another shared detail in the characterization of the two heroines. Dorinda and Scarlett are both following in the footsteps of a female relative of the generation before their mothers'. Dorinda's great-aunt, for whom she was named, had tried to commit suicide after she was rejected by her first love interest, but when rescued, she, like Dorinda, "sobered down and married somebody else and was as sensible as anybody until the day of her death" (102). Scarlett's grandmother "married three times and had any number of duels fought over her and she wore rouge and the most shockingly low-cut dresses" (680), all of which Scarlett repeats in the course of her life.

Surprisingly, given the characterization of Nathan, Dorinda's marriage to him is also similar to Scarlett's third marriage to the quite different Rhett Butler. Both women must be talked into the marriage and assured that their new husbands will not interfere with their work. Tonette L. Bond's reading of the purpose for Dorinda's marriage to Nathan—"to gain a strong partner to help her achieve permanence for her ideal" (571)—can be applied to Scarlett's reason for agreeing to marry Rhett. Also, Dorinda realizes that Nathan "was at her mercy because he cared while she was indifferent," and thus that she "would be always . . . the stronger of the two" (374). Though Rhett makes sure that Scarlett does not realize it, he, too, is at a disadvantage in their relationship because he loves her. And in the fates of Scarlett and Rhett, the reader will learn that she is ultimately "the stronger of the two."

Jan Zlotnik Schmidt's assessment of Nathan and Dorinda's marriage is also remarkably applicable to Scarlett's third marriage, as well as her first two: "Obsessed by her memories of love, Dorinda destroys any possibility of anything more than a platonic union with Nathan Pedlar." Schmidt believes that "Dorinda's desire for revenge [against Jason] has produced her sterile marriage and stunted her emotional growth" (128). Similarly, Scarlett remains obsessed with Ashley all during her marriage to Rhett, so that, although their marriage (like her other two marriages) is consummated (unlike Dorinda and Nathan's), Scarlett only participates in the sex act as a wifely duty. And Scarlett's constant love for Ashley hinders her maturation.

Schmidt terms the effect that buying Five Oaks has on Dorinda "aphrodisiacal." The night of their purchase is the "one real moment of communion" Dorinda has with Nathan. Schmidt concludes from this episode that at this point in the novel "Dorinda's character growth is [still] incomplete" (128). Somewhat similar to this event, with Schmidt's reading of it, is the "one real moment of communion" between Scarlett and Rhett during their night of violent lovemaking. Thus, this episode is also evidence of Scarlett's undeveloped character, since she is attracted to Rhett's ability to overpower her. She is still longing to return to her former childhood state when she was not the one in the position of power with so many responsibilities and dependents.

Also connecting these two events are the events that precede each. During the auctioning of Five Oaks, Dorinda struggles to keep her mind from recalling the past, realizing that only the present matters. Similarly, earlier in the day that ends with Rhett carrying Scarlett upstairs in hopes of getting Ashley out of her mind once and for all, Scarlett and Ashley had talked about the past, at which time she thinks, "'I shouldn't have let him make me look back. . . . I was right when I said I'd never look back. It hurts too much, it drags at your heart till you can't ever do anything else except look back'" (925). Like Dorinda, she realizes that "[n]o one could go forward with a load of aching memories" (924).

During this night of momentary closeness between the Pedlars, Dorinda realizes that her husband "is worth twenty of Jason," but fails in her attempts "to say something affectionate" to him (393). Similarly, after the "wild mad night" of passion (940), Scarlett and Rhett are unable to communicate their true feelings for each other. Later, Scarlett tells Rhett that that night "'must have been when I first knew I cared about you. . . . I never was happy about Ashley after that'" (1031). In contrast, however, whereas Dorinda is "sure that [Nathan] understood her mood and was touched by its gentleness" and the two talked together late into the night about their plans for the future of their farm (394), Scarlett and Rhett completely misunderstand each other when next they meet. Still, it is not until the night of Nathan's death that Dorinda misses him and realizes how much she has grown to like him over the years, just as Scarlett did not realize until after she had banished Rhett from her bedroom that she would miss their nightly talks, and she does not determine until she is on the way home from Melanie's deathbed that she loves Rhett. Like Dorinda, she will soon learn that it is too late for this to matter to him.

Jan Schmidt remarks upon the consequences of Dorinda's "emotional frigidity," which "is life-denying for Dorinda" and "demands . . . an unfair self-abnegation" from Nathan. Nathan's death, then, she argues, "provides Dorinda with the final realizations necessary for character building" (129), just as Rhett's abandonment of Scarlett does at the end of Mitchell's novel. But before achieving this insight, Dorinda transforms her deceased husband in much the same romantic way she had transformed Jason years before: after Nathan's heroic death, "it was impossible that she should ever think of [him] as unromantically as she thought of him while he was alive. Death had not only ennobled, it had superbly exalted him" (442). Even years later the narrator remarks that though it "was true that she had missed love[,] . . . after all, it was something to have married a hero. Nathan's victorious death had filled the aching void in her heart. Where the human being had failed her, the heroic legend had satisfied" (456). Consequently, "the years after [his] death were the richest and happiest of her life" (446). She had her work and a hero, too—and one who would not interfere with her work. However, Schmidt criticizes Dorinda's "depend[ence] upon this legend to provide 'a sense of purpose in existence'" because "she is not searching within herself for the dimensions of her own legend" (129). Indeed, it is not until several years after Nathan's death, when Dorinda painfully contemplates her life as it really was in light of what she had not had in it—love—that Dorinda becomes completely satisfied with herself and what she *has* accomplished with her land.

At the end of *Gone with the Wind,* we see Scarlett begin a similar transformation of Rhett. As Rhett observes, "'it's written plainly on your face. Something, someone has made you realize that the unfortunate Mr. Wilkes is too large a mouthful of Dead Sea fruit for even you to chew. And that same something has suddenly set my charms before you in a new and attractive light'" (1027). Further on, he adds, "'I see you are contemplating the transfer of your tempestuous affections from Ashley to me'" (1033). Rhett is right, and not only does this notion undermine the idea that Scarlett really does love Rhett after all, but also the reader realizes that it would be better for Scarlett if she were to recognize her own value, rather than turn her attention to another man and begin another obsessive quest for his love.

At the end of both novels the heroines find their original knights in shining armor in their care, dependent upon them for survival. When Dorinda sees Jason in the poorhouse, "all connection between him and the man she had once loved was severed" (488). And once he is in her care, she realizes that "[w]hether he had loved her or not made no difference. . . . How futile, how unnecessary, it had all been,—her love, her suffering, her bitterness" (492–93). Like Dorinda, Scarlett does not want the responsibility of taking care of Ashley now that Melanie is dead: "'But, just the same I've got him round my neck for the rest of my life. As long as I live I'll have to look after him. . . . And if I hadn't promised Melly, . . . I wouldn't care if I never saw him again'" (1017). She is at first disgusted with Ashley for realizing only now that his wife is dead that he actually loved Melanie all along, but then pity for him replaces her anger, which she soon turns upon herself for not realizing long ago that "her love, her suffering, her bitterness" could all have been avoided had she realized the truth about Ashley sooner. According to Dawson Gaillard, "In discarding the illusion, the image from the past [of Ashley], Scarlett discards completely her girlhood; she becomes an adult, the point toward which the novel has been moving" (17). Her insight, late though it is, indicates that she, unlike Rhett, is developing finally, rather than regressing. At the end of the novel, in contrast to Rhett's backward view, she is looking toward "Tomorrow."

After leaving Ashley, Scarlett hurries home to Rhett, and as she rushes through the streets in the fog, she realizes that her nightmare has come true. She believes, however, that when she reaches Rhett she will finally find the haven that she has always felt was out there. But she is soon to learn otherwise. And yet, the realization of her nightmare in all its horror, including not being able to finally reach security, can be read positively when it is compared to the positive manifestation of Dorinda's "nightmare dream of ploughing under the thistles" and then the actual event—when Dorinda works to reclaim the land of Five Oaks from the broomsedge and pine (401). Dorinda's rejuvenation of Five Oaks reminds the reader that Scarlett, too, reclaimed land from destruction just after a waking nightmare of finding her home ravaged and the survivors dependent upon her for sustenance. It was in those days of running Tara that she most revealed her strength and endurance. Now, when the nightmare is repeated by Scarlett's arrival home to learn that Rhett, like her mother, will not relieve her of her responsibilities, she determines to return to Tara, where the reader feels sure she can again be strong.

The reader must not see Rhett's rejection of Scarlett as indicative that he, too, is triumphant at the novel's end. A comparison between Rhett and Jason at this point, in its illumination of the final image of Mitchell's hero, reveals otherwise. Thus, using Barren Ground, rather than Selznick's film, as an intertext recalls Rhett's condition at the end of the novel (which Selznick ignored in his depiction of this final scene between Scarlett and Rhett). As with Jason, Rhett's drinking since Bonnie's death has taken a significant toll on his appearance: "He was untidy now, where once he had been well groomed. . . . Whisky was showing in his face and the hard line of his long jaw was being obscured under an unhealthy bloat and puffs rising under his blood shot eyes. His big body with its hard swelling muscles looked soft and slack and his waist line began to thicken" (1001). This description is quite similar to Jason's condition toward the end of the novel: "He looked [like] an old man, for his skin was drawn and wrinkled, the pouches under his eyes were inflamed with purple, and there were clusters of congested veins in his cheeks" (450). Scarlett returns home from Melanie's deathbed to find Rhett

> sunken in his chair, his suit wrinkling untidily against his thickening waist, every line of him proclaiming the ruin of a fine body and the coarsening of a strong face. Drink and dissipation had done their work on the coin-clear profile and now it was no longer the head of a young pagan prince on new-minted gold but a decadent, tired Caesar on copper debased by long usage. (1024–25)

His final speech to her, which has long been interpreted (thanks, in large part, to the still impeccably dressed and self-controlled Clark Gable's delivery of it in the movie, followed by his walking out and closing the door on Vivien Leigh's Scarlett) as Rhett's triumph over Scarlett, provides further evidence of his complete destruction: he is looking and heading backwards toward the old southern values he had rejected early in his life for their hypocrisy and self-destructiveness. Scarlett, in contrast, like Dorinda, is still holding up, in spite of the many tragedies she has endured in the course of her lifetime. Indeed, if one compares the hardships that Scarlett and Dorinda overcome during their lifetimes with those suffered by Rhett and Jason, the men's troubles—including the death of Bonnie, since Scarlett has also lost her daughter, as well as many more members of her family—pale in comparison, and yet it is these men who are destroyed by the end of the two novels.

But before emerging triumphant, both women must go through some moments of agonizing contemplation, which contribute to the ambiguous ending of both novels. As Jason lies dying, Dorinda realizes that she has never known him, and now she can never know him (497). After Jason's death, she mourns her lost youth and "the love that she had never had" (504). She wishes she could relive her life differently, and "because it was too late and her youth had gone, she felt that the only thing that made life worth living was the love that she had never known and the happiness that she had missed" (507). She recalls Jason "as he was when she had first loved him. Though she tried to think of him as broken, ruined, and repellent, through some perversity of recollection he returned to her in the radiance of that old summer. . . . Success, achievement, victory over fate, all these things were nothing beside that imperishable illusion" (508). She revokes her early contention that "[t]here must be something in life besides love" (192, 245) with the thought that "[l]ove was the only thing that made life desirable," and she despairs in this notion since "love was irrevocably lost to her" (508).

Scarlett also realizes that she "had never understood either of the men she had loved and so she had lost them both" (1036). Like Dorinda, as she rushes home to him, she is thinking of a former Rhett, "who had strong arms to hold her, a broad chest to pillow her tired head, jeering laughter to pull her affairs into proper perspective" (1021). Dieter Meindl agrees "that the man she resolves to win back is no longer the man she loves, who represents to her the promise that life can be mastered and peace be found. . . . What Scarlett, after her pursuit of a knightly Ashley existing only in her imagination, finally purposes to do is to hunt for just another phantom, a Rhett who is no more" (421). Even after seeing and talking with him, she believes that with "the sound of his feet dying away in the upper hall was dying the last thing in the world that mattered" (1036). Like Dorinda, she tries an oft-repeated motto—"I'll think of it tomorrow"—but it, too, fails, leaving her desperate to get Rhett back, even though she, too, recognizes "that there was no appeal to emotion or reason which would turn that cool brain from its verdict . . . that he had meant every word he said" (1036).

The morning after Dorinda's painful night of self-evaluation, she emerges strong again:

> The storm and the hag-ridden dreams of the night were over, and the land which she had forgotten was waiting to take her back to its heart. Endurance. Fortitude. The spirit of the land was flowing into her, and her own spirit, strengthened and refreshed, was flowing out again toward life. This was the permanent self, she knew. (509)

She recalls old Matthew's words about the land, and takes comfort from her own experience with the truth of them. Thus, as Frederick P. W. McDowell explains, although "Dorinda occasionally feels that she may have paid too high a price for her success, . . . such misgivings are, for the most part, momentary." He sees Dorinda as "both victor and victim in her struggle with the soil," in that "the grimness of her existence on the land is offset by her sense of a kinship with its strength"

(151). And, as Linda W. Wagner has noted, "Dorinda's reward—for her life of affirmation and deprivation—is not fairy-tale happiness, . . . but a kind of constancy, a satisfaction with herself" (76).

Similarly, Scarlett also finally recognizes the high price she has paid to insure herself and her family against ever being hungry again. Since Rhett's departure with Bonnie earlier and even more so since Bonnie's death and Rhett's increasing distance, she has felt lonely and questioned the value of her new lifestyle and friends. Now that she has lost both Melanie and Rhett, she is in despair. But she, too, finds a "bulwark against the rising tide of pain" within her by recalling Tara: "She had gone back to Tara once in fear and defeat and she had emerged from its sheltering walls strong and armed for victory. What she had done once, somehow—please God, she could do again! . . . She thought of Tara and it was as if a gentle cool hand were stealing over her heart" (1036). As Dawson Gaillard points out, Tara is a "boon" superior to Rhett's love (12), which Gaillard sees as debilitating, in that Rhett treats Scarlett like a little girl. Therefore, although the reader's sense of Scarlett's development is somewhat undermined by her longing for Mammy's arms and her plan to come up with a scheme to get Rhett back, Scarlett is still more triumphant than Rhett. Whereas he is returning to the restrictive codes of the Old South, she, as Gaillard notes, "is free to exert her own vital self" (18). And like Dorinda, who believes in the end that "[t]he best of life . . . was ahead of her" (510), Scarlett is looking toward tomorrow. Furthermore, the reader should recall that it was at Tara that "the girl with her sachet and dancing slippers had slipped away," leaving "a woman with sharp green eyes, who counted pennies and turned her hands to many menial tasks, a woman to whom nothing was left from the wreckage except the indestructible red earth on which she stood" (490). From this earlier passage, one can find support for the idea that Scarlett will conquer again the frivolities of her recent lifestyle and recall, like Dorinda, the value of working with the land. Therefore, neither is Mitchell's book a traditional romance novel: as pointed out by Helen Taylor, "the happy ending involves not a man but a piece of property/land" (131).

Like the two novels' endings, their titles are somewhat ambiguous. As Linda Wagner points out, Glasgow "found that readers sometimes misread the title *Barren Ground* (and viewed Dorinda Oakley as defeated instead of productive)" (94).[4] Wagner writes: "Childless as she is, Dorinda herself might be termed *barren*, but Glasgow shows clearly that Dorinda has never been a barren woman: she has known passion, she has conceived. And what she wrests from the generally unyielding land is fruit, success, promise for the future—the opposite of barrenness" (74).

Glasgow's title, whether it refers to Old Farm or to Dorinda, is ironic by the end of the novel, since neither is ultimately barren. At the same time, it sets the stage for the state of affairs at the novel's beginning, describing as it does the condition of the land before Dorinda's hard work. In Mitchell's title's reference to the Old South (which is what is "gone"), it, too, sets the stage for the novel's beginning. And like *Barren Ground*, *Gone with the Wind* could refer to both the old way of life and the old Scarlett. But this title is not intended to evoke nostalgia for the past, as does the music playing in the background as the title appears on the screen in Selznick's movie. We might remember here that Mitchell originally entitled her manuscript *Tomorrow Is Another Day*, and changed it upon her publisher's suggestion because there were several books with titles beginning with "tomorrow." The former title certainly looks toward the future, and the present title, which is what matters in the long run, attests to the fact that the old days are *gone*.

The reviews and early criticism of *Barren Ground* perceived Dorinda Oakley's life as a failure;[5] however, in more recent years, critics have begun to view Dorinda more positively. A similar development can be found in the criticism of Scarlett O'Hara. Still, she has been criticized more often than not, and critics continue to show why she deserves the negative fate that they infer from the end of the novel. But eleven years before Margaret Mitchell's publication of *Gone with the Wind*, Ellen Glasgow had shown in *Barren Ground* that being alone is not necessarily a punishment, particularly when one has an occupation about which she feels passionately. Examining Scarlett's life in comparison to Dorinda's, then, should remind those who still express doubts about Scarlett's ultimate development and triumph that ending up without a man is not necessarily evidence of failure.

In *Barren Ground* Glasgow succeeded in breaking away from southern literary conventions of the era of plantation fiction, as the reviewer for the *New York Times* proposed she had (Brock 2) and as she believed she had (*ACM* 152). She does not glorify the "remnants of an older civilization, of a dying culture" about which she writes. Rather, she shows that "they had outlived their usefulness" (*ACM* 155). Her focus, then, is on the question of whether "the wasting malady [was] incurable." From the past does come "some deep instinct for survival" (*ACM* 156), which could be put to good use to stop the decline, as Dorinda does. In spite of the tendency of critics to classify *Gone with the Wind* as plantation fiction in the tradition of John Pendleton Kennedy or as a romance novel, it, too, defies the southern literary conventions found in plantation novels (with the exception of its portrayal of blacks)—even the glorification of the past. Although it classifies the destruction of the old order as a *Götterdämmerung,* its sympathies lie more with the survivors than with those who are destroyed. And, as Darden Pyron argues, "The novel rejects the past as a legitimate source of authority" (584). It focuses on the present, as Scarlett O'Hara struggles to survive, and looks forward to the future, when she will be rewarded for her strength and perseverance, rather than punished for her defiance of old southern codes of behavior.

Notes

1. Criticizing the character of Dorinda, Glasgow's biographer, E. Stanly Godbold, Jr., calls her "a sexless Scarlet [*sic*] O'Hara against a setting less dramatic than the Civil War and Reconstruction and without the accompaniment of a Rhett Butler." He continues, "The selfish personality, the feeling of being wounded by circumstances, the bitter determination to rise above tragedy, and the ultimate turn to the land as a source of strength are shared by both characters" (148). Elizabeth Jane Harrison compares Dorinda to Scarlett for "steal[ing] the role of hero from the male characters" and thus having to "'atone' for this sin" (32). She also compares Scarlett to Dorinda, as well as Glasgow's Ada Fincastle, for "return[ing] to the land . . . in order to recover her strength and identity" (43). Harrison later contrasts Scarlett and Dorinda on the basis of Scarlett's "climb to power in Atlanta [which] results not from meaningful work, like Dorinda's, but from her manipulation and exploitation of the labor of others" (58).

2. Scarlett does bear Charles's son, but the child does little to slow his mother down, as indicated by the small role he plays in the novel.

3. Harrison also makes an interesting connection between Nathan and Dorinda's relationship and Scarlett's relationship with Will Benteen (57).

4. Louis D. Rubin, Jr., for example, believes that "*Barren Ground* is an aptly named novel. Dorinda's life is a progressive espousal of barrenness" (26).

5. In the *New York Times Book Review,* H. I. Brock says Dorinda is "drearily triumphant" as "a prosperous woman dairy farmer who made barren ground bear rich pasturage and paid the price of it in her own barren life" (2). Jessie Hopkins, reviewer for the *Atlanta Journal Magazine,* notes similarly that although "Dorinda succeeds in conquering the barren soil of her home, . . . she cannot apply the same determination to retrieve her own barren life" (20). And critic John Edward Hardy believes that the "outcome of [Dorinda's] life is meant to be tragic," since "the fertility of the land [is] secured at the expense of human sterility" (245).

Works Cited

Bond, Tonette L. "Pastoral Transformations in *Barren Ground*." *Mississippi Quarterly* 32 (1979): 565–76.

Brock, H. I. "Southern Romance Is Dead." Rev. of *Barren Ground*. *New York Times Book Review* 12 Apr. 1925, sec. 3: 2.

Edwards, Anne. *Road to Tara: The Life of Margaret Mitchell*. New York: Ticknor, 1983.

Gaillard, Dawson. "*Gone with the Wind* as Bildungsroman; or, Why Did Rhett Butler Really Leave Scarlett O'Hara?" *Georgia Review* 28 (1974): 9–18.

Glasgow, Ellen. *A Certain Measure: An Interpretation of Prose Fiction*. New York: Harcourt, 1938.

———. *Barren Ground*. Garden City: Doubleday, 1925.

Godbold, E. Stanly, Jr. *Ellen Glasgow and the Woman Within*. Baton Rouge: Louisiana State UP, 1972.

Granberry, Edwin. "The Private Life of Margaret Mitchell." Gone with the Wind *as Book and Film*. Ed. Richard Harwell. New York: Paragon, 1983. 46–55.

Hardy, John Edward. "Ellen Glasgow." *Southern Renascence: The Literature of the Modern South*. Ed. Louis D. Rubin, Jr., and Robert D. Jacobs. Baltimore: Johns Hopkins P, 1953. 236–50.

Harrison, Elizabeth Jane. *Female Pastoral: Women Writers Re-Visioning the American South*. Knoxville: U of Tennessee P, 1991.

Harwell, Richard, ed. *Margaret Mitchell's* Gone with the Wind *Letters, 1936–1949*. New York: Macmillan, 1986.

Hopkins, Jessie. Rev. of *Barren Ground*. *Atlanta Journal Magazine* 3 May 1925: 20.

Levin, Amy. "Matters of Canon: Reappraising *Gone with the Wind*." *Proteus* 6.1 (1989): 32–36.

McDowell, Frederick P. W. *Ellen Glasgow and the Ironic Art of Fiction*. Madison: U of Wisconsin P, 1960.

Meindl, Dieter. "A Reappraisal of Margaret Mitchell's *Gone with the Wind*." *Mississippi Quarterly* 34 (1981): 414–34.

Mitchell, Margaret. *Gone with the Wind*. New York: Macmillan, 1936.

———. "Margaret Mitchell." Gone with the Wind *as Book and Film*. Ed. Richard Harwell. New York: Paragon, 1983. 37–38.

Pickrel, Paul. "*Vanity Fair* in America: *The House of Mirth* and *Gone with the Wind*." *American Literature* 59 (1987): 37–57.

Pyron, Darden Asbury. "*Gone with the Wind* and the Southern Cultural Awakening." *The Virginia Quarterly Review* 62 (1986): 565–87.

Rubin, Louis D., Jr. *No Place on Earth: Ellen Glasgow, James Branch Cabell, and Richmond-in-Virginia*. Austin: U of Texas P, 1959.

Runyon, Keith. "Mr. Mitchell Remembers Margaret." Gone with the Wind *as Book and Film*. Ed. Richard Harwell. New York: Paragon, 1983. 77–82.

Schefski, Harold K. "Margaret Mitchell: *Gone with the Wind* and *War and Peace*." Gone with the Wind *as Book and Film*. Ed. Richard Harwell. New York: Paragon, 1983. 229–43.

Schmidt, Jan Zlotnik. "Ellen Glasgow's Heroic Legends: A Study of *Life and Gabriella, Barren Ground,* and *Vein of Iron*." *Tennessee Studies in Literature* 26 (1981): 117–41.

Taylor, Helen. "*Gone with the Wind:* The Mammy of Them All." *The Progress of Romance: The Politics of Popular Fiction*. Ed. Jean Radford. History Workshop Series. New York: Routledge, 1986. 113–36.

Wagner, Linda W. *Ellen Glasgow: Beyond Convention*. Austin: U of Texas P, 1982.

Wood, Gerald. "From *The Clansman* and *Birth of a Nation* to *Gone with the Wind:* The Loss of American Innocence." *Recasting:* Gone with the Wind *in American Culture*. Ed. Darden Asbury Pyron. Miami: U Presses of Florida, 1983. 123–36.

"Telling the Truth about Themselves"
Women, Form and Idea in *The Romantic Comedians*

Caroline King Barnard Hall

In her preface to *The Romantic Comedians*, Ellen Glasgow calls her novel "one of those happy marriages of form and idea" (*Measure* 211) in which she is concerned with "valid evidence of the imagination" and "sound psychology" (213). It is, she notes, "a morality play" (216) reflecting "the upheaval of the post-war decade" (218) in which "happiness-hunters travel perpetually on roads that are circular and lead back again to the beginning" (216). Glasgow comments further in her preface to *The Sheltered Life* that "the concluding paragraph of *The Romantic Comedians* echoed the keynote of the book, and reflected the ironic mood" (*Measure* 207). These observations suggest a means both for examining the design and value system of *The Romantic Comedians* and for elucidating its feminist concerns.

Reading Glasgow's preface to *The Romantic Comedians*, one is impressed by the author's apparent delight in "the wings of my comic spirit" (*Measure* 212). Her novel is intellectual high comedy that, as C. Hugh Holman defines it, "arouses 'thoughtful' laughter by exhibiting the inconsistencies and incongruities of human nature and by displaying the follies of social manners" (*Handbook* 213). It is indeed, as Glasgow herself points out, a "comedy of manners" (*Measure* 212) in which social folly is unmasked by witty dialogue, epigram, irony, and understatement. *The Romantic Comedians* is also, of course, a romantic comedy, and the outlines of this genre are instructive. Traditionally offering serious love complicated by great difficulty as its central interest, romantic comedy resolves its difficulties and leads to a happy ending. In case of doubt, then, we are invited to view Glasgow's plot resolution as happy, or at least felicitous, remembering the close relationship of laughter to tears.

Glasgow opens her *Romantic Comedians* preface by announcing her novel to be the "tragicomedy of a happiness-hunter" (*Measure* 211), and she soon designates this central figure to be the novel's protagonist, Judge Gamaliel Honeywell. Judge Honeywell is an elderly male chivalric figure of a type familiar in Glasgow's fiction; Glasgow describes him in her preface as "a collective portrait of several Virginians of an older school, who are still unafraid to call themselves gentlemen" (215). He is a respectable, conservative, sixty-five-year-old widower who exhibits the virtues of "moderation, dignity, reserve, equanimity" (217). Much of the narrative takes his point of view through indirect discourse, interior monologue, or reverie, and as a result of this intimate relationship that narrative perspective establishes between him and the reader, the Judge is the character who seems calculated most to engage the reader's understanding. Glasgow's sympathy for him is demonstrated in many ways but none more dramatically than in passages describing his "miraculous visitation[s]" (*Comedians* 327). These appear twice in the novel at moments when, knowing he must relinquish his new, one-sided love, the Judge's loss becomes the material of epiphany:

> [T]here was a break in the clouds and light streamed into his mind. A faint, thin vibration, clear as the ringing of bells and luminous as the sunrise, quivered about him. . . . For a single point of eternity, beyond time, beyond space, beyond good and evil, he surrendered to this incorruptible harmony, to this cloudless substance of being. Light? Music? Ecstasy? God? Or merely a rainbow mist of illusion? (254)

And as Louis Auchincloss points out (16), Glasgow herself, after learning of the impending death of her love "Gerald," relates a similar experience:

> Light streamed through me, after anguish, and for one instant of awareness, if but for that one instant, I felt pure ecstasy. In a single blinding flash of illumination, I knew blessedness. I was a part of the spirit that moved in the light and the wind and the grass. . . . Spirit? Matter? Imagination? Or a fantasy of tortured nerves? (*Woman* 166)

Since Glasgow is surely serious about the value of her own experience, she appears serious as well about the value of her character's. Nevertheless, at the same time that she takes great care to paint Judge Honeywell as a sensitive, admirable, and courtly gentleman, she also exposes him to ridicule. The last sentence in the description of each mystical experience ("Or merely a rainbow mist of illusion?" "Or a fantasy of tortured nerves?") is key, for these wry, ironic interrogatives undermine the relevance and gravity of the event both for the author and for her character. The main elements of the novel's plot concern the Judge's struggle to recapture youth and love, beginning in the opening pages when he feels an "urgent . . . craving of the withered heart to be green again" (5). The reader surely sympathizes with such an impulse even though it may turn out to be no more than a "rainbow mist." But it is "illusion" (or maybe "tortured nerves") after all; the Judge's cravings are the stuff of comedy.[1]

Although Judge Honeywell prides himself on his perception and sensitivity, believing that he has not, "like the community of which he [is] a part, lost the faculty of self-criticism" (3), his acuity fails him where women are concerned. He is jealous, possessive, and snobbish; before marrying Cordelia, he broke his engagement to Amanda Lightfoot after he quarreled with her for dancing "too often with a young man of attractive appearance but undesirable progenitors" (12). He is self-deluded and sexist; Amanda, now fifty-eight, "had been a beautiful woman; she was still beautiful for her age; but . . . beautiful women who were no longer young had ceased to interest him" (53). Furthermore, in his opinion, Amanda must "have put the thought of love outside of her life" (58), since "no woman approaching sixty would permit herself to cling to a romantic illusion" (199). Yet he "remind[s] himself that at sixty-five he [is] too young to renounce the innocent pleasures of life . . . ; that he [is] indeed, thanks to his frugal habits, at least twenty years younger than most men of his age" (72). He is selfish and obtuse; when his new young wife wishes to redecorate his house (now their house), he wants her to make no changes. "No, what he desired was that each object should remain where Cordelia had placed it, in the precise spot, unaltered in feature yet illumined in aspect by Annabel's girlish charm" (183). He is egotistical and shortsighted; now that he visits only her grave, he sometimes thinks of Cordelia, his wife of thirty-six years, as having been "perfect," a "housekeeper" who took "excellent care of him and his health" (6). Yet while he is relieved "never again [to] be obliged to sit opposite to that unselfish solicitude" (7), and while he muses that "the worst of all possible worlds would be one invented by good women" (78), he remains unable to envision or to function in a world more to his liking. He considers himself "as helpless without Cordelia as a bird with a broken wing" (4–5).

Such imagery provides one key to the value system of this novel, for the narrator assigns to several characters the traits of earthbound birds, either captive or injured and thereby unable to fly free. The obsequious Bella Upchurch, "who had made a precarious though eminently respectable living by nursing the vanities of her own and her late husband's male relatives" (17), is often described as a pigeon or a dove that never flies. She has "dove's eyes" (17); she "coos" (20); she gazes "like a pretty pigeon into Judge Honeywell's face" (21). "For hours, she could twitter merrily in her discreet and entertaining fashion; for she was too wise ever to be original and too tactful ever to argue" (221). Judge Honeywell, reports the narrator, views himself as a "caged eagle," "a spirit restless, craving, eternally unsatisfied, yet with a wild comedy in its despair." "Perhaps," he muses, ". . . the fault lay in himself, not in circumstances. . . . Perhaps he had skimmed too lightly over the glazed surface of inherited wisdom" (205). He feels that "downy wings were fluttering within his heart, imprisoned and trying to break free" (42). And he believes that Annabel Upchurch can help him to fly free again, since she moves in a "flying rhythm" and has "winged eyebrows" (19). Amanda Lightfoot, "[s]erene, unselfish, with the reminiscence of a vanished day in her face and figure," is symbolized by her canaries in "gilded bird-cages" (143); her "first canary was a gift from dear Cordelia" (119), and both Cordelia and she belong to "that fortunate generation of women who had no need to think, since everything was decided for them by the feelings of a lady and the Episcopal Church" (143). These doves, canaries, and eagles live in cages of their own making; each is a captive of tradition and gentility; all are unable to fly through the failure of their own vision and imagination.

If the Judge and the other imprisoned birds are held captive by a "rainbow mist of illusion," we find freedom, energy, life, and common sense in the female point of view. Women frequently offer corrections to the Judge's faults, sometimes in witty dialogue and sometimes in ironic narrative comment. Judge Honeywell is vain, feeling "confident that he looked . . . at least twenty years younger" than his twin sister, Edmonia Bredalbane (26). "[R]emember," he tells her, "that a man remains young longer than a woman of the same age." Replies Edmonia, "I wonder what lascivious old male first invented that theory?" (27). He is "deeply moved" by his observation that Amanda Lightfoot has become a "frustrated" woman because "she had never known the complete joy of belonging to some good man" (34). After the narrator deflates this pretension by showing the Judge's immodest proclivity for being "deeply moved" by his own "conventional" ideas, Mrs. Bredalbane completes the job: "[T]he trouble with women who have never married," she tells her brother, "is that you don't realize how little there is to it until you've tried it at least once or twice" (36). As the Judge's marriage to Annabel Upchurch fails, the narrator reports his musings to us:

> There are women, he had always known (having a wide theoretical knowledge of character) who, though virtuous by instinct, recognize no ultimate authority beyond emotion. These women, he had dimly

surmised, might have their own exalted standards, however conflicting they appeared to a balanced mind where sober reason was in the ascendant. . . . To Judge Honeywell, . . . to this perfect pattern of the conventional mind, it appeared that all women, except Cordelia, inhabited some misty area between inspiration and lunacy. (217–18)

Here Glasgow sets up a witty parody of male "reason" and power. Because women who "recognize no ultimate authority beyond emotion" confound Judge Honeywell, he adopts the familiar male attitude of believing them ill or mad rather than seeing them (as we may see them or as they may see themselves) as repressed or oppressed. Yet the Judge, in an ironic reversal, believes himself ill. Bored by Amanda, infatuated with Annabel, the Judge seeks precisely the help that male characters have often sought for their melancholic wives: he visits his doctor.

Nothing troubled him, but, perhaps—yes, but this shifting sensation— this indefinite feeling that he was losing control of his faculties. Nothing but these—well, these spells of loose thinking. . . . Lack of discipline, lack of precision, lack of proper coördination. These absurd and vagrant fantasies now—what else could you call them? (123)

Glasgow's placing of this particular male character in this historically female position demonstrates both his and its absurdity.

Further, the novel is full of women who decline to recognize male authority ("ultimate authority"), who make no sense to the male mind ("balanced mind," "conventional mind"), and who occupy that familiar place of original, iconoclastic women, the "misty area between inspiration and lunacy." All are mysterious to Judge Honeywell, who "had never acquired the new habit of thinking of women as detached beings" (203). Bella Upchurch is a transitional figure who allows herself to be ruled by traditional attitudes but knows their shortcomings. "If I were Annabel," she muses, "I'd think twice before I gave up landscape gardening for the richest man in the world" (159). Returning alone to the "cheerful welcome" of her cat, canary (she keeps a caged bird), lighted candles, and fragrant kitchen, she thinks, "And this . . . is what they call loneliness." Observes the narrator: "She sighed happily; there was no crisis here. There was no wild youth. . . . there was no sentimental age. There was nothing more agitating than the tranquil immunity of a mind that had finished with love" (305). Although Annabel Upchurch is heedless, changeable, and brashly insensitive, her directness and energy are appealing. "I want it now. I want my life, Mother," she says to Bella. "This will pass, dear," her mother replies. "Think of other women." Answers Annabel, "You were all afraid of life, and you called your fear virtue" (297). Annabel Upchurch is one of two birds in the novel that fly; she is "as light and graceful as a swallow in the air" (19). The other flying bird is Glasgow's winged comic spirit.

Edmonia Bredalbane strikes the narrative's most positive and comic note of female independence. Recalling her youth in Queenborough, she says, "It took courage to face a ducking in those days, and so long as you were different from the wasp-waisted morality of the period, it scarcely mattered whether you were a saint or a sinner, for both got the same punishment" (311). She is straightforward and truthful; the narrator describes her as "[l]arge, raw-boned, with strong, plain features" and "an expression of genuine humour." She has "the courage of her appetites" and has "feared to be stout in age as little as she had feared to be scandalous in youth" (16). "An intrepid woman of liberal views and loose behavior," she has "indulged herself through life in that branch of conduct which was familiar to ancient moralists as nature in man and depravity in woman" (7). This male-female duality is replicated in Mrs. Bredalbane's relationship to Judge Honeywell. Since she is his twin sister, we are invited to arrange the narrative according to twin principles, correcting the irony of what is meant by "nature in man" and "depravity in woman" and judging Gamaliel Honeywell by the same standards he uses to judge his sister. Both pursue a "young mooncalf," as the Judge dubs Edmonia's husband. Both, in very different senses, lose their "modesty" and abandon the safety of "orthodox beliefs and the conventional standards," as he accuses her of doing (9).

Edmonia Bredalbane, Annabel Upchurch, and often Bella Upchurch are new women, "detached beings" whom the narrator fills with life and interest, whose comments and observations shine and sparkle while correcting stuffiness and pretension, who reject "the orthodox beliefs and the conventional standards." And it is precisely those beliefs and standards that this comedy of manners targets. One cause of the demise of traditional values is the war, which, thinks Judge Honeywell, "had shaken everything but the unalterable laws of biology" (8). The narrator ascribes to Bella Upchurch a similar view: "It seemed to her that there were no longer any moral properties left in the world. Experience was reduced to the sum of pure egoism" (300). Thinking of the difficulty of her daughter's marriage to the Judge, Bella summarizes this position:

> Never . . . had she felt so urgently the need of a strong moral support. Religion, yes, but even more than religion, she craved the efficacious belief in reticence, in refinement, in perfect behaviour. If the world

continued to grow away, not only from God, but from good breeding as well, what, she wondered despondently, could be trusted to keep wives contented and the working classes in order? (193–94)

Glasgow weaves into her novel a texture of nostalgia and correcting wit, of wistful longing for pre–World War I values and clear understanding of their present irrelevance, of old male standards and new female iconoclasm. And central to her ironic rendering of the failure of traditional forms and beliefs is her employment of a subtext that amplifies the novel's theme and meaning and informs its structure. Glasgow must have known T. S. Eliot's *The Waste Land* (1922) before writing *The Romantic Comedians* (1926), for she appears to allude to Eliot when describing those symptoms of sexual anxiety and postwar breakdown of values that Eliot explores in his poem.[2] There is, for example, a moment in the novel where Judge Honeywell realizes the futility of reaching his new wife either emotionally or physically. Begging her to spend the night with him ("I love to have you near me. . . . You don't know how much it means to me . . . just for to-night? . . . I want you with me, but—" [211–12]), he sees her aversion for him and feels the pain of rejection. "Then, as he made a despairing grasp at her, she slipped away from his outstretched arms and across the floor to the adjoining room" (212). This sequence echoes the content and atmosphere of a scene in Eliot's "A Game of Chess": "'My nerves are bad to-night. Yes, bad. Stay with me./ Speak to me.'"

This allusion relates to another that also concerns the relationship of Judge Honeywell and Annabel. Having decided to run off with a much younger man because if she "cannot have love, [she'd] rather die" (288), Annabel refuses to hear her mother's arguments for staying with the Judge. Thinks Bella,

> It all came back . . . to the lost idea of duty. . . . She remembered hearing once of an aunt of her mother's who had been restrained from the fatal step by pondering Goldsmith's mournful advice to lovely woman. Well, if Goldsmith was a convenient household remedy in her grandmother's time, Mrs. Upchurch could only regret that the world had passed away from such simple antidotes to sin. (288)

The well-known Goldsmith citation, from the comedy of manners *The Vicar of Wakefield*, refers to the seduction of a young woman by an aristocratic, older male libertine. Shortly after the affair, the young woman sings the following "melancholy air":

When lovely woman stoops to folly,
>   And finds too late that men betray,
What charm can soothe her melancholy,
>   What art can wash her guilt away?

The only art her guilt to cover,
>   To hide her shame from every eye,
To give repentance to her lover,
>   And wring his bosom—is to die.

Glasgow's new woman neither defines her situation as comparable to the lovely woman's nor values Goldsmith's "art." Not a betrayed victim, Annabel Upchurch, who is something of a betrayer herself, is free to fly away. Furthermore, since neither the Goldsmith heroine nor Annabel wishes to (or does) sacrifice herself for her older, unworthy lover, neither is restrained by the outmoded fate of the song's "lovely woman." The Annabel—Judge Honeywell allusion is complicated further in *The Waste Land,* where love is reduced to a casual, commercial encounter and where Eliot alludes directly to Goldsmith:

She turns and looks a moment in the glass,
Hardly aware of her departed lover; . . .
When lovely woman stoops to folly and
Paces about her room again, alone,
She smoothes her hair with automatic hand,
And puts a record on the gramophone.

As in Eliot's wasteland, the postwar world of Judge Honeywell and Annabel Upchurch lacks meaning and value, and it ends in despair. Also, as in Eliot's wasteland but with very different emphasis, Glasgow places a male at the center of her imagery of meaninglessness and emotional poverty. If love has been reduced to its physical character in Eliot's poem, it has met a similar fate in Glasgow's novel, for Judge Honeywell's attraction to Annabel is shown by imagery to be merely physical fever. Waltzing with Annabel, feeling her "fragile body . . . helpless and clinging," the Judge experiences "this instinct of fatherhood, which, bursting suddenly from a seed of sympathy, had shot up like the fairy beanstalk in his mind—this prodigious instinct absorbed all that was tender, as well as all that was sublime, in his nature" (67). Talking with Annabel, he has "again the strange feeling of freshness . . . as if he were plunging into a virgin wilderness of experience" (70). Annabel may be as selfish and unconcerned with Judge Honeywell's feelings as Eliot's "lovely woman" is with those of her "departed lover." Yet the Judge is equally as unconcerned with Annabel's hopes and wishes, making Annabel as much the Judge's victim as Goldsmith's Olivia is Squire Thornhill's. And the Judge is as lascivious and ineffectual as his counterparts in Goldsmith and Eliot. Seen in a postwar context, all of Glasgow's characters are happiness hunters, and her novel concerns "the brittle nature of human happiness" (245). Glasgow gives the meaning and words of her title to Bella Upchurch:

> [I]t seemed to her that even the insidious irony of the modern point of view had scarcely damaged the popular superstition that love and happiness are interchangeable terms. . . . Judge Honeywell with his law and learning; Amanda with her exalted character and her simple wit; Annabel with her artless sophistication; . . . all this company of happiness-hunters appeared to be little better than a troupe of romantic comedians. (269)

Glasgow's further ironic use of *The Waste Land* is the one to which she must be referring in her prefatory remarks that her "happiness-hunters travel perpetually on roads that are circular and lead back again to the beginning" (216) and that her novel's "concluding paragraph . . . echoe[s] the keynote of the book, and reflect[s] the ironic mood" (207). *The Romantic Comedians* opens in spring, on Easter Sunday, as Judge Honeywell visits his first wife's grave. The sky is "a glimmering April blue," "fresh young leaves [are] sprinkling the gnarled old trees," and April is "burgeoning within" him (2). At Cordelia's graveside, experiencing and recollecting the "resurrection of Spring," he remembers another "April night when he had rushed to Amanda and implored her to go away with him" (13). "Only her steadfast virtue" and "her unswerving devotion to duty . . . had saved them both from disaster" (13). This time, however, there will be no one of steadfast virtue and unswerving devotion to duty to save him from his April stirrings. Annabel, of course, is associated with April: as the Judge's infatuation with her grows, he dreams of young girls dancing around him "beneath greenish skies" in "April meadows," then retreating "into the iridescent mist of April" (47).

The novel closes in April one year later, as Judge Honeywell bids farewell to his second wife and looks upon his young nurse as a potential candidate for wife number three and as Glasgow manipulates mood and tone to toy with the readers' expectations. Judge Honeywell has returned from New York, ill and dejected after his confrontation with and release of Annabel; he has gone to bed with his hot water bottle and feels he has "one foot in the grave already" (339). As he drifts in and out of consciousness and "his past life rushe[s] by him on the waves of an immense stream of illusion" (342), we anticipate with his physical death the conclusion of the novel's motif of the ephemeral, illusory na- ture of human perception and understanding.[3] We also feel great sym- pathy for the noble, old, rejected gentleman. But wait. In his delirium he is a child again waiting for his mother to tuck him into bed—but this ministering angel turns out to be his nurse, who is "[g]entle and young," "[f]resh, spotless, and womanly, in her white uniform, with the competent hands of a physician and the wise and tender touch of a mother" (345). Snapping back to full consciousness, he thinks, "There is the woman I ought to have married!" (345). And as his "vital sap" rises again, he realizes, "Spring is here, and I am feeling almost as young as I felt last year!" (346). Then follows the concluding paragraph that Glasgow describes as echoing the novel's "keynote": "Suddenly, be- neath the dark sunset, an apocalyptic light rained from the sky, and in this light all the tender little leaves of April were whispering together" (346).

April is Glasgow's keynote, April tied closely to Judge Honeywell and his epiphanies. And this keynote must bring to mind the opening lines of Eliot's *Waste Land:* "April is the cruellest month, . . . mixing / Memory and desire, stirring / Dull roots with spring rain." As C. Hugh Holman and others have pointed out, "those lines define in miniature the central fable of the Queenborough novels, and Miss Glasgow's emphasis on April cannot be accidental" (*Glasgow* 122). Those lines also describe the novel's circular structure and underscore its irony. As Linda W. Wagner notes, Glasgow's "interest" at this point in her career "lay in observing the cyclic and recurring patterns of romantic attraction" and in showing people's responses to "spring's dangerous liberation" (81–82). April is indeed the "cruellest month" for Glasgow's protago- nist, "mixing memory and desire," blind to the foolishness of his posi- tion, eternally hopeful of "stirring" his "dull roots," whose efforts to recapture youth by wooing young women are bound to fail. Eliot's wasteland has become a subject for comedy, filling in the outlines of a world in which the traditional underpinnings of love, faith, and hope have failed. And Glasgow's allusions to *The Waste Land* call attention to the postwar, modern condition *and* to the masculine point of view as sources of this cultural failure.

For if one cause for the demise of traditional values in this modern- ist wasteland is the war, another cause is the bankruptcy of male authority. The world that Glasgow has chosen to create in *The Romantic Comedians* is a world of women in orbit around one elderly Virginia gentleman about whom she appears to feel ambivalent. Yet the relative positions that these characters assume demonstrate the impoverishment and absurdity of conventional male views and the failure of the male imagination. Judge Honeywell does not esteem women of his own age and social standing either because they bore him by playing the subservient female role too well (Amanda Lightfoot, Cordelia Honeywell) or because they threaten him by failing to play it well enough (Edmonia Bredalbane, Bella Upchurch). His pursuit of the youthful, outspoken Annabel (together with the impending pursuit of his nurse) is rooted not in enlightened awareness but in vanity and egotism. He is driven by sexual energy and challenged by the prospect of subduing her to his will.

Annabel's story ends with the apparent victory of a new woman over old misogynist tradition. She flies off to Europe (throughout the novel the location of license, freedom, and escape) with Dabney Birdsong, a sketchily rendered new man who seems neither threatened by females who eschew traditional roles nor daunted by strong women. The narrator twice calls him a "strange young man" (268, 270); his strangeness lies probably in his newness. Glasgow even gives him androgynous traits; Bella Upchurch sees him as the young boy she remembers who had beautiful, long curls. But does the name "Dabney Birdsong" suggest that Dabney will remain a fitting companion for Annabel, the novel's only flying bird? Or is he companion, rather, to Glasgow's winged comic spirit, a precursor to George Birdsong in the third novel of Glasgow's Queenborough trilogy, a dashing, duplicitous character who betrays (remember the fate of Goldsmith's lovely woman) and destroys his wife? The novel's circular structure may point wittily and ironically not only to the return of Judge Honeywell's April stirrings but also to the recurrence of Annabel's springtime sexual alliance, or of Dabney Birdsong's. The action of this romantic comedy continues, circularly, into an uncertain and perhaps comically repetitious future.

Yet another cause for the demise of traditional values in this modernist wasteland is the new female power. However much the novel's new women may appear to view their freedom as a mixed blessing, they nevertheless embrace it with gusto, for they realize that they can be free not by assisting in the perpetuation of male standards but by engaging in self-discovery and self-creation. Like Eliot's females removed from the control of a male author (in both *The Waste Land* and "Prufrock"), Glasgow's new women are confident, unsentimental, and confounding to men. But in Glasgow's sexual exchanges, the laughter of the female characters, the narrator, and the author echoes beyond Eliot's brittle females and somber theme, deflating pretension, undermining male authority, and unbalancing postwar disillusionment. Says Bella Upchurch to her daughter, "There isn't any age, my dear, when men can't be [in love]. I'm not sure about women, because it has taken a world war to make women begin telling the truth about themselves, and they haven't told half yet" (287).

In *The Romantic Comedians*, the narrator (surely female, surely promulgating Glasgow's own point of view) and her female characters tell the truth. These women of flesh and of the imagination tell the truth about themselves and about their social and personal predicaments (even the women characters arrested in prewar attitudes tell the truth about themselves with the help of narrative irony). They also tell the truth about men, principally about one man, mainly about his hopes and insecurities and his anachronistic convictions and sexist beliefs, affording the distance for comedy by seeing that man more clearly than he does or could see himself. In calling attention to the absurdity of Judge Honeywell's point of view by means of literary allusion, ironic commentary, imagery, and circular structure, Glasgow shows the impotence of male authority. The truth these women tell demonstrates all the features to which Glasgow calls attention in her prefatory remarks; truth *is* "the upheaval of the post-war decade," and the telling of that truth is comic and witty, focused on manners and rooted in current events, ironic, and psychologically sound.

The Romantic Comedians is a romantic comedy whose happiness hunters redefine the serious love at its center. It is a comedy of manners that explores the options of women living in a wasteland and straining against the forces of twentieth-century disintegration. It is a morality play that exposes the paucity of inherited wisdom and the failure of prewar, male-dominated structures. And it is a "happy marriage of form and idea" (*Measure* 211) whose "delicate laughter with ironic echoes" (214) instructs and delights.

Notes

1. See also, for example, Linda W. Wagner's comment (in *Ellen Glasgow* 81) that in *The Romantic Comedians* "the Anderson figure (Judge Honeywell) is mocked rather than villainized." Or Kathryn Lee Seidel's discussion of satire in Glasgow's Queenborough trilogy, in which Judge Honeywell is "an entirely comic yet sympathetic character," an "unheroic parody of the hero," and "the fool who brings about his own punishment" ("The Comic Male" 18).

2. Carrington C. Tutwiler, Jr., Glasgow's nephew, reports in his *Catalogue of the Library of Ellen Glasgow* (7.87) that Glasgow owned several of Eliot's works, among them *The Waste Land* (New York: Boni, 1922).

3. Or we anticipate the conclusion, as Kathryn Lee Seidel puts it, of the novel's theme of "the victimization of the protagonist by the sexual impulse" (*Southern Belle* 86).

Works Cited

Auchincloss, Louis. *Ellen Glasgow*. Minneapolis: U of Minnesota P, 1964.

Glasgow, Ellen. "*The Romantic Comedians.*" *A Certain Measure: An Interpretation of Prose Fiction*. New York: Harcourt, 1943. 211–23.

———. "*The Sheltered Life.*" *A Certain Measure*. 189–210.

———. *The Romantic Comedians*. Garden City: Doubleday, 1926.

———. *The Woman Within*. New York: Harcourt, 1954.

Holman, C. Hugh. "The Comedies of Manners." *Ellen Glasgow: Centennial Essays*. Ed. M. Thomas Inge. Charlottesville: UP of Virginia, 1976. 108–28.

———. *A Handbook to Literature*. 4th ed. Indianapolis: Bobbs, 1980.

Seidel, Kathryn Lee. "The Comic Male: Satire in Ellen Glasgow's Queenborough Trilogy." *Southern Quarterly* 23.4 (Summer 1985): 15–26.

———. *The Southern Belle in the American Novel*. Tampa: U of South Florida P, 1985.

Tutwiler, Carrington C., Jr. *A Catalogue of the Library of Ellen Glasgow*. Charlottesville: Bibliographical Society of the U of Virginia, 1969.

Wagner, Linda W. *Ellen Glasgow: Beyond Convention*. Austin: U of Texas P, 1982.

Glasgow's Time in *The Sheltered Life*

Linda Wagner-Martin

If there is anything that readers of Ellen Glasgow's works agree on, it's the fact that she thought of herself as an anomaly. And she was, at least compared with many of her well-born, southern women friends, whose lives fed importantly into hers—and into her fiction—throughout her lifetime. It was the friendship of these devoted women relatives and friends that brought Glasgow to see how central to her life—to all women's lives—same-sex friendships were. As early as her 1913 novel, *Virginia,* she says of Virginia Pendleton and Susan Treadwell's love for each other, in phrases reminiscent of Carroll Smith-Rosenberg's findings: "they were intimate with that full and perfect intimacy which exists only between two women who trust each other" (517).

Glasgow began life immersed in women's experience, and many of the peak emotional events of her life occurred with other women: her mother, and the traumatic discovery of her husband's long-term affair with a mulatto lover; her sisters, especially Rebe and Cary—with whom Glasgow lived after the suicide of Cary's husband, until Cary's death from cancer in 1911—and countless good women friends in Richmond, New York, and Maine. In Glasgow's life, as in her fiction, heterosexual romance broke into that largely matriarchal lifestyle with the suddenness, and the threat, of an assault. Ellen Glasgow never married. She separated herself from her betraying father (and, accordingly, from the church); from the married man who was her first passion (a seven-year-long one); and from the two men to whom she later became engaged.

Reasonably, given this personal history, Glasgow lived an imaginative life that was also matriarchal. Few of the women protagonists in

---

With thanks to Kristeva for her concept of "women's time."

her fiction are married, even though the convention she was working in was often the romance novel. If protagonists marry, they usually do so at the end of the narrative, so that the reader does not have to see them as married and, probably, subordinate. Rather, Glasgow's women protagonists are often independent—and sometimes martyred. Cultural imperatives sometimes win out: Susan Treadwell, who wants nothing more than to go to college, ends up caring for her abused mother and waiting years for the man she loves to understand that he loves her. John Henry finally proposes, only to have her mother's health deteriorate. Susan's moment of independence comes when she confronts her powerful father to *tell* him she is marrying. (Years before, when she had *asked* him if she could go to college, he had said no.) His choice now is only whether John Henry will move in with the Treadwell family or whether Belinda, his wife, should make her home elsewhere, with Susan and John Henry. Susan is one of the few women in Glasgow's galaxy of protagonists who is able to demand both the passion of marriage to a man she loves and the right to fulfill her daughterly responsibility to her mother. She creates a matriarchal world, one in which nothing is dour or stinting.

Susan Treadwell is a key character because in many of Glasgow's early and middle novels, she pits a possibly destructive heterosexual romance against a supportive same-sex relationship. Male characters become invaders of the sane (if dull) matriarchal world, yet those male characters are seldom drawn as evil but rather as prizes for Glasgow's wistful women. No reviewer of her time saw Glasgow as writing feminist utopian fiction (what a matriarchal world without the male invasion might be like) or even noticed the fact that she was constructing a series of matriarchal worlds. In every one of her novels, the way to a positive resolution either was found, or could have been found, in women's bonding, in knowledge as drawn from women's intuition, and in the centrality of women's wisdom about both life values and time.

Ideas that sound most like Julia Kristeva's concepts of women's worlds and time are clearest in Glasgow's 1932 novel, *The Sheltered Life*, and go a long way toward explaining the narrative problems in that brilliant but sometimes troublesome book. In her opening scene, of the naive Jenny Blair Archbald lamenting the pokiness of Meg and Jo March in Alcott's *Little Women*, she affirms her own uniqueness ("but I'm different, I'm different") and also forms what Kristeva would later describe as "monumental time," an engulfing rhythm that includes chronological time but is not dependent on it (471). Jenny Blair's mystical experience with nature also acts to unify all parts of herself:

The book dropped from her hands, while her startled gaze flew to the topmost branch of the old sycamore in the garden. Deep pulsations of light were flooding the world. Very thin and clear through the May afternoon, there was the chime of distant bells striking the hour. Somewhere, without or within, a miracle had occurred. At the age of nine years and seven months, she had encountered the second important event in human experience. She was discovering her hidden self as once before, in some long forgotten past, she had discovered her body. "I don't care. I'm different," she repeated exultantly. (3–4)

Jenny may be only nine, but she already knows all she needs to know. She knows more than the men in the novel, her Grandfather Archbald and—later—her would-be lover, George Birdsong, and she shares what she knows with the book's enigmatic heroine, Eva Birdsong. It is, in fact, their shared knowledge that allows Eva to shape her anger into act; it is the preemption of Jennie Blair's "self" that is George Birdsong's greatest evil and the direct cause of his death.

Glasgow emphasizes this sacral relationship with self—both its attainment and its loss—throughout the book. She intensifies Jenny's joy through this self-knowledge in chapter 1; but she also places General Archbald, with all his financial and social power, in conflict with it: it is her grandfather who pays her for reading *Little Women*. It is General Archbald who "answers" all the household's questions, who provides the construct of information that keeps all the women in it—for the household, except for the General, is female—in the paternalistic protection that they, as women, "need." Early in *The Sheltered Life*, Jenny defies that protection, but she quickly learns that she, too, needs it when she goes roller-skating in the black section of Queenborough, falls, and is carried into the house of Memoria, the Birdsongs' laundress. There, to her surprise, she finds George Birdsong, and in the pact of secrecy he establishes with the adoring child begins Jenny Blair's co-optation. Her physical adventure (her mother and aunts would be shocked that she had skated so far, and in the black section of town) ends ironically in her emotional enslavement to the handsome George, a scene Glasgow describes at great length. Returning home, Jenny Blair tells her grandfather how "good" George Birdsong is (he has given her a kiss to seal their secret), and when she next visits Eva Birdsong, her erstwhile idol, she changes her loving refrain about Eva to this: "She is like roses and lilies. . . . She is like roses and lilies together—roses and lilies. . . . But I like Mr. Birdsong best. I like him best because we've a secret together" (70–71). Responsive to the message of her "required" reading and of her household, in which all women are desperate for marriage, Jenny Blair has been coerced by those sheltering maternal forces to succumb to male manipulation. She covers for George and his affair with Memoria. Worse, Jenny begins the flirtation that eventually leads to her complete enthrallment. George Birdsong, despite his name, is not what Annis Pratt would ever term a "green world lover." Rather than developing what she had already come to understand, on the first page of the book—her hidden self and her body—Jenny Blair becomes the slave of her friend Eva's betraying husband. She never again knows the same kind of "joy" she experienced as a child; she never again can express herself truthfully to anyone because the "secret" has taken over her identity and her life. She is only the girl/woman who has a secret with George Birdsong, and that secret is pervasively, invasively, sexual.

The Sheltered Life works on many levels of irony, but it also works as a poignant lament for the lost "garden" of female self-sufficiency, and as such it is a culmination of many of Glasgow's earlier works. Glasgow structures the work so that the reader attends to many of the patriarchal power alignments in society. For information of any kind, Jenny Blair goes increasingly to her grandfather, even though Glasgow shows from the start that Archbald lives in some isolated dream world of heterosexual romance. He does not move away from the deteriorating neighborhood, for example, because he wants to remain close to Eva Birdsong; yet he condones her husband's infidelities—even though they are literally killing Eva—because the male double standard is such an approved part of his social world. Jenny Blair gives up her knowledge of monumental time in order to be able to live within her grandfather's linear time. Glasgow begins the novel with Jenny immersed in what Kristeva terms "the massive presence of a monumental temporality, without cleavage or escape, which has so little to do with linear time (which passes) that the very word 'temporality' hardly fits: All-encompassing and infinite like imaginary space" (473).

Yet from this clear beginning, Glasgow shows Jenny Blair doing exactly as Kristeva describes: renouncing her "female subjectivity." As Kristeva notes, "female subjectivity as it gives itself up to intuition becomes a problem with respect to a certain conception of time: time as project, teleology, linear and prospective unfolding; time as departure, progression, and arrival—in other words, the time of history" (473). Glasgow's novel is nothing more in its second half than these departures and reunions, Jenny Blair's time spent waiting for George Birdsong's acknowledgment, his caress, his kiss. Time in *The Sheltered Life* passes filled with seemingly reassuring words: George's words, General Archbald's words, and the all too seldom heard Eva's words. Eva, as might be expected in this culture, has difficulty saying things straight out because what she is forced to say undermines—declares valueless—her own existence. In contrast, George and General Archbald, through lying, talk a great deal as they reinscribe their behavior as appropriate. Again, Kristeva: "It might also be added that this linear time is that of language considered as the enunciation of sentences (noun + verb; topic-comment; beginning-ending), and that this time rests on its own stumbling block, which is also the stumbling block of that enunciation—death" (473).

All the explaining, rationalizing, and manipulation of speech in this novel, echoed so pitifully by the maturing (yet growing down) Jenny Blair, pales to nothing beside Eva Birdsong's final act. Seen in a passionate embrace with George, Jenny Blair is caught between the ecstasy of his avowal and the meaning—wordless as it is—of Eva Birdsong's gaze. George tells her:

> "I do care. You can see that I care. Haven't I cared for months? Haven't I cared until I am almost out of my mind?" His arms were round her, and looking up she saw a single vein beating like a pulse in his forehead. "You know I care," he said over and over, as if he were suffocated by words, and in his voice, too, she felt the throbbing of anguish.
>
> Then, suddenly, while her whole being vibrated, a shudder jerked through his muscles, and she was left there, alone and abandoned, as his arms dropped from her body. From the horror in his face, she knew, before she spun round, that Mrs. Birdsong was looking at them out of the dusk in the library. (390)

Words interrupted by the gaze, Jenny Blair casts her beloved "Eva" into the role of "Mrs. Birdsong," the married woman as adversary. The protected young woman is bereft, but her emptiness is nothing compared with the desiccation Glasgow depicts for Eva Birdsong:

> Frozen, expressionless, grey as a shadow, she smiled through them and beyond them to the empty horizon. For an instant time paused. Then she said in a voice that was as vacant as her smile, "George, I want you," and turned slowly back into the room. Without a rustle, as soundlessly as she had come, she turned away, and was sucked in by the twilight. (390–91)

Eva's words are sexual, though she appears as a ghost, silent, evanescent, moving outside human time, so fragile that she is "sucked in" by her surroundings. Jenny's reactions, to follow, chart her recognition of Eva's anger, her realization of the falsity of language, and of her own corrupt existence outside both time and space.

> "No! No!" Jenny Blair cried, and flung out her hand, as if she were push-
> ing aside a moment too terrible to be borne. She was alone and deserted
> in space. Without a word to her, without so much as a look, George
> had followed his wife into the house. (391)

Jenny Blair's knowledge, her being brought back to the state of monumental time, of all knowledge, through the gaze, the act of comprehending—separate from, sometimes betrayed by, the existence of linear time and language—this is the true ending of Glasgow's fine novel. That the rest of the book is filled with words, apologies, lies, as grandfather, doctor, and Jenny Blair herself try to create a scene other than the one that exists—and deserves to exist, as truth—is more of Glasgow's deft irony.

That same irony led to her mistitling the three sections of the novel, and it is the middle section, devoted to General Archbald's story, that has caused so many critical problems. It was only 1932, and Glasgow was still deferential about novelistic conventions. She labeled each of the three parts of the book as if from a patriarchal perspective (or perhaps the irony of her labeling was a part of the subversive text she often managed to write). Part 1, the clearest statement of the maturing female sense of self, is entitled "The Age of Make-Believe." (By the end of the section, of course, Jenny Blair is well on her way to her enslavement to Birdsong.) I would rather call it "The Education of Jenny [Henry] Archbald [Adams]."

Part 2, the story of General Archbald's mockingly sad relinquishment of passion for the mandates of polite society, is called "The Deep Past"—and it is that, so deep, so immured in tradition and pastness, in the rigid forms of the patriarchy, that Archbald can do nothing but live out his years in obeisance to those sterile social forms. Of Archbald's self-pitying reminiscence, again consider Kristeva's words as she says that many of us are trapped in "obsessional time": "The hysteric (either male or female) who suffers from reminiscences would, rather, recognize his or her self in the anterior temporal modalities: cyclical or monumental" (473). Rather than "The Deep Past," this segment might have been titled with either of Glasgow's other two section titles—"The Age of Make-Believe" or simply "Illusion."

The last, "Illusion," with its biting applicability to everyone—Eva, General Archbald, George, and Jenny Blair—ends with the shockingly realistic scene, and the death, of the patriarch, George, *blood* on his lips here rather than words, murdered by the woman he had "protected" and "loved" for such a long lifetime.

Glasgow gives us a probing story, a strangely contemporary story, especially in Eva's evolution to self through her love for someone other than herself, her love for her only "child," Jenny Blair. The bond between the two is the heart of the novel; in many places, it becomes the "plot." Again, Kristeva: "The arrival of the child . . . leads the mother into the labyrinths of an experience that, without the child, she would only rarely encounter: love for an other. Not for herself, nor for an identical being, and still less for another person with whom 'I' fuse (love or sexual passion). But the slow, difficult, and delightful apprenticeship in attentiveness, gentleness, forgetting oneself" (482). Eva comes to understand her own life by trying to explain it—and all women's lives—to Jenny Blair. She thinks she is sharing her hard-won, bitter wisdom with this girl who is her surrogate, same-sex, constant friend/child. She is giving Jenny Blair all that she has to give. The tragedy of Jenny Blair's co-optation by the very man who has ruined and devalued *her* life is the event Eva cannot blink from her gaze.

What of the question of Eva's murdering George? Again, Kristeva:

> Let us remember here that Hegel distinguished between female right (familial and religious) and male law (civil and political). If our societies know well the uses and abuses of male law, it must also be recognized that female right is designated, for the moment, by a blank. (481)

We return to the pervasive question of the woman writer's inscribing a traditional form and text with her own message, using disguise and subtext to signal meanings that might read differently for male and female readers, sympathetic readers and unsympathetic. It is hardly accidental that Glasgow often wrote about young, developing women; that she shaped the *bildungsroman* into a female story; that she focused her ostensibly domestic novels into more gender-based structures, so that she could come again and again to the basic truth that this novel, and many others of hers, presents. In Kristeva's language, Glasgow's primary concern is with "the complexity of the female experience, with all that this complexity comprises in joy and pain" (481).

The use of a child in fiction allows the writer to show a full complement of maternal qualities. As Kristeva claims, "studies on the acquisition of the symbolic function by children show that the permanence and quality of maternal love condition the appearance of the first spatial references which induce the child's laugh and then induce the entire range of symbolic manifestations which lead eventually to sign and syntax" (472). Our language, our joy, our mental processes—what more would a woman writer care about, want to give readers information about, in her own surrogate child, her fiction? For Glasgow knew, as does Kristeva, who wrote in another 1980s essay, "My Memory's Hyperbole":

> The eruptions, encounters, loves, passions, as well as the more or less liberated or controlled eroticism that have shaped each person's biography constitute, I am convinced, the deepest influence on an individual path. (275)

And finally, no matter what our geographical or chronological experiences in space and time, we are all brought back into "the only continent we had never left: internal experience."

Ellen Glasgow brings us back to that continent through deft structuring, ironic yet seemingly straightforward dialogue, and an indictment of the patriarchy—complete with its love of linear time—that makes *The Sheltered Life* a novel remarkable for its insights and its timelessness.

Works Cited

Glasgow, Ellen. *The Sheltered Life.* Garden City: Doubleday, 1932.

———. *Virginia.* Garden City: Doubleday, 1913.

Kristeva, Julia. "My Memory's Hyperbole." Trans. Athena Viscusi. *The Female Autograph.* Ed. Domna C. Stanton. New York: New York Literary Forum, 1984. 261–76.

———. "Women's Time." *Critical Theory since 1965.* Ed. Hazard Adams and Leroy Searle. Tallahassee: Florida State UP, 1986. 469–84.

Pratt, Annis V. *Archetypal Patterns in Women's Fiction.* Bloomington: Indiana UP, 1981.

Consciousness, Gender, and Animal Signs in *Barren Ground* and *Vein of Iron*

Catherine Rainwater

Several of Ellen Glasgow's novels, especially *Barren Ground* (1925) and *Vein of Iron* (1935), are replete with animal tropes and references. Many of Glasgow's characters not only show affection for their dogs, horses, sheep, and chickens, but also seem to embody traits of the animals they tend. In turn, some of the animals in Glasgow's novels have such fully developed personalities that they appear almost like minor characters. Glasgow's fondness for animals is well known. As her reading in science and philosophy reveals, however, her interest in animals extends far beyond ordinary attachment to pets.[1]

Glasgow's fiction, her personal writings, and most overtly, her review of Virginia Woolf's *Flush: A Biography* (of Elizabeth Barrett Browning's dog) indicate that she saw in animals evidence of consciousness and subjective states unacknowledged by most human observers. Glasgow writes:

> With her firm, swift strokes, Mrs. Woolf has stripped away all the thinking and the talking about life, and has dealt with the sight, sound, touch, taste and smell of life itself. . . . [S]he has crossed the imaginary boundaries of psychology, and has portrayed a sensitive and emotional but inarticulate being. . . . To one who has observed canine psychology from earliest childhood, who has studied the responses of animals not in a laboratory, where fear paralyzes the mind and distorts the personality, but in a long association so free and natural that it has been possible, in some instances, to establish a means of communication woven partly of sounds or signs and partly of intuitions—to such an observer Mrs. Woolf's narrative will appear remarkable for its fidelity. (Raper, *Reasonable Doubts* 184–85)

These comments suggest that like the ethicist Mary Midgley, Glasgow sees human ignorance about the consciousness of the animal Other as insufficient grounds for denying the existence of such consciousness, which reveals itself "to one who . . . observe[s]." Indeed, some of the most unique narrative features of Glasgow's texts focus reader attention on the act of observing animals. Glasgow's remarks on Woolf's book also suggest her sense of a cognitive link between animals and human beings, many of whose differences, she implies, are exaggerated by the "imaginary boundaries of psychology."

In entertaining this notion, she anticipates the views of such contemporary figures as Paul Shepard, ethologist, and Thomas Sebeok, semiotician and pioneer in the field of "zoosemiotics."[2] Shepard argues that humans and animals share many of the same cognitive traits and that, indeed, human consciousness arose and evolved partially through human interactive observation of animals. According to Shepard, animals are important "in the growth and development of the human person, and in [the development of] those most priceless qualities which we lump together as 'mind.' . . . [A]nimal images and forms . . . [shape] personality, identity, and social consciousness. Animals are among the first inhabitants of the mind's eye" (2), and they "help to secure the polarity between the self and nonself" (24). In essence, Shepard posits a fundamental relationship between animals and humans that speaks volumes about the human (and animal) negotiation of identity and Otherness.

Along comparable avenues of inquiry, Sebeok has defined "specular semiotics" as the practice of generating meaning by looking at objects (including animals) in the world; such exterior objects become "iconic spatial expressions" of meaning and are often internalized as representations of self. These representations help one to construct and maintain the "*Umwelt*" or "self-world," which includes one's interior reality as well as a sense of the reality of "the-world-about-me" (Sebeok, *American Signatures* 43, 181).[3]

Much of Glasgow's writing suggests a keen awareness of such complexity in the human relationship to animals as Shepard and Sebeok investigate in their works. Indeed, throughout her life, Glasgow was fascinated by Darwin's apparent concern with animal consciousness and the implications of Darwin's thought for an expanded, pan-species morality. She was also well aware that the Western rationalist tradition led scientists and philosophers of her own and other eras to ignore this vein of Darwin's thought (which has, in fact, been pursued only in fairly recent years by ethologists).[4] Objecting particularly to Spinoza's quintessentially rationalist arguments concerning animals, Glasgow writes in her copy of his works that "the weakness of almost all Western philosophy" is the "belief that man is of a different creation from the rest of Nature" (Tutwiler 1.30). In an essay called "I Believe" (1938), Glasgow reiterates this conviction and hopes that Darwinism may one day lead human beings to "extend [justice] even into the animal kingdom" (Raper, *Reasonable Doubts* 230).[5]

Over the years, the relationship of "man," and especially of woman, to "the rest of Nature" and "the animal kingdom" apparently commands increased amounts of Glasgow's attention. A semiotic network of animal references unites nearly all of her novels, especially *Barren Ground* and *Vein of Iron*. Focusing on Glasgow's animal signs discloses a subtle textual level of her novels; at this level she most profoundly considers various enigmas of consciousness that interest her as an avid reader of philosophy, religion, science, and evolutionary theory. These preoccupy her as a female author struggling to think and write against the rationalistic, patriarchal grain of the early twentieth-century American milieu.[6]

Animal signs occur at key junctures in *Barren Ground* and *Vein of Iron:*

1. when the stability of self and world is threatened;
2. when a self confronts the subjectivity of the Other (especially the male Other) and finds it inaccessible to communication;
3. when women characters and narrators (some of whom are, arguably, personae of Glasgow herself) begin to empower themselves and to transcend socially and culturally imposed female silence; and
4. when a character struggles toward a conscious philosophy of compassion for humanity.

In each case, Glasgow's narrative preoccupation with animal signs amounts to a form of "specular semiotics" that highlights her sense of the fundamental importance of the act of looking at animals in the cognitive process of sustaining interior and exterior reality.

From her first novel, *The Descendant* (1897), begun when she was only eighteen, to her last, *In This Our Life* (1941), Glasgow pursues questions about consciousness and human identity.[7] Beginning with the tormented Michael Akershem in *The Descendant*, Glasgow's protagonists are variously perplexed by the sudden turns of fate that shatter their sense of external reality as well as their confidence in an internally stable self. Perhaps more emphatically than any of Glasgow's other novels, *Barren Ground* suggests that consciousness and the sense of a distinctive "self" are not the same and that, indeed, the sense of a coherent, unassailable personal identity is only a fragile, though useful, illusion. Her reading of David Hume, in particular, may have led her to investigate the ways in which "sensation" and "habit" (words on which her narrators repeatedly dwell) evoke an illusory sense of a discrete self that is coterminous with consciousness.[8] Animal signs are a chief means through which Glasgow inscribes and negotiates perceived threats to the stability of self and *Umwelt*.

Early in *Barren Ground*, Dorinda Oakley discovers the vulnerability of self to alien, frequently hostile forces:

> By some accident, for which nothing in her past experience had prepared her, all the laws of her being, thought, will, memory, habit, were suspended. In their place a force which was stronger than all these things together, a force with which she had never reckoned before, dominated her being. *The powers of life had seized her as an eagle seizes its prey.* (29; emphasis added)

Though this passage refers specifically to Dorinda's sudden awareness of being in love, Glasgow represents this awareness in terms not much different from those describing purely negative experience. Emphasizing the uncomfortable *phenomenon of a break* with a familiar past rather than the positive or negative *nature of the break*, Glasgow inscribes Dorinda's experience within a predator-prey code that runs throughout the text and suggests that sudden change of any kind can make one feel like a victim who has lost control (or perhaps only the illusion of control) over her destiny.

This code of predator and prey likewise emerges in *Vein of Iron*. Ada Fincastle discovers how ephemeral one's sense of self can be when she learns that her fiancé, Ralph, will marry another woman. Ada

> stared through tears at a soaring hawk, which swooped suddenly, flashed downward like a curved blade in the air, and seized a small bird—or it may have been one of Aunt Meggie's chickens—in its claws before it swept upward and onward. And she felt that the same claws had seized her heart out of her breast, and had swept away with it over the sunny land, over the tranquil blue of the hills. Until this moment of anguish, she had felt that she was a part of the Valley, of its religion, its traditions, its unspoken laws, as well as of its fields and streams and friendly mountains. (161)

These passages from *Barren Ground* and *Vein of Iron* emphasize a sudden rupture in the flow of experience that alters a character's feelings of stability and belonging. Abruptly, such characters become aware of irreversible separation and difference from the world and the self of

only a moment before. Thus Glasgow suggests that while consciousness flows on continuously, its constructions—self, world, Other—may
disintegrate without warning.

At such moments, her characters often engage in acts of specular
semiosis. They organize, interpret, and imagistically express the sensation of threat in terms of the iconized, primordial experience of being
either predator or prey. Thus they reconstruct or shore up the *Umwelt*
through specular semiosis involving iconized animal behavior. Indeed,
according to Shepard and other animal behaviorists, identifying oneself with either predator or prey helps "to secure the polarity between
the self and nonself" (Shepard 24), and thus to decide on appropriate
reactions. (Shepard points out that intelligent predators do not search
at random, but "define" themselves as predators partly by looking for
signs of the prey; likewise, intelligent prey see the signs of the predator
and often develop strategies for escape that "define" their prey status.
Both activities show how one entity's identity partially derives from its
response to the Other.)

Barren Ground and *Vein of Iron* are especially rich in examples of
Glasgow's management of animal signs to "secure the polarity between
[a character's or narrator's] self and nonself" (Shepard 24). Glasgow
frequently presents to the reader a perceiving consciousness (usually a
narrator) who describes characters defining themselves or others in the
role of the prey, usually small, domesticated, or otherwise vulnerable animals. In the previously quoted passages, the narrators equate Dorinda and
Ada with "prey" (the threatened self) seized by an eagle and a hawk (the
threatening nonself), respectively.

In *Barren Ground*, we also learn that Dorinda finds sympathy for
her inarticulate, passive father as she compares his "humble, friendly eyes"
to "the eyes of a dog that is uncertain whether he is about to receive a pat
or a blow" (54). Furthermore, the narrator describes Dorinda herself as "a
mouse in the trap of life" (56) whom "solitude," a predatory "beast," lies
"waiting for the right moment to spring and devour" (57). Such passages
illustrate the narrator's tendency to represent threatening situations in
terms of iconized animal images and, as we shall presently see, to deal
with such situations in ways that empower (or re-empower) the "prey."

One particular passage in *Barren Ground* clearly exemplifies such an
act of self-definition and self-empowerment through looking at animals.
Sitting at family prayers one evening, Dorinda feels especially "trapped":

> Motionless, in her broken splint-seated chair, scarcely daring to breathe,
> Dorinda felt as if she were floating out of the scene into some world of
> intenser reality. . . . She saw Joshua bending forward . . . his eyes fixed

in a pathetic groping stare, as if he were trying to follow the words. The look was familiar to her; she had seen it in the wistful expressions of Rambler [the dog] and of Dan and Beersheba, the horses. . . . On opposite sides of the fireplace, Josiah and Rufus [her brothers] were dozing. . . . Curled on the rag carpet, Rambler and Flossie [the cat] watched each other with wary intentness, Rambler contemplative and tolerant, Flossie suspicious and superior. The glow and stillness of the room enclosed the group in a circle that was like the shadow of a magic lantern. . . . Outside, in the fields, a dog barked, and Rambler raised his long, serious head from the rug and listened. (47)

The faces and attitudes of her parents and brothers evoke Dorinda's internalized, sympathetic images of animals. In her father she sees the look of dogs and horses, and she sees her brothers "curled" up, much like the dog and cat, within the "circle." Conversely, she looks at the animals and sees in them the mirror reflections of her own and other human family members' perceived qualities. (Rambler is "contemplative and tolerant," and Flossie is "suspicious and superior.")

This passage also implies that looking at animals is for Glasgow a way not only of interpreting but also of negotiating human problems. The family circle is too confining for Dorinda. Generally impatient with religion and wanting to escape the "trap" of the farm, Dorinda fears and resents this domestic routine because it threatens to define her entire life and thus to deny her autonomy and identity. Like the dog's, Dorinda's attention is drawn by compelling forces "in the fields" outside the domestic scene—Rambler's by the literal call of another dog, and Dorinda's by the emotional call of Jason Greylock, with whom she has recently fallen in love and will later meet "in the fields." Since the narrator has already attributed to Rambler a "contemplative and tolerant" personality, the semiotic equation of Dorinda with Rambler— through their mutual distraction—inscribes Dorinda with those same traits and justifies her feelings of domestic discontent. Her desire to escape to the "fields" of romance is the desire of a thoughtful and reasonable entity, unnaturally confined within the "family circle." Though Dorinda's guilt prevents her from justifying her rebellion in human terms, the narrator makes justification available through another—animal—frame of reference or, in other words, through an act of specular semiosis. Dorinda sees her own situation reflected in the situation of the family animals, in whom she can justify rebellion against suffocating domesticity.

Through an allusion to a magic lantern, an early type of image-projection device, this same passage also implies Glasgow's awareness of the specular-semiotic characteristics of consciousness. Glasgow's reference to "the shadow of a magic lantern" is an apt metaphor for human consciousness engaged in specular semiosis; the perceiver looks to the external world of visible forms, which are internalized as iconic representations of concepts and qualities associated with such forms. These representations are, in turn, "projected" outwardly again as part of an interpretive frame of reference for organizing experience. Thus Glasgow's narrator organizes the narrative world through animal signs that are a means used by the "magic lantern" of consciousness to conceptualize and resolve problems in the external world.

Semiotic "projections" or transfers of traits or experiences between animals and humans are often Glasgow's means of negotiating a critical moment, in this case Dorinda's moment of desire to escape the trap of her domestic existence for the fields of romance and adventure. Later, however, we will see how in *Barren Ground* and *Vein of Iron,* animal signs also indicate a transformation of the desire for flight into a desire for autonomy within a revised domestic scene. Within this revised scene, Glasgow's female protagonists see themselves not as trapped but, on the contrary, as dominant figures in control of their worlds. They have sacrificed adventure for a security which implies compromise with but not submission to a dominant Other (whether this Other is a person, such as a husband, or a place, such as a farm).

Even richer in animal references than *Barren Ground, Vein of Iron* likewise represents and manages crises of stability through animal signs. Furthermore, in the latter novel, animal signs reveal Glasgow's attempts to investigate and sometimes to reduce the liminal space between the self and an Other who is perceived as a threat to the self. In the opening pages of the novel, the integrity of Ada's self is threatened by Toby, a retarded boy who reminds her of a "rabbit" and whom she fears because she identifies with him as an existential victim. One day, young Ada defends Toby from the other children who taunt and humiliate him:

> In a flash of vision it seemed to her that she and Toby had changed places, that they [the children] were chasing her over the fields. . . .
> But it wasn't the first time she had felt like this. Last summer she had seen a rabbit torn to pieces by hounds . . . and she had heard it cry out like a baby. She had watched its eyes throbbing with fear and pain, like small, terrified hearts. (Glasgow, *Vein of Iron* 4–5)

Reducing the distance between the otherwise "repulsive" Other (Toby) and Ada, the narrator shows us how Ada first imagines Toby as a small, defenseless animal, with whom she can sympathize. Ada reminds herself that Toby is "a creature like herself . . . born, as she and an animal were born, to crave joy, to suffer loss, and to know nothing beyond" (166). Ada overcomes revulsion and *fear of* Toby by understanding a *fear* she shares *with* him. In Ada's eyes, she and the retarded child share a common status as "prey": "Horror waited everywhere to pounce upon happiness, as the hawk had pounced upon the small bird" (167–68).

Such passages suggest that for Glasgow, despite the obvious violence inherent in animal life, the animal world is more easily comprehended than the human world. Perhaps because the fundamental relationships among animals are apparently more clearly delineated (as in predator-prey relations) than those among humans, animals often seem to represent for Glasgow a lesser extreme of alterity than do other humans. Ironically (as we shall presently see), animal alterity might appear less extreme to Glasgow because of animals' conspicuous lack of verbal language. Indeed, in many instances rewarding our speculation, Glasgow's narrators negotiate crises of human communication through a semiotic system of animal signs *re-presenting* human behavior and situations and, simultaneously, mediating and reducing the threat posed by the noncommunicative Other. Thus it is hardly surprising that in *Barren Ground* and *Vein of Iron,* novels in which males are typically represented as noncommunicative, issues of gender-difference are likewise frequently negotiated through animal signs.

Animal signs display important semiotic functions at moments when a self (usually female) confronts the subjectivity of the human Other, especially a male, and finds it apparently inaccessible to communication. Glasgow's animal signs often function to reduce male Otherness in relation to a female perceiver; understanding male behavior in animal terms apparently renders less infuriating such males' inability or refusal to communicate in spoken language.

As we have seen, Glasgow's review of Virginia Woolf's *Flush: A Biography* suggests that having no spoken language does not necessarily make animals absolutely Other to humans. Indeed, the review implies that she finds animals perhaps more comprehensible and certainly more sympathetic than humans, despite or possibly owing to animals' lack of verbal language. Glasgow admires Woolf for "cross[ing] the imaginary boundaries of psychology," for "stripp[ing] away all the thinking and the talking about life," and for "deal[ing] with the sight, sound, touch, taste and smell of life itself" (Raper, *Reasonable Doubts* 184). She credits Woolf with recognizing some fundamental ground of experience or dimension of sentient life that, unlike spoken language, is common to human and nonhuman entities alike.

Glasgow's works repeatedly depict characters, especially female characters, longing for a state of transparent knowledge of an Other such as Glasgow describes in this review of Woolf's book. These characters often find that the same capacity for language that makes human communication possible also, ironically, prevents such transparent human relationships. Glasgow shows how humans (particularly males) seem inevitably to use language and its semiotic supplement, silence, deliberately to impose barriers to communication. In *Barren Ground,* Jason's lies, verbal evasions, and finally his almost total silence lead Dorinda to conclude that human reserve is "impenetrable" (497); and in *Vein of Iron,* Ralph marries Janet instead of Ada because of a lie that he covers with silence. However, in both books, Glasgow treats gender-oriented communication problems within a semiotic frame of reference composed of animal signs. Within this frame of reference, male failure to communicate becomes much less a source of frustration when it is identified with animal silence. Once again, Glasgow's recourse to animal signs reduces the distance between a self and a threatening or unknowable Other and reintroduces stability to an *Umwelt* under siege by otherwise inexplicable forces.

In *Barren Ground,* for example, Dorinda returns to the farm from New York when her father is ill: "How immeasurably far away he seemed! How futile was any endeavor to reach him! Then she remembered that he had always been far away, that he had always stood just outside the circle in which they lived, as if he were a member of some affectionate but inarticulate animal kingdom" (261). Dorinda's recollection replaces frustration with a wordless empathy between her and Joshua, as in the old days when Dorinda saw her father "talking to [his horses] . . . in the tone a man uses only to the creatures who speak and understand the intimate language of his heart" (95).

In Glasgow's universe, communication problems characterize males precisely because most men apparently seem to Glasgow not only less capable of communicating but also less willing to communicate than women. In *Barren Ground,* even Dorinda's favorite stepson, John Abner, irritates her because, like Glasgow's typical male, he resists Dorinda's efforts to discuss important issues but, nevertheless, expects to be understood: "Although he said little, for he was never a great talker, she had observed that his face wore a look of severe disapprobation" (474). Fortunately, John Abner, like Dorinda's father, shares some animal traits that help Dorinda to overlook his gender traits. He is an endearing "lame duck" (342). He has a great sympathy with animals ("one of the strongest bonds between" him and Dorinda [360–61]), and he resembles his father, Nathan, who has eyes like a gentle dog (355).

John Abner and other sympathetically portrayed males in Glasgow's fiction are often semiotically equated with animals—a favorable equation in Glasgow's narrative universe. Indeed, partially because Jason Greylock has no animal traits, Dorinda concludes after many years that he is completely inaccessible. As Jason dies of acute alcoholism, he sits all day in the sun, rarely speaking. Unlike the distance between Dorinda and her dying father, however, the distance between Dorinda and Jason cannot be diminished through recourse to animal signs, for Jason is a male without any animal "language" of the "heart." Dorinda speaks to Jason only to inquire, "parrot-like" (497), whether he feels pain; his inaccessibility transforms *her*, but not him, into an "animal"—a bird that is conventionally associated with humanlike but apparently noncommunicative speech.

Difficulties of communication are similarly represented through animal signs in *Vein of Iron*. Ralph and his wife, Janet, "quarreled like bluejays" (188). Meanwhile, Ada keeps silent about her grief over the loss of Ralph to Janet. Her father, John Fincastle (one of Glasgow's idealized male characters who *does* communicate), expresses sympathy for his silent daughter in animal terms: "He felt her suffering as he felt the inarticulate distress of a child or an animal" (125). Later, when Ada is pregnant, unwed, and a shame to her mother and grandmother, John advises her to "walk with sheep instead of human beings for the next few months. There is something companionable about animals, even about sheep, that human beings lack" (251). Ultimately adopting a kind of mystical silence as a response to life, John decides shortly before he dies that "[p]ure philosophy," like the language of companionable animals, "is a wordless thing" (427).

All good men in *Barren Ground* and *Vein of Iron* are, like John, identified with animals and represented through animal signs by Glasgow's narrators. In the latter novel, Otto Bergen emerges as one of Glasgow's most significant male characters, despite his minor role in the plot. The discourse describing him signals a major transformation of Glasgow's attitude toward the "trap" of domesticity and of both male and female roles within the domestic scene.

The Bergens are Ada's favorite neighbors. The narrator explains that Otto Bergen exhibited

> the German friendliness for animals. His workshop in the basement sheltered, to the delight of Ranny and other children on the block, a variety of pets he had rescued from ill-treatment. Not only was there his superb parrot on its stand, but the big cage contained a whole community of trained white mice. He was never seen apart from his slender little dachshund, Hans, with a coat like brown satin and a long wise head, as flawless and fine as a cameo. (Glasgow, *Vein of Iron* 297)

Typical of Glasgow's depiction of sympathetic males, Otto is represented primarily through his association with animals. He has a devoted dog companion, rescues abused pets, and protects and trains a community of white mice.

Despite their confinement, Otto's animals are nevertheless depicted not as "trapped" but as cheerfully domesticated. Moreover, as a compassionate caretaker of animals, Otto resembles a benevolent, godlike figure in a revised, domestic universe. He is a "round, genial man, with a pleasant smile" who has "transformed a grimy back yard into the only flower garden in Mulberry Street" (280). Such descriptions of Otto Bergen and his household imply a transformation of Glasgow's earlier-expressed negative attitudes toward domesticity. Indeed, particularly in its conclusion, *Vein of Iron* suggests an ideal, female-dominated human order based on the example of Otto Bergen and his pets.

In the closing pages of *Vein of Iron,* congenial language positively representing animal domestic community describes Ralph and Ada's reconciliation after long years of emotional estrangement. Recalling Dorinda in *Barren Ground,* who ultimately rejects the city for the farm, Ralph and Ada return to Ada's old home to resume the rural life of their youth. However, a wild "menagerie" (*Vein of Iron* 458) has invaded the long-unoccupied farm house, and a "fantasy of impotence, of failure . . . ha[s] built its nest in the lower levels of [Ralph's] consciousness" (365). Just as the invasion of the house by wild creatures results from disruption of the Fincastle family's domestic scene, Ralph's physical and emotional illness partly results from disrupted domestic relations: he marries the wrong woman, goes off to war, and later (after divorce and remarriage to Ada) has an affair with one of Otto Bergen's daughters. All of these problems are semiotically condensed in the image of a wild bird's nest in the otherwise domesticated "house" of Ralph's mind and in the image of the "menagerie" in the farmhouse.

Ralph and Ada attempt to renovate the old house and to repair their marriage and Ralph's mind—all acts of domestic restoration. Driving the inappropriate occupants (wild bird and "nest") from the "lower levels" of Ralph's "consciousness" and from the actual house means restoring wildness to its proper place on the margins of domesticity. Moreover, this act of restoration clearly establishes Ada as the dominant figure in the domestic scene. Like John Abner and Jason in *Barren Ground,* Ralph is incapacitated and requires Ada's benevolent caretaking.

Such scenes of revised and restored domestic order place previously victimized female characters in positions of power. Glasgow devises a narrative order reflecting the ideal order of the farm, presided over by a female, compassionate steward of domesticated animals, including

noncommunicative but sympathetic males. The narrator and her female characters, as articulate wielders of domestic power, preside over
an "affectionate but inarticulate animal kingdom" (*Barren Ground* 261),
much like the idealized Otto Bergen presides over a house full of pets.

Glasgow's traffic in animal signs suggests the specular-semiotic process
by which her narrators establish this narrative order of revised, female-
centered domestication. We may trace a pattern of animal signs showing
how, gradually, Glasgow's narrators attempt to drive "wildness" to the
margins of the narrative universe. The predator-prey code, so prevalent
in the opening chapters of both books, is gradually balanced by the
tender-and-tended code: the "tender" is most often a powerful female,
while the "tended" include both animals and inarticulate but sympathetic males. In *Barren Ground,* for example, Dorinda ultimately prevails
over a "lame duck" stepson who, like a domestic animal, contributes to
the human community but also requires its care. She is also in the position to choose whether and when Bob Ellgood, whom she sees as a
"sleek, mild-mannered Jersey bull" (283), will be a part of her life. Likewise, in *Vein of Iron,* Ada tends Ralph, now a benign, uncommunicative
male in need of her care, specifically in need of her help to overcome
"impotence"—a result of his "wild" transgressions against domesticity—
that had "built its nest" in his mind.

Establishing an ideal order of gynecocentric domesticity, Glasgow's
animal signs further signal the beginning of female transcendence of
socially and culturally imposed silence. Her narrative order might also
hint at the shape of Glasgow's own *Umwelt,* as well as at the process
by which she sought to sustain it. Glasgow is justifiably equated with
the narrating voices of most of her novels. The earliest of these novels
suggest that she struggled to imagine free and outspoken female characters and to break free of the stereotypes of female behavior that she
apparently accepted as a young woman. For example, in *The Descendant,* her first novel, a rebellious "new woman" type of character gives
up her career for an exploitative male and suffers silently as a victim of
love. In *The Voice of the People* (1900), published three years later, an
intelligent, strong woman nevertheless chooses (appropriately, it is implied, though not without some hesitation) a traditional, southern female
role over a nonconformist marriage beneath her social class. By age 52,
however, when Glasgow writes *Barren Ground,* her ideas about women
have decidedly altered. Her protagonists such as Dorinda and (ten years
later) Ada not only make independent choices and decisions, they also
speak their minds even when they are likely to be censured for it.

Semiotically forecasting such actions and speech, references to the
voices of animals often occur at strategic moments in both *Barren*

Ground and *Vein of Iron* when female characters are poised to reject traditional female behavior and silence. When Dorinda learns that Jason has married Geneva, she at first feels like an animal victim, suffering a "dumbness" like "paralysis," while only "instinct . . . remain[s] alive in her" (*Barren Ground* 149). Gradually, however, sheer force of will drives her to Jason's house. Along the way, she hears the "hoot of an owl, followed presently by another; but the cries seemed to be a part of the inner voice which was urging her on" (162). Though Dorinda ultimately suppresses the upsurging wildness suggested by the call of the owl (she does not kill Jason), this incident marks the beginning of a series of Dorinda's independent actions. These actions lead ultimately to the establishment of her orderly farm world, where wild things (including threatening males) exist outside the female-controlled boundaries of the domestic scene.

Years later, Jason's death threatens Dorinda's domestic tranquility and control, for it brings on a flood of unpleasant memories of youth. When Jason dies, she hears a sheep "bleating somewhere in the meadow, and it seemed to her that the sound filled the universe" (500–501). Later, depressed and lying in bed, Dorinda hears the sound of the wind "like a pack of wolves in the meadow" (508). These animal voices recall Dorinda's vulnerability as "prey." Within the semiotic network of animal signs established throughout the novel, the voices of the wolf and sheep (predator and prey) signify a threat to be overcome by an empowered female refusing to be a victim. Unsurprisingly, Dorinda soon recovers, declaring herself even more secure and independent than before. Indeed, she is more independent, for the deaths of Jason and, earlier, of Nathan have altogether freed her from male Others whose power always threatened to eclipse her own.

Ada's independent acts and decisions in *Vein of Iron* likewise often occur within a semiotic network of references to animal voices. Ada spends a clandestine weekend alone with Ralph, home on leave from the war, in a cabin in the woods: "'Is that the hoot of an owl?'" she inquires of Ralph, "'Or is it the ghost of Grandmother Tod's Indian lover?'" (*Vein of Iron* 213). The voice of the owl signals Ada's and Ralph's rebellion against Ralph's domestic entrapment with Janet, as well as their surrender to wildness and passion (recalling Grandmother Tod's). Ultimately, this wildness and its consequences (a child named Ranny) come under the control of Ada as the dominant figure in Glasgow's ideal domestic scene containing Ralph, Ada, and Ranny in the restored Fincastle home. Just as Dorinda in *Barren Ground* finally presides over a universe in which wildness is driven to the margins, Ada likewise eventually prevails in a world in which wild things are driven from the "house" and back into the fields where they belong.

References to animal voices in *Barren Ground* and *Vein of Iron* often signal the rise of female, articulate power over inarticulate males and the establishment of a female-dominated domestic world in which men are tolerable owing to their animal-like silence and nonverbal means of communication (such as Joshua's "language" of the "heart" shared with his horses). However, both novels suggest that female patterns of communication are far more conducive to the good life than are male patterns of reserve. Female (and a few male) articulate characters become the outspoken proponents of compassion as the supreme human value in a world that reduces animals and humans alike to the status of prey.

Accordingly, animal signs figure significantly in passages throughout both novels in which characters struggle to adopt and articulate this value. In *Vein of Iron*, John Fincastle adopts a Schopenhauerian type of compassion defined in terms of what the articulate may feel for the inarticulate.[9] Several times in the novel, the words of Schopenhauer echo in John's memory: "May all that have life be delivered from suffering" (*Vein of Iron* 414, 448). At the conclusion of the novel, Ada has adopted her father's compassionate philosophy and treats what he always called the "human flock" as sheep (11). Apparently, for Glasgow, such compassion first originates in a sympathy for animals that her characters psychologically, and her texts semiotically, transfer to humans. Indeed, in *Vein of Iron*, several passages repeat the narrator's idea that when viewed from afar or near-sightedly, humans and sheep are indistinguishable (12, 80).

In *Barren Ground* we have also seen how Dorinda's feelings frequently soften toward human beings, to whom she can relate as she relates to animals. Though Jason Greylock commands as little sympathy from Dorinda as anyone possibly can ("'I have no sympathy to waste on him,'" she declares [*Barren Ground* 466]), in the end she cannot allow him to die in the poorhouse, in the "*livery* of dependence" (484; emphasis added). She finds compassion for him at last by seeing him as a fettered animal—a horse in "livery."

In Glasgow's narratives, animal signs often mark sites of human developmental crisis and resolution leading to an ethics of compassion in a female-centered, domesticated universe. Such animal signs are the measure of and the instrument for negotiating perceived danger to a self by a threatening world or a threatening Other. For Glasgow, identification with nonhuman creatures is a key to developing compassion for human creatures. This narrative universe of animal signs suggests the cognitive process by which Glasgow herself might have dealt with her own fears and feelings of "difference." Apparently, the feeling that led Glasgow to reject Spinoza's philosophy because it denies animal sentience is the same feeling that shaped her compassionate response to the human condition—the feeling that one is, after all, no "different . . . from the rest of [suffering] Nature" (Tutwiler 1.30).

Notes

1. Glasgow's extensive reading in a number of subjects, including Darwinism, is well documented in her own fictional works and her autobiography, *The Woman Within*. The heavily annotated volumes in her library also reflect the amount of, and her critical engagement with, her reading. For a list of works in Glasgow's library and an account of her annotations in each, see Tutwiler. For a sense of the range of Glasgow's interests in philosophy, see also Rainwater, Raper, and Westbrook.

2. Sebeok's numerous works on zoosemiotics are listed and self-critically reviewed in *American Signatures: Semiotic Inquiry and Method*. Key works on the semiotics of self also include *Sign, Self, and Society* and *The Sign and Its Masters*.

3. On the subject of humans looking at animals and constructing self and world, see also Berger. See also J. R. Raper's "Once More to the Mirror: Glasgow's Technique in *The Sheltered Life* and Reader-Response Criticism" for a parallel discussion of how Heinz Kohut's psychological theory of "self-objects" applies to Glasgow's writing.

4. On the subject of recent reconsiderations of Darwin, see Midgley and Rachels.

5. Glasgow might also have run across this idea in W. E. H. Lecky's book, *The History of European Morals*, which she owned and mentions in her autobiography.

6. On Glasgow's narrative manner of working out philosophical problems, see Rainwater.

7. For a study of self in *Barren Ground*, see Wagner. For remarks on the "self" of Glasgow's autobiography and its relationship to Glasgow's characters, see Chandler. Finally, for a study of Glasgow's identity vis-à-vis the women's movement, see Scura.

8. Glasgow's reading of Hume is documented throughout her autobiography.

9. Glasgow refers to the impact of Schopenhauer's ideas on her own thinking in *The Woman Within*. *Barren Ground* and *Vein of Iron* both contain direct allusions to Schopenhauer. I am indebted to William J. Scheick for my understanding of Schopenhauerian compassion. See his *Fictional Structure and Ethics: The Turn-of-the-Century English Novel*.

Works Cited

Berger, John. "Why Look at Animals." *About Looking.* New York: Pantheon, 1980. 1–26.

Chandler, Marilyn R. "Healing the Woman Within: Therapeutic Aspects of Ellen Glasgow's Autobiography." *Located Lives: Place and Idea in Southern Autobiography.* Ed. J. Bill Berry. Athens: U of Georgia P, 1990. 93–106.

Glasgow, Ellen. *Barren Ground.* 1925. San Diego: Harcourt, 1985.

———. *Ellen Glasgow's Reasonable Doubts: A Collection of Her Writings.* Ed. Julius Rowan Raper. Baton Rouge: Louisiana State UP, 1988.

———. *Vein of Iron.* New York: Harcourt, 1935.

———. *The Woman Within.* New York: Harcourt, 1954.

Midgley, Mary. *Animals and Why They Matter.* Athens: U of Georgia P, 1983.

Rachels, James. *Created from Animals: The Moral Implications of Darwinism.* New York: Oxford UP, 1990.

Rainwater, Catherine. "Narration as Pragmatism in Ellen Glasgow's *Barren Ground.*" *American Literature* 63 (1991): 664–82.

Raper, Julius Rowan. "Once More to the Mirror: Glasgow's Technique in *The Sheltered Life* and Reader-Response Criticism." *Modern American Fiction: Form and Function.* Ed. Thomas Daniel Young. Baton Rouge: Louisiana State UP, 1989. 136–55.

———. *Without Shelter: The Early Career of Ellen Glasgow.* Baton Rouge: Louisiana State UP, 1971.

Scheick, William J. *Fictional Structure and Ethics: The Turn-of-the-Century English Novel.* Athens: U of Georgia P, 1990.

Scura, Dorothy M. "A Knowledge in the Heart: Ellen Glasgow, The Women's Movement, and *Virginia.*" *American Literary Realism 1870–1910* 22.2 (1990): 30–43.

Sebeok, Thomas A. *American Signatures: Semiotic Inquiry and Method.* Ed. Iris Smith. Norman: U of Oklahoma P, 1991.

———. *The Sign and Its Masters.* 2nd ed. Lanham, MD: UP of America, 1989.

———. *Sign, Self, and Society.* Ed. Benjamin Lee and Greg Urban. Berlin: Mouton de Gruyter, 1989.

Shepard, Paul. *Thinking Animals: Animals and the Development of Human Intelligence.* New York: Viking, 1978.

Tutwiler, Carrington C., Jr. *A Catalogue of the Library of Ellen Glasgow.* Charlottesville: Bibliographical Society of the U of Virginia, 1969.

Wagner, Linda W. "*Barren Ground*'s Vein of Iron: Dorinda Oakley and Some Concepts of the Heroine in 1925." *Mississippi Quarterly* 32 (1979): 553–64.

———. *Ellen Glasgow: Beyond Convention.* Austin: U of Texas P, 1982.

Westbrook, Perry D. *Free Will and Determinism in American Literature.* Rutherford: Fairleigh Dickinson UP, 1979.

Coming Home
Glasgow's Last Two Novels

Helen Fiddyment Levy

There is in every human being, I think, a native country of the mind,
where, protected by inaccessible barriers, the sensitive dream life
may exist safely. Frequently, the fields within are no more
than an extension of some lost and remembered earlier surroundings.
—*A Certain Measure*

[Kate Oliver's] nature is rooted in some hidden identity with the land.
She has the gift of creation. Whatever she touches lives and thrives.
—*Beyond Defeat*

Although Ellen Glasgow's last novels, *In This Our Life* (1941) and *Beyond Defeat: The Epilogue to an Era* (1966), have often been slighted by critics, their composition in fact allowed her to resolve the perceived conflict between her own literary art and her gender.[1] The posthumously published *Beyond Defeat* in particular deserves a renewed examination because in its plot, characterization, and pictorial language it suggests that Glasgow at last found a faith in the future that merged female identity and independent creativity. Its creation freed her at last from the nagging influence of her father's perceived cruel patriarchal religion of "red images" and "the sacrifice of the lamb"; it gave an affirmative answer to the questions generated by the "anxiety of influence" (*WW* 72).[2]

Of *In This Our Life* Glasgow wrote, "The scene, then, in this book is the intrinsic life of a community, as portrayed through the group consciousness" (*ACM* 250). These books, or more correctly *this* book—J. R. Raper argues persuasively that the two novels should be published as one volume—center on the human community rather than the individual (192). *Beyond Defeat* shifts even more markedly than *Vein of Iron* and *In This Our Life* from an emphasis on the individual's struggle with social and natural environment to an examination of an ideal community. Despite her insistence that the individualistic faith of *Barren Ground* embodied her final philosophy, *Beyond Defeat* suggests that Glasgow at last found refuge in a visionary pastoral home place presided over by an elder wise woman, an American icon (*WW* 271).

The discussion of Glasgow's female home place in the two last novels proceeds from my understanding of several sources in sociology and anthropology. First, along with other modern American women writers such as Sarah Orne Jewett, Willa Cather, Katherine Anne Porter, Alice Walker, Eudora Welty, and Gloria Naylor, Ellen Glasgow responds to aspects of modernity that Max Weber formulates as integral to the process of social rationalization. Those most pertinent to the present discussion are the demand for the erasure of received traditional identities and methods of passing on knowledge (the craft tradition), the increasing organization of the social structure to maximize economic productivity and to reward individual success, and the objectification of nature into malleable material for individual and corporate exploitation. The movement toward the large-scale rationalized bureaucratic society appears in *In This Our Life* through the pronouncements of the dominant male material achiever William Fitzroy and through the practices and relationships of his supporting impersonal social organizations, the corporation and the urban family. The drive for more efficient inner and outer control of the worker-citizen implies a cultural devaluation and even denial of the biological processes of the female body, particularly as it is involved in what Sara Ruddick calls "birthing labor" (191).

Weber's idea of increased impersonal social control dovetails neatly with the observations of anthropologist Mary Douglas. Stating that different sorts of social matrixes generate particular patterns of language, Douglas in *Natural Symbols* describes the dynamic by which the mature industrial society, a variation of the "Big Man" society, generates an elaborated language code, which I call the associational language. The always innovating language centers on the individual (as opposed to the group), allowing him or her to "make his [or her] own intentions explicit, to elucidate general principles" (44). Language serves to emphasize separation of the individual from the rest of the social order. This language is strongest at the social center, the professional, managerial, and entrepreneurial classes to which the author belongs. Glasgow represents the "competitive cosmology" (Douglas 160) by her depiction of the city of Queenborough and its bureaucratic institutions, the adoption service conducted by Louisa Littlepage, and the corporation headed by William Fitzroy. In this social order each individual attempts to impose his or, much less often, her personality on the group, and, as Fitzroy understands all too well, stupidity is the only sin.

In contrast, Douglas, building on the work of Basil Bernstein, posits a second language, the restricted code, which I call the local language. It partakes of the immediacy and the inclusiveness of ritual.[3] These communications have, as Douglas explains, "a double purpose: They convey information, yes, but they also express the social system, embellish and reinforce it. The second function is the dominant one" (44). The shorthand verbal communication assumes the ongoing, face-to-face relations of the stable community. The bonding, and bounding, local language is found in face-to-face groups. These local groups, families, and small-scale communities, for example, are located far from the individualistic competition at the social center that generates the associational language.[4] Kate Oliver's home place exists far from that center, and *Beyond Defeat*'s pictorial language shares the goals of that language.

The human being shaped by the local language will feel the communal context as a crucial part of his or her identity, with language constantly reinforcing the relationships of the community and assuming their continuance throughout a lifetime; in contrast, the individual molded by the associational language will experience life as a free agent, unconstrained by the duties, traditions, and history of the group. Freed from received communal definitions and categories, the individual is defined increasingly through a specialized vocational identity with the correspondingly exclusive, abstract jargon of the insider. Early in her career, Glasgow realized her connection to the elaborated language of the German philosophers and Darwin, a pattern of thought and language reflected in the plot and characterization of her early novels. Only later did she realize that her love of literature had arisen from her female family:

> I hunted for the worn volume inherited from my grandfather's library, and taught myself, with infinite patience, to spell out the words on the printed page. But I have never forgotten how the glorious adventures seemed to grow stale and flatten out when I read them in cold and faded print, deprived of the magical tones of my Aunt Rebecca's voice. (*ACM* 166–67)

Filled with the flat, dim printed pages of the male canon, her grandfather's library now appears as a repository of times past and gone, of traditions alien and irrelevant. Its influence is replaced by the true source of Glasgow's creativity, the sound of the beloved female voice bringing

ballads and stories to full, immediate life and revitalizing even the male
literature itself. The language and imagery of *Beyond Defeat* suggests
Glasgow's search for a mother tongue that will both address her scattered readership and reproduce the communal feelings of the woman-
centered homeland. Through the loss of Aunt Rebecca's voice for so
many years, Glasgow comes to realize the loss of the local language
and the retreat of literature from immediate consequence to the reader's
life. The public language of cultural differentiation makes woman's
communal experience of personally transmitted knowledge harder to
portray. As the pleadings of the intellectual language of the modern
center sound ever more faint and distant, the woman's voice within
calls the dying author more urgently and immediately.

As ritual evolves to local language to personal memory, it falls in
danger of shrinking to the private vision, to being captured in the net
of individualism—thus the recourse to mythic and religious symbolism that elevates even the most private of moments into an ongoing
community. Incantations, conventional metaphor, religious and biblical references, orally transmitted legends, folk stories, songs—all these
indicate the communal didactic intent in many modern American
women's writings. Like her sisters, Glasgow redeems ancient communal references from paternalistic bias. By recourse to these still-shared
references, she hopes to achieve the bonding effect of local language and
even more to evoke the exaltation and complete participation felt by each
member participating in communal ritual. The pictorial language rein-
forces the meaning of the goddess figure, giving the woman's literature a
depth beyond individual experience, a path out of modern solipsism.[5]

Glasgow brings the reader fully into the sun-dappled world of Hunter's
Fare. The binding immediate emotion of ritual, which has its residue in
such conventional communal forms as the pastoral and the epic, appears here in the pictorial passages and in the implications of a life
transcending existing social reality. One quote will illustrate Glasgow's
style and intent:

> While he rested there, in the hushed life of the hour, warmed by
> the sun, and by the bitter-sweet tang of autumn, it seemed to him that
> he was caught and held in some slow drift of time. Barred with a pat-
> tern of light and shade, the terraces appeared to rise and fall, and to
> settle back, silently, under the blown grass. Within this stillness, the
> wind moved, the grass bent and straightened, the fall of leaves broke
> and scattered. All these separate motions were imprisoned here, now,
> in the crystal globe of this instant. But, beyond this sphere of eternity,
> above, below, around the encircled moment, he felt that changeless,

perpetual rhythm of time passing. Clouds and light, air and water, tree and flower, all were drifting. Even the wild geese, ranging far overhead, through the bright hollow of afternoon, appeared to float, like shadows, in a liquid medium. For it was the closing season of an abundant earth, when nature, serene and effortless, was drifting into the long pause of winter. . . .

A voice called, and he started up. Awaking from his sleep, which was not sleep, he remembered that outside this stillness, this peace, this crystal globe, the retarded evolution of men had turned back on itself, and was, even now, devouring its own children. (*BD* 119; ellipses Glasgow's)

Several features of this passage show Glasgow's extra-rational, otherworldly intent. First, there is the intent to take the reader to a place beyond human time: the attempt to hold immediately the moment "imprisoned here, now, in the crystal globe of this instant," the explicit reference to the distant horror, the "evolution of men" like Saturn or time devouring the children, and the movement of the flora and fauna "drifting, like shadows, in a liquid medium." The reference to the now-irrelevant "evolution" may well be a rejection of her earlier rational belief in benevolent evolution in the natural and social world (*WW* 92). Logic is confounded by movement within stillness, by the "sleep which is not sleep," by the passing of time within the enclosed bubble of the eternal autumn moment. The sounds of the words themselves underline the meaning; the long vowels, the sibilant consonants slow the passage, suggesting the movement into the golden season before death. Finally, there is the rhetorical triple phrase, "this stillness, this peace, this crystal globe," which attempts to enclose the scene and the feelings in one sentence just as all eternity is collapsed into one glowing moment. Nature transcends the physical world, flowing into the ocean of identity as Asa's being ebbs and flows at once, breathing with the universe (the play of shadow and light, the rise and fall of the terraces, the bending and straightening of the grass). This is death, but death without fear. A sense of well-earned rest after long labor and abundant harvest comes to Asa as the waves of time and nature flow toward eternity. He feels, and we feel, a part of the ongoing existence that Kate Oliver represents. Like the author, we have come home.

As Raper argues, the intent of *Beyond Defeat* is that of "wisdom literature" (192), a mode of expression requiring another critical approach from that taken to realistic fiction. With its emphasis on "liturgical cadence" and "stress on vision," the novel must be placed, Raper points out, alongside religious works centering on the male deities Zeus, Vishnu, and the "mystic's God" (192). He concludes that its ritual structure unites it with those works addressing the central dramas of existence such as Aeschylus's tragedies or medieval quest tales, thus "it should be judged upon its style and vision" (192).

To what end does Glasgow create this homeland? The writing of this last book, as I say, allowed Glasgow to address a number of issues that had long troubled her. Not only does it address eschatological issues for the author, but it also examines her longstanding concerns centered on woman's roles and creativity. The ideal female-created homeland Glasgow envisions in the last two books centers on a reconstitution of the family that redeems the paternalistic, hierarchical family. Unlike that family, Kate's family welcomes and honors all people; Glasgow insists that Kate, the ideal mother, supplies the ongoing strength that enlivens the American future represented by Timothy and by Roy and by the male and female generations who will return to Kate and the land. Kate's lifetime, like those of Cather's Antonia, Naylor's Miranda Day, or Jewett's Mrs. Todd, will not be measured by the clocks of the flimsy city house nor by the timesheets of the efficient factory. She exists in a time beyond present reality, the time of the constantly renewing natural world, the time of the sunset pastoral.

Kate dispensing food to her "family," Kate walking among the swaying grain, Kate standing in the autumn sun—all these scenes center on pictorial images that glow with the patina of time-honored sources, enlarging the reader's emotional parameters and escaping the individualized language that Glasgow as a modern author uses. More than simple nostalgia, *Beyond Defeat* lives instead as a picture of an exemplary community transcending the material competition and the individual life.

To underline her communal, ritualistic intent, Glasgow contrasts the two social matrixes in characterization and plot. The avaricious families and the jerry-built houses hovering in the expanding shadow of the master of Queenborough dominate the first novel; the loving family and the enduring home emerging from Kate Oliver's labors appear at the center of the second. William Fitzroy, "the biggest man in the South" (*ITOL* 4), who rules the fallen city contrasts with Kate, the "great [female] companion" (173), who creates the golden pastoral. Through the writing of *Beyond Defeat,* Glasgow transcends the victimization that threatens her strongest female protagonists. She creates a home presided over by a wise woman who overcomes aging and loss to form a haven in nature that welcomes refugees from the urban wasteland.

The novels share twin protagonists. Asa Timberlake, a decent man, and his beloved daughter Roy find themselves isolated even within their own family, pushed aside by the wealth and power of Uncle William Fitzroy. Their histories illustrate the effect of social environment on even the strongest individual. Asa in the first book is bitter, detached, discouraged, just as Roy is self-obsessed, harried, and hopeless. Linda Wagner notes the similarity of Roy's attitudes to those of Glasgow's authorially identified social observers such as Asa and John Fincastle. The incidents of Roy's life find parallels in Glasgow's life at the time of the novel's composition. Like Glasgow, Roy feels herself dispirited by war, violence, and shattered relationships. At the beginning of *Beyond Defeat*, Roy, like the author herself, has emerged from a critical illness so grave that the attending doctor calls it a "Resurrection of the body" (6). Through this circumstance, Glasgow prepares us for the rebirth this novel intends to effect.

Dominating private life as thoroughly as public life, Fitzroy has, in effect, claimed Asa's home and family and reshaped them in his own acquisitive image, just as he has changed the established business practices of Queenborough. He furnishes the house in which the Timberlakes live; he permits Asa's wife and his niece Lavinia to recline in easy invalidism, and he serves as indulgent benefactor of Asa's other daughter, Stanley. His economic dominance allows Fitzroy to remain a "pillar" of the community despite his well-known failures as husband and employer. Fitzroy's portrait holds more than a hint of the rapacious predator as he "caws," "brays," "snorts," and "bellows." He characterizes desirable women in culinary terms as "tender" and "plump," and Asa notes William's tendency to grasp at any young woman who comes within his reach (*ITOL* 202, 56). The "father" of this evil trinity also achieves self-gratification from the "child," who, as Asa's own son observes, really belongs to Fitzroy (62). Glasgow adds a suggestion of venality to the emotional incest; when Uncle William gives Stanley a handsome wedding check, he demands a kiss on the lips from the "minx" (56). Upon Stanley's elopement with Roy's husband—yet another incestuous incident indicating Queenborough's moral anarchy—Fitzroy opines that she needs a "'sound whipping.'. . . His sly chuckle held a lustful note" (203). Asa sums it up: "I wonder how much of his anger with Stanley . . . is mere jealousy in a perverted form?" (203).

Asa's contrast of the earlier paternalistic entrepreneur with Fitzroy's bureaucratic impersonality surely reflects Glasgow's opinion. "In the old days his [Asa's] father had known the name and face of every man he employed. . . . One had dealt with flesh and blood, not with a list of printed names at the top of a page" (*ITOL* 9–10). Fitzroy represents the impersonal bureaucratic forces which now increasingly control the individual. As a representative "Big Man" of the complex social order, Fitzroy directs its bureaucracies, but he himself is not constrained by their proliferating rules nor by social disapproval. Roy remarks, "But there's too much of Uncle William. He seems to get all over the place" (*ITOL* 43).

The "mother" of Fitzroy's "family," Lavinia Timberlake, is a self-indulgent invalid who rules through complaint. As numerous commentators have noted, Lavinia represents the old, aristocratic tradition now depicted as a "fraud" (*ITOL* 51). Her description suggests the decline of that social pattern:

> Her large, heavy, composed face, in which disposition had long since triumphed over contour and feature, appeared to him to hang there, like a moon in a sullen sky. . . . Her spreading figure, unconfined by an old-fashioned wrapper of purple challis, seemed to fill the entire space of the couch. (*ITOL* 45–46)

Her large, loose mind, the source of Glasgow's evasive idealism, marks her as the conventional mother of Queenborough's modern age who is clad in an old royal purple robe. In her desire to stop time, to live in the "old days," she will not allow Stanley to progress into womanhood: "I shall always feel that she is my baby" (157). Her attempt to live through her daughter's dominance over men contrasts with the willingness of the good "mother," Kate Oliver, to encourage the independence of the members of her family. So strong is her stubborn conventionality that she directs her other daughter and her grandchild to the urban bureaucracies because the remaining family "could never feel that a child born out of marriage is a member of—of our connection" (*BD* 46).

Men adore the third member of the Queenborough "family," Stanley, characterized by Glasgow as a "soulless little pleasure-seeker" (*ACM* 259). Described as a "doll," a "baby," an "effigy," and a "child," the deadly Stanley has been transformed into a mannequin for the male material-achiever's wealth, just as she is shrunken into a child to preserve the youth of a grasping matriarch (*ITOL* 283). Stanley is created by male desire and feminine weakness. Neither "father" nor "mother" in Queenborough can allow or imagine mature womanliness. One man after another, young or old, seeks Stanley as the prize in the social competition, and she uses and destroys them all—except for Uncle William Fitzroy, her "father" and most powerful suitor.

The Fitzroy "family" displays Glasgow's opinion of the ills infecting Queenborough. The calculating relationships of Fitzroy, Lavinia, and Stanley produce only death, heartache, and sterility. Fitzroy buys Stanley's attentions and lives as a jealous *voyeur* in her romantic adventures; Lavinia, for her part, seeks continually to foster the relationship between her daughter and Fitzroy for her own emotional and financial purposes; and Stanley in her turn approaches her "family" only as an opportunity for self-advancement. Despite their blood ties, there is no abiding, heartfelt bond. Unlike Kate's ongoing dynamic homeland, their house falls with Fitzroy's death.

At the beginning of *Beyond Defeat,* Roy remarks that "Uncle William, who used to boast that he carried the world in his pocket, was dead, with all his proud world in ruins" (21); as Douglas observes, the Big Man's "magic" lasts only as long as his strength holds, that is, for the span of the individual life. After Fitzroy's death, Lavinia dies and Stanley seeks out her true homeland, Hollywood, with her destined mate, a movie producer. Roy returns to a moribund city with her illegitimate child, seeking shelter. Asa has found peace working on Hunter's Fare, the female pastoral. Glasgow indicates forthrightly that the farm exists in an ideal landscape: "As Roy went up the long slope, she felt . . . as if time were running down, and she had walked into another life and another world" (105). The landscape of the dying dream underlines descriptive passages as Glasgow evokes the pastoral mode with Kate as a nature demigoddess:

> Around them, there was the low, perpetual humming of autumn, the vibration of innumerable small voices. The wind had turned, and they were sheltered by the huge overhanging boughs of the cedars. Through the sifting pollen of milkweed, Roy looked eagerly down the white road ahead, where Pat and Percy raced homeward. On the left, in an endless meadow, sheep were cropping lazily among uninterested cattle. (68)

The outcasts of Fitzroy's temporal realm come to be healed at Hunter's Fare, a place located in the pastoral distance. "Still ahead, and within sight, but just out of reach, and always a little farther away, fading, but not ever disappearing, was freedom" (*ITOL* 467). Through the use of the pastoral mode and the visual passages, Glasgow attains a new voice that approaches the inclusive communal effect of ritual and rejects the linear, individualized narrative. Although Glasgow evokes the setting and mood of the traditional male mode, she nonetheless rejects the detached, contemplative attitude associated with the pastoral, which Raymond Williams describes as that "of the scientist or the tourist, rather than of the working countryman" (20). The author refuses to allow the reader to objectify this experience, to treat it as mere entertainment. The author concentrates instead on woman's role in actively shaping the pastoral landscape, integrating manual and mental labor, men and women, and nature and culture in an organic, peaceable kingdom.

In both books Kate Oliver appears as the mature nature mother who partakes of the "natural harmony in earth or air" (*BD* 82). She stands at the quiet center of *Beyond Defeat* with Queenborough as the framing wasteland. No lost Fisher King impoverishes the modern world; instead, the exile of the "Gaea-Rhea-Demeter figure" leads to its fall (Raper 188). From her first appearance in *In This Our Life*, Kate embodies the harvest home as she transfigures the "whole world" with "the flushed air of October" (181). Her smile is "as genial as autumn" and her "large, warm hand" is "burned as brown as the soil" (181). Like the autumn she represents, Kate emanates with the glow that lights the coming dark. She shares the huge size of all outdoors with such American demigoddesses as Jewett's Mrs. Todd, the conservator of woman's lore of *The Country of the Pointed Firs*, Porter's Aunt Eliza, the huge nature seer of "The Fig Tree," and Cather's Alexandra, the guardian of the land in *O Pioneers!*

> "Fly! Fly! Fly!" Timothy was jumping up and down, while a cloud of larks rose, with a whirring noise, from the powdery bloom of a near meadow. In the midst of the startled flock, a tall upright figure, in blue overalls, moved swiftly, as if it obeyed some natural harmony in earth or air. "That must be Mrs. Oliver," Roy said. "She looks as if she were a part of the autumn."
>
> "She is that," Craig answered, watching the asters and life-everlasting divide into a path. "But it is true of her in all seasons. I thought that about her in the spring. Not because she looks young. She isn't youthful. She is elemental." (*BD* 82)

Like those other female seers, Kate herself has no biological children. Creative care, not physical birth, is the crux of Kate's female creativity. Kate becomes the true mother all these lost Queenborough inhabitants miss just as she becomes the author of the farm's fruitfulness. Through fictional circumstance Glasgow implies that creativity resides in women, a genius that complements their biological identity.

As Glasgow had done in *Vein of Iron*, she amended American history in *Beyond Defeat* to reflect woman's contribution. Glasgow recounts the founding of Hunter's Fare, an old Virginia home built by Kate's family before the Revolution (110). Like the ideal homelands in Welty's *Golden Apples*, Cather's *My Antonia*, Naylor's *Mama Day*, and Jewett's *Country of the Pointed Firs*, Glasgow's female pastoral shows that the true American homeland exists in the neighborhood of loving inhabitants created and guided by the wisdom of the ideal mother. Glasgow depicts Hunter's Fare as the embodiment of an authentic American tradition exemplified by the description of the house itself.

In its old-fashioned, abundant roses, its weathered brick, and its Georgian porch, Glasgow draws a solid, long-established home. This domestic and natural ideal preserves the traditions of grace that diminish in Lavinia's Queenborough to mere propriety or shrink in Fitzroy's factory to bare efficiency. As we sit down to the simple, plentiful dinner with the "family," we glimpse a true land of milk and honey with the earth giving back its fruits as generously as Kate herself dispenses them. Hunter's Fare fulfills the ideal of the American earth as a place for new beginnings. Fitzroy's arrogant, ostentatious Fitzroyal and, even more, the cramped, chilly structure given over to his satellite "family" invite no one. In contrast, Kate's venerable house, filled with books, friends, and of course dogs, gathers in the weak, the lost, and the discarded. Here is the ideal New World homeland: not the Technicolor fantasies of the westering male individual, not the gray daydream of "feminine" conventionality, but instead the glowing image of the healing female pastoral.

Kate rejects the limited, dependent female roles allowed women in both traditional and industrial Queenborough. Unlike Queenborough's desexed upper-class ladies or genderless happiness hunters, she accepts no limitations on her womanliness imposed by either patriarch or tycoon. Her creativity in the house complements her work in the fields. She undertakes both domestic and agricultural labor as gracefully as she realizes her vision of the homeland. In this organic world, other lines drawn by the vocationally differentiated large-scale social order are erased: for example, Glasgow embeds labor within the rest of life as she blends domestic and natural space. As with Welty, Walker, Naylor, Jewett, and Cather, the home place merges with nature. "Below the river front of the house, the almost obliterated terraces fell away to the scalloped edge of the James" (BD 81). Kate's domesticity offers no threat to the green world, but instead woman's care serves to bring nature to fruition.

Suggesting that womanliness is an active force for enrichment of both nature and culture, Kate's creation of Hunter's Fare demonstrates that she expresses herself both through the work of her female body and the creativity of her feminine imagination. Through the characterization of *Beyond Defeat*, Glasgow overcomes the formulation identified by Sherry Ortner in which woman is to man as nature is to culture. The author escapes the categories of that paradigm through recourse to the pastoral mode and domestic ideal, through the artistic use of language, and through the summoning of its strong, womanly creator. The "barren ground" of Virginia realizes its fruitfulness not by the struggle of an isolated individual against nature, but by the cooperative efforts of Kate's rejoined family working with domesticated nature.

The novel contains none of the legendary Glasgow wit, nor does it appeal to abstract intellectual systems. Instead, Glasgow writes in a cadenced, deliberate visionary voice. In *Vein of Iron,* she had attempted to reach "the speech of the heart, not the language of the mind"; she now sought an expanded vision through this language (*ACM* 178). Glasgow attempted to break the causal assumptions of the linear narrative and create the network of ongoing personal relationships that form the home place. In its pace, its language, and its larger-than-life heroine, the author reached for a vision of the ideal not unlike those portraits of human possibility drawn in much male religious and secular literature. Glasgow seeks the mythic reverberations through incantatory phrases and conventional descriptions and characterization, marks of the attempt to bring the emotions and solidarity of ritual to the modern prose narrative. Unlike her earlier novels, the characterization and the solemnity of the writing itself attempt to summon the reader's full feeling participation and belief to the home place. The brutality of war, the horror of marauding children, the degradation of nature, and the desolation of houses that are no homes—all are left behind. In Kate's idyllic homeland, the life of the relentless factory and the cold house Asa remembered as "purgatory" is forgotten as the Land of Canaan is envisioned. Amid the fears and violence of a world war, Kate's American home place fulfills, as does Antonia's farm at the end of Cather's *My Antonia* (1918), the biblical prophecy:

> And he shall judge among many people, and rebuke strong nations afar off; and they shall beat their swords into plowshares, and their spears into pruning-hooks; nation shall not lift up a sword against nation, neither shall they learn war any more. But they shall sit every man under his vine and under his fig tree; and none shall make them afraid: for the mouth of the LORD of hosts hath spoken it. (Micah 4: 3–4)

The woman's homeland can realize the Edenic dream of American nature. America's democratic promise will be realized by rejecting both traditional and modern male-dominated hierarchies for an egalitarian homeland. At the end the male tycoon and the female victim are dead, making way for a new world.[6]

Far from being the last effort of a dying author, the visionary sequel looks forward serenely to the future and the passing of the generations. Facing her death, the author determined to address the questions that haunted her since she as a young woman refused to worship her father's angry, distant patriarch. At the end of the lives of John Fincastle in *Vein of Iron* and Victoria Littlepage in *They Stooped to Folly,* Glasgow had drawn the image of the mother transfigured into Jungian archetype. In the last book, Kate is no mere dark maternal face glimmering in a window to eternity, but a living, compelling female personality. With her elemental nature and ample stature, Kate is drawn by Glasgow as a nature goddess, female energy personified, which suffuses all creation. Unlike the jealous male deity Glasgow put aside in her youth, Kate engenders feelings of love, of harvest, of reward. As Kate herself observes about her care of the land, and as Glasgow must have felt about her own creative labors, "Then I tell myself the end may yet be easier than the beginning" (*BD* 86). In the last account, Glasgow found the language that allowed her to balance her female identity with the profession of authorship. After the false spring of *Barren Ground*, Ellen Glasgow at last found her way home to the figure of the elder wise woman, Mother Autumn.

Notes

Quotations from Ellen Glasgow, *Beyond Defeat: Epilogue to an Era* (Charlottesville: UP of Virginia, 1966), are used by permission.

1. This argument may be found in another form in my *Fiction of the Home Place: Jewett, Cather, Glasgow, Porter, Welty, Naylor.*

2. Sandra Gilbert and Susan Gubar frame the fundamental question that haunts women writers: "[W]hat if the male generative power is not just the only legitimate power but the only power there is?" (7). Glasgow answers this with the creation of Kate and the autumnal homeland.

3. Robert Nelson discusses Cather's use of pictographic language in *Willa Cather and France: In Search of the Lost Language.* It considers the evocative, visual language, which comes close to ritual itself, as an attempt to reclaim the "lost language" of immediate emotional communication. In *Beyond Defeat* Glasgow uses fictional strategies parallel to those employed by Cather to achieve the communal bonding of ritual.

4. Ritual in our innovative modern society often means a habitual action, but, in the sense I use it, it is a system of compressed symbols. These communications are characterized by exact repetitions of action and verbal formulae intended to promote solidarity across the range of a small-scale culture.

5. It may help to think of these two types of social arrangements in terms of Ferdinand Toennies's concept of *Gemeinschaft* and *Gesellschaft.* These concepts are models; each social order deviates from the model, but the distinctions are nonetheless useful roadmaps to guide the discussion on the relationship of literature to culture.

6. Earlier, indeed, Glasgow had imagined an agrarian solution for a strong female protagonist and for her state in *Barren Ground*. Finally, however, that
novel rested on an individualistic "Big Man" framework, depicting a rural en-
clave dependent on the beliefs and financial support of the rationalistic, tech-
nocratic urban center—there, the Northern economic center New York itself.

Works Cited

Cather, Willa Sibert. *My Antonia*. 1918. Boston: Sentry/Houghton, n.d.

———. *O Pioneers!* 1913. Boston: Sentry/Houghton, 1962.

Douglas, Mary. *Natural Symbols: Explorations in Cosmology*. 1970. New York: Vin-
tage/Random, 1973.

Gilbert, Sandra M., and Susan Gubar. *The Madwoman in the Attic: The Woman Writer
and the Nineteenth-Century Literary Imagination*. New Haven: Yale UP, 1979.

Glasgow, Ellen. *Barren Ground*. Garden City: Doubleday, 1925.

———. *Beyond Defeat: An Epilogue to an Era*. Ed. Luther Y. Gore. Charlottesville:
UP of Virginia, 1966.

———. *A Certain Measure: An Interpretation of Prose Fiction*. New York: Harcourt,
1943.

———. *The Deliverance*. New York: Doubleday, 1904.

———. *In This Our Life*. New York: Harcourt, 1941.

———. *Vein of Iron*. New York: Harcourt, 1935.

———. *The Woman Within: An Autobiography*. 1954. New York: Hill, 1980.

Jewett, Sarah Orne. *The Country of the Pointed Firs*. 1896. New York: Penguin, 1977.

Levy, Helen Fiddyment. *Fiction of the Home Place: Jewett, Cather, Glasgow, Porter,
Welty, and Naylor*. Jackson: UP of Mississippi, 1992.

Micah. The Holy Bible. King James Version.

Naylor, Gloria. *Mama Day*. 1988. New York: Vintage/Random, 1989.

Nelson, Robert J. *Willa Cather and France: In Search of the Lost Language*. Urbana:
U of Illinois P, 1988.

Ortner, Sherry. "Is Female to Male as Nature is to Culture?" *Women, Culture, and
Society*. Ed. Michelle Zimbalist Rosaldo and Louise Lamphere. Palo Alto:
Stanford UP, 1974. 67–87.

Porter, Katherine Anne. "The Old Order." *The Collected Stories of Katherine Anne
Porter*. 1965. New York: Harcourt, 1972. 321–68.

Raper, Julius Rowan. *From the Sunken Garden: The Fiction of Ellen Glasgow, 1916–
1945*. Baton Rouge: Louisiana State UP, 1980.

Ruddick, Sara. *Maternal Thinking: Toward a Politics of Peace*. 1989. New York:
Ballantine, 1990.

Toennies, Ferdinand. *Community and Association*. Trans. Charles P. Loomis. London: Routledge, 1955.

Wagner, Linda W. *Ellen Glasgow: Beyond Convention.* Austin: U of Texas P, 1982.

Walker, Alice. *The Temple of My Familiar.* New York: Harcourt, 1989.

Weber, Max. *Economy and Society: An Outline of Interpretative Sociology.* 3 vols. Trans. Ephraim Fischoff et al. New York: Bedminster, 1968.

Welty, Eudora. *The Golden Apples.* 1949. New York: Harcourt, n.d.

Williams, Raymond. *The Country and the City.* New York: Oxford UP, 1973.

Bibliography

Works by Ellen Glasgow

Novels

The Descendant. New York: Harper, 1897.
Phases of an Inferior Planet. New York: Harper, 1898.
The Voice of the People. New York: Doubleday, 1900.
The Battle-Ground. New York: Doubleday, 1902.
The Deliverance. New York: Doubleday, 1904.
The Wheel of Life. New York: Doubleday, 1906.
The Ancient Law. New York: Doubleday, 1908.
The Romance of a Plain Man. New York: Macmillan, 1909.
The Miller of Old Church. Garden City: Doubleday, 1911.
Virginia. Garden City: Doubleday, 1913.
Life and Gabriella. Garden City: Doubleday, 1916.
The Builders. Garden City: Doubleday, 1919.
One Man in His Time. Garden City: Doubleday, 1922.
Barren Ground. Garden City: Doubleday, 1925.
The Romantic Comedians. Garden City: Doubleday, 1926.
They Stooped to Folly. Garden City: Doubleday, 1929.
The Sheltered Life. Garden City: Doubleday, 1932.
Vein of Iron. New York: Harcourt, 1935.
In This Our Life. New York: Harcourt, 1941.

Other Works

The Freeman and Other Poems. New York: Doubleday, 1902.

The Shadowy Third and Other Stories. Garden City: Doubleday, 1923.

A Certain Measure: An Interpretation of Prose Fiction. 1938. New York: Harcourt, 1943.

The Woman Within. New York: Harcourt, 1954.

Letters of Ellen Glasgow. Ed. Blair Rouse. New York: Harcourt, 1958.

The Collected Stories of Ellen Glasgow. Ed. Richard K. Meeker. Baton Rouge: Louisiana State UP, 1963.

Beyond Defeat: An Epilogue to an Era. Ed. Luther Y. Gore. Charlottesville: UP of Virginia, 1966.

Ellen Glasgow's Reasonable Doubts: A Collection of Her Writings. Ed. Julius Rowan Raper. Baton Rouge: Louisiana State UP, 1988.

Secondary Works

Ammons, Elizabeth. *Conflicting Stories: American Women Writers at the Turn into the Twentieth Century.* New York: Oxford UP, 1991.

Anderson, Mary Castiglie. "Cultural Archetype and the Female Hero: Nature and Will in Ellen Glasgow's *Barren Ground.*" *Modern Fiction Studies* 28 (Autumn 1982): 383–93.

Atteberry, Phillip D. "Ellen Glasgow and the Sentimental Novel of Virginia." *Southern Quarterly* 23.4 (Summer 1985): 5–14.

Auchincloss, Louis. *Ellen Glasgow.* Minneapolis: U of Minnesota P, 1964.

Brantley, Will. *Feminine Sense in Southern Memoir: Smith, Glasgow, Welty, Hellman, Porter, and Hurston.* Jackson: UP of Mississippi, 1993.

Bunselmeyer, J. E. "Ellen Glasgow's 'Flexible' Style." *Centennial Review* 28.2 (1984): 112–28.

Dillard, R. H. W. "On Ellen Glasgow's *The Battle-Ground.*" *Classics of Civil War Fiction.* Ed. David Madden and Peggy Bach. Jackson: UP of Mississippi, 1991. 63–82.

Donovan, Josephine. *After the Fall: The Demeter-Persephone Myth in Wharton, Cather, and Glasgow.* University Park: Pennsylvania State UP, 1989.

Godbold, E. Stanly, Jr. *Ellen Glasgow and the Woman Within.* Baton Rouge: Louisiana State UP, 1972.

Harrison, Elizabeth Jane. *Female Pastoral: Women Writers Re- Visioning the American South.* Knoxville: U of Tennessee P, 1991.

Holman, C. Hugh. "April in Queenborough: Ellen Glasgow's Comedies of Manners." *Sewanee Review* 82 (Spring 1974): 264-83.

————. *Three Modes of Southern Fiction: Ellen Glasgow, William Faulkner, Thomas Wolfe.* Athens: U of Georgia P, 1966.

Inge, M. Thomas, ed. *Ellen Glasgow: Centennial Essays.* Charlottesville: UP of Virginia, 1976.

Jones, Anne Goodwyn. *Tomorrow Is Another Day: The Woman Writer in the South, 1859–1936.* Baton Rouge: Louisiana State UP, 1981.

Kelly, William W., ed. *Ellen Glasgow: A Bibliography.* Charlottesville: UP of Virginia, 1964.

Levy, Helen Fiddyment. *Fiction of the Home Place: Jewett, Cather, Glasgow, Porter, Welty, and Naylor.* Jackson: UP of Mississippi, 1992.

MacDonald, Edgar E., and Tonette Bond Inge, eds. *Ellen Glasgow: A Reference Guide.* Boston: Hall, 1986.

MacKethan, Lucinda H. *Daughters of Time: Creating Woman's Voice in Southern Story.* Lamar Memorial Lectures, No. 32. Athens: U of Georgia P, 1990.

McDowell, Frederick P. W. *Ellen Glasgow and the Ironic Art of Fiction.* 1960; rpt. Madison: U of Wisconsin P, 1963.

Rainwater, Catherine. "Narration as Pragmatism in Ellen Glasgow's *Barren Ground.*" *American Literature* 63 (1991): 664–82.

Raper, Julius Rowan. "Ambivalence toward Authority: A Look at Glasgow's Library, 1890–1906." *Mississippi Quarterly* 31.1 (Winter 1977–78): 5–16.

————. *From the Sunken Garden: The Fiction of Ellen Glasgow, 1916–1945.* Baton Rouge: Louisiana State UP, 1980.

————. *Without Shelter: The Early Career of Ellen Glasgow.* Baton Rouge: Louisiana State UP, 1971.

Rouse, Blair. *Ellen Glasgow.* Twayne's United States Authors Series. New York: Twayne, 1962.

Schmidt, Jan Zlotnik. "Ellen Glasgow's Heroic Legends: A Study of *Life and Gabriella, Barren Ground,* and *Vein of Iron.*" *Tennessee Studies in Literature* 26 (1981): 117–41.

Scura, Dorothy M. "A Knowledge in the Heart: Ellen Glasgow, the Women's Movement, and *Virginia.*" *American Literary Realism 1870–1910* 22.2 (Winter 1990): 30–43.

————. *Ellen Glasgow: The Contemporary Reviews.* Cambridge: Cambridge UP, 1992.

Seidel, Kathryn Lee. *The Southern Belle in the American Novel.* Tampa: U of South Florida P, 1985.

Tutwiler, Carrington C., Jr. *A Catalogue of the Library of Ellen Glasgow.* Charlottesville: Bibliographical Society of the U of Virginia, 1969.

Wagner, Linda W. "*Barren Ground*'s Vein of Iron: Dorinda Oakley and Some Concepts of the Heroine in 1925." *Mississippi Quarterly* 32 (1979): 553–64.

————. *Ellen Glasgow: Beyond Convention.* Austin: U of Texas P, 1982.

Contributors

PHILLIP D. ATTEBERRY is assistant professor of English at the University of Pittsburgh, Titusville. He has published a variety of essays on English and American literature, most recently in *Studies in the Novel* and *Nineteenth-Century Prose*. He is currently at work on a book about mainstream jazz.

MARGARET D. BAUER is a visiting assistant professor of English at Texas A&M University. She has published articles in *College Language Association Journal, Southern Literary Journal, Louisiana Literature, Mississippi Studies in English,* and *South Central Review* on Ellen Gilchrist, Zora Neale Hurston, Alice Walker, William Faulkner, and Mark Twain.

STEPHANIE R. BRANSON is assistant professor of English and director of women's studies at the University of Wisconsin, Platteville. She has published on Isak Dinesen in *Short Story* and has an article forthcoming on Ellen Glasgow, Edith Wharton, and Eudora Welty in *American Women Short Story Writers: A Critical Collection.*

MARTHA E. COOK is professor of English at Longwood College in Virginia. Coeditor of *Resources for American Literary Study* from 1980 to 1986, she has published articles on twentieth-century Southern literature in *Southern Review, Southern Literary Journal,* and *Mississippi Quarterly* and in several recent collections. She held a Fulbright lectureship in southern literature at the University of Waikato in Hamilton, New Zealand, in 1987.

SUSAN GOODMAN is assistant professor at the University of Delaware. She is the author of *Edith Wharton's Women: Friends and Rivals* and numerous articles and papers on Wharton as well as other women writers. She is at work on a biographical-critical study of Glasgow.

CAROLINE KING BARNARD HALL is associate professor of English at Pennsylvania State University, Beaver Campus. She is the author of *Sylvia Plath* and *Anne Sexton*. She has served as a senior Fulbright lecturer in twentieth-century American literature and women's studies at the John F. Kennedy Institute of the Free University of Berlin, the University of Copenhagen, and the University of Klagenfurt, Austria.

TERENCE ALLAN HOAGWOOD, professor of English at Texas A&M University, is the author of *Prophecy and the Philosophy of Mind, Skepticism and Ideology, Byron's Dialectic, Fictionality and History,* and articles on the poetry of Elinor Wylie and numerous other writers. He is also the editor of several books, including most recently Elizabeth Smith's *The Brethren: A Poem in Four Books* and Charlotte Smith's *Beachy Head, with Other Poems.*

HELEN FIDDYMENT LEVY is a lecturer at George Mason University. She is the author of *Fiction of the Home Place: Jewett, Cather, Glasgow, Porter, Welty, and Naylor.* She has published essays and presented papers on several women writers, including Glasgow.

LUCINDA H. MACKETHAN is professor of English at North Carolina State University. She is author of *The Dream of Arcady: Place and Time in Southern Literature* and *Daughters of Time: Creating Woman's Voice in Southern Story.* Her essays on southern and African-American writers have appeared in *Southern Review, Southern Literary Journal,* and *Mississippi Quarterly.*

PAMELA R. MATTHEWS is assistant professor of English and director of women's studies at Texas A&M University. Her research focuses on American women writers of the late nineteenth and early twentieth centuries. She is the author of *Ellen Glasgow and a Woman's Traditions* and is working on an edition of Glasgow's correspondence. Her current book in progress is entitled *We Dream of Her Often: Joan of Arc in America.*

CATHERINE RAINWATER is associate professor of English at St. Edward's University in Austin, Texas. Her recent publications include essays in *Philological Quarterly, American Literature,* and *Texas Studies in Literature and Language* on such writers as Mary Cholmondeley, Louise Erdrich, Toni Morrison, Leslie Marmon Silko, and Ellen Glasgow. Her essay on Erdrich's novels won the Foerster Prize from the MLA in 1990. She is also coeditor of two books, including *Contemporary American Women Writers: Narrative Strategies.* At present, she is working on a book concerning the semiotics of contemporary Native American narrative.

JULIUS ROWAN RAPER is professor of English at the University of North Carolina, Chapel Hill. He is author of *Without Shelter: The Early Career of Ellen Glasgow, From the Sunken Garden: The Fiction of Ellen Glasgow, 1916–1945,* and *Narcissus from Rubble: Competing Models of Character in Contemporary British and American Fiction.* He is the editor of *Ellen Glasgow's Reasonable Doubts: A Collection of Her Writings* and co-editor of *Lawrence Durrell: Comprehending the Whole.* At present he is writing a study of Lawrence Durrell.

FRANCESCA SAWAYA is an assistant professor at Illinois State University, Normal. She has published articles on Sarah Orne Jewett and James Fenimore Cooper. Her work-in-progress is a study of domesticity, feminism, and nationalism in regional women's writing.

DOROTHY M. SCURA is professor of English at University of Tennessee, Knoxville. She is editor of *Henry James, 1960–1974: A Reference Guide, Conversations with Tom Wolfe,* and *Ellen Glasgow: The Contemporary Reviews.* She is author of numerous articles and presentations on Ellen Glasgow, James Branch Cabell, Doris Betts, and various southern women writers.

LINDA WAGNER-MARTIN is Hanes Professor of English and Comparative Literature at University of North Carolina, Chapel Hill. She is completing a family biography of Gertrude, Michael, Leo and the other Steins and coediting *The Oxford Companion to Women's Writing in the United States.* She is also writing a sequel to her *Modern American Novel, 1914–1945.* Author of *Ellen Glasgow: Beyond Convention* and *Sylvia Plath: A Biography,* she has also published many books on twentieth-century writers. Her most recent work is *Telling Women's Lives: The New Biography.*

NANCY A. WALKER is professor of English and director of women's studies at Vanderbilt University. She is the author of *A Very Serious Thing: Women's Humor and American Culture, Feminist Alternatives: Irony and Fantasy in the Contemporary Novel by Women,* and *Fanny Fern.* She is currently editor for the Rachel Maddux volumes published by the University of Tennessee Press, and she has edited a critical edition of Kate Chopin's *The Awakening* for St. Martin's Press.

Index